IN THE EMPEROR'S SERVICE

Wallenstein's Army, 1625–1634

Laurence Spring

'This is the Century of the Soldier', Fulvio Testi, Poet, 1641

Helion & Company

The series editor would like to thank Michał Paradowski for his advice and help with illustrations for this book.

Helion & Company Limited
Unit 8 Amherst Business Centre
Budbrooke Road
Warwick
CV34 5WE
England
Tel. 01926 499 619
Fax 0121 711 4075
Email: info@helion.co.uk
Website: www.helion.co.uk
Twitter: @helionbooks
Visit our blog at http://blog.helion.co.uk/

Published by Helion & Company 2019
Designed and typeset by Serena Jones
Cover designed by Paul Hewitt, Battlefield Design (www.battlefield-design.co.uk)
Printed by Henry Ling Limited, Dorchester, Dorset

ISBN 978-1-911628-56-9

British Library Cataloguing-in-Publication Data.
A catalogue record for this book is available from the British Library.

For details of other military history titles published by Helion & Company Limited, contact the above address, or visit our website: http://www.helion.co.uk

We always welcome receiving book proposals from prospective authors.

Contents

List of Illustrations & Maps

Illustrations

Maps

Acknowledgements

I would like to thank the staff of the The National Archives at Kew, the British Library, the Shakespeare Birthplace Trust Library, the Bibliothèque Nationale in Paris, the Statni Oblastni Archive in Zamrsku, the Bavarian Main Archives and the LVR Archivberstung and Forbildungszeitum at Pulheim, Germany for all their assistance.

I would also like to thank Mark Allen for supplying illustrations of the regimental colours and Serena Jones for proof reading the text of this book.

Chronology

1618

May 23	The Defenestration of Prague marking the beginning of the Thirty Years' War.

1620

November 8	The Bohemian Rebels are defeated at the Battle of the White Mountain near Prague.

1625

July 25	Wallenstein promoted to commander of the Imperialist forces.

1626

April 20	Wallenstein defeats Count Ernst von Mansfeld at the Battle of Dessau Bridge.
August 27	Wallenstein and Johan von Tilly, general of the Catholic League's forces, defeat Christian IV of Denmark's Army at Lutter am Baremberg.

1627

September 1	Wallenstein and Tilly join forces to put down the Peasant Revolts in Laurenberg.
November	Wallenstein gains control of Lower Pomerania and Rygen Island.

1628

May 23	Wallenstein lays siege to Stralsund, Mecklenburg.
August 3	Wallenstein abandons the siege of Stralsund.
September 2	Wallenstein defeats the Danes at Wollgast on the Baltic Coast.

1629

Arnim is sent to Poland with an army of about 10-12,000 to assist King Sigismund of Poland in his fight against Sweden, but the majority die of sickness and hunger.

March 6	Ferdinand II issues the Edict of Restitution.
May 22	Emperor Ferdinand II concludes peace with King Christian IV of Denmark.

1630

June 24	Gustavus Adolphus of Sweden lands in Pomerania
August 18	Ferdinand II dismisses Wallenstein at the Diet of Regensburg.

1631

December	Ferdinand recalls Wallenstein

1632

May	Wallensteins drives the Saxons out of Bohemia.
August	Gustavus Adolphus set up a fortified camp at Nuremberg and is besieged by Wallenstein, who sets up his own fortified encampment.
September 3	Gustavus Adolphus assaults Wallenstein in his fortified encampment at the Alte Veste.
November 16	Although Gustavus Adolphus is killed during the battle of Lutzen, Wallenstein is narrowly defeated.

1633

October 20	Wallenstein defeats a Swedish Army at Steinau, on the Oder in Silesia.

1634

January 24	Ferdinand II dismisses Wallenstein as commander-in-chief of the Imperialist Army and appoints his son, Ferdinand, King of the Romans, in his place.
February 25	Wallenstein is assassinated at Eger.

Introduction

Albrecht Wenzel Eusebius von Waldstein, better known to history as Wallenstein, was born on 24 September 1583 in Hermsdorf (Hermanitz) in Bohemia, the son of Protestant parents who despite enjoying noble status were not wealthy. At the age of 12, upon his father's death, Wallenstein inherited the title of Baron. Little is known of his childhood, but his mother also died when he was young. He attended the University at Altdorf near Nuremberg, but was expelled after a year for nearly beating his manservant to death. He decided to travel, but returned to Bohemia in 1602 and enlisted into Imperial service when the war broke out between the Holy Roman Empire and the Ottoman Empire, which was known as the 'Long War'. To further his military career, in 1606 he converted to Catholicism and in 1609 he married the wealthy Lukrezia Nekšová, who died five years later. At the time of outbreak of the Bohemian Revolt on 23 May 1618 he had risen to the rank of colonel, raising two regiments of cavalry for Ferdinand, which were both at the Battle of the White Mountain on 8 November 1620 where the Bohemian Army was heavily defeated. However, Wallenstein was not present at the battle due to ill health.

With the wealth he had inherited from his wife he was able to buy up large estates of the nobility who had sided with the Bohemian rebels. These estates had been undervalued by Emperor Ferdinand's officials for a quick sale since the Emperor needed the money to pay for the recent campaign and quell other rebellious rulers, such as Frederick V, who had recently been deposed as King of Bohemia; his Electorate of Palatinate had been confiscated. With his allies Christian von Brunswick and the Count von Mansfeld the war would continue and draw in other rulers such as Christian IV of Denmark and Gustavus Adolphus of Sweden.

The continuation of the war was good news for Wallenstein who continued to be climb the promotion ladder of the Imperialist Army and when in 1625 the most senior commander of the army retired, he was chosen to replace Hieronymus Caraffa, the Marquis of Montenegro. On 7 April 1625, the Emperor Ferdinand appointed Wallenstein commander-in-chief of 'all his [the Emperor's] troops currently in the Holy Roman Empire and the Netherlands, as well as those that may be sent to him'. This is usually seen as the beginning of the Imperialist Army, but this is incorrect, as the oldest regiment in the army had been raised in 1616 and the army had been in the field since 1618. At the beginning of 1624 the Imperialist Army was composed of nine regiments of horse and 11 regiments of foot. Wallenstein is said to have introduced uniformity within the regiments and even to have chosen the weapons himself. However, uniformity within regiments had been known for decades before Wallenstein became commander-in-chief of the Imperialist forces, and he left most of the choosing of weapons to his subordinates. In fact no contemporary source suggests that Wallenstein's Army was any different to those of armies of other nations. The only comments which were made, were how was he going to fill the ranks of his regiments from all the commissions he had issued. Initially he had promised to raise 50,000 men, but this was reduced to 20,000 men since he found it difficult to raise such as large number of men in a short space of time.

1. Albrecht von Wallenstein. Pieter de Jode (I), after Anthony van Dyck, 1628–1670 (Rijksmuseum)

Certainly Ferdinand needed such a large army because despite the Bohemian rebels being defeated and the Palatinate being overrun, the Emperor still needed to defeat Bethlen Gabor's forces from Hungary and Transylvania and in 1625 Christian IV of Denmark sided with the Protestant cause in what would become known as the 'Danish period' of the war. However, it was as the Duke of Holstein rather than the King of Denmark, that Christian initially entered the fray, since the Danish government would not support the ambitions of their king. Even so, Christian still had vast resources he could count on including several Scottish regiments, including that commanded by Lieutenant Colonel Robert Monro. It would not be until Wallenstein threatened Denmark itself that the Danish mobilised their forces.[1]

To help finance their war effort an army could impose taxes on the local population, especially if they were in hostile territory, in which case a soldier would be more likely to get paid. However, as with other armies this 'contribution system' only worked when it controlled large areas of land. When it lost control of these territories, as in 1645, the system broke down and Maximilian had to rely on his own finances to keep the army in the field.

Contributions, or 'Brandschatzung', had been used to pay an army since medieval times, if not before, but the Thirty Years' War saw it expanded like never before. As one would expect, it was unpopular with the local inhabitants. The commander of an army or his 'Brandmeister' would calculate what a town or village should pay, and this sum would be divided into the number of persons who were to pay the contribution. Commanders preferred that it was a monetary payment so that they could pay their troops, but payments

1 Peter Wilson, *The Thirty Years War: A Sourcebook* (Basingstoke: Palgrave Macmillan, 2010), p.103; Alphons Freiherr von Wrede, *Geschichte der K. und K. Wehrmacht* (Vienna: L.W. Seidel, 1898), vol. 2, pp.12, 96.

2. Emperor Ferdinand II. Cornelis Danckerts (I), 1613–1656 (Rijksmuseum)

in the form of provisions or clothes were also known. However, contributions were also made in kind, such as silverware etc., in which case the commanders would have to exchange this for money and so they would not get its full value. If a town or village refused to pay their contributions then force would be used.[2]

Such was its unpopularity that during his first generalate Wallenstein needed the Emperor's permission to levy a contribution on any town, but in practice he often ignored Ferdinand's orders. Therefore the more territory that was conquered the more income a general had, on the other hand when an area was being fought over, it might have to pay contributions to both sides.

However, these contributions were still not enough and Ferdinand had to rely on subsidies from the Pope to finance his armies. In 1631 the Papacy contributed 27,000 gulden, and in 1633 25,000 thalers, although on 4 October 1631 Spain paid a staggering 300,000 gulden to Wallenstein.

Wallenstein was unpopular with enemies not only on the other side, but also within the Catholic hierarchy insomuch that the Emperor was forced to dismiss his general, although by this time Ferdinand believed that the war was as good as over since with the defeat of Christian of Denmark there were very few enemy armies left in the field. Command of his army passed to Count Johan von Tilly who also commanded the Army of the Catholic League, which meant that now Tilly had to report to two masters, Emperor Ferdinand II and Maximilian of Bavaria. However, in 1630 there was once more a foreign intervention, this time by Gustavus Adolphus of Sweden, who defeated Tilly's veteran army at the Battle of Breitenfeld. The Emperor had no choice but to recall Wallenstein, who set about raising regiments for his new army, and granted him new powers which according to *Theatrum Europaeum* were:

> That the Duke of Friedland be not only His Roman Imperial Majesty's, but also the Austrian house's and the crown of Spain's generalissimo.
>
> That the generalship be conferred upon him *absolutissima forma*
>
> That His Imperial Majesty should not appear in person with the army and even less should he have personal command over it, instead when the kingdom of Bohemia recovers and is conquered again, the king should reside in Prague and

2 Fritz Redlich, 'Contributions in the Thirty Years' War', *English Historical Review*, Dec. 1959 vol. 12, issue 2, p.251.

> Don Balthasar shall supply 12,000 men to protect Bohemia to remain there until a universal peace has stabilised the Holy Roman Empire. For he, the Duke of Friedland, finds that the Bohemians must have a real ruler with the personal presence of their king in their own country. In this way the Emperor and his general will be protected all the more from rebellion.
>
> He should have as security an Imperial pledge on an Austrian hereditary territory as recompense for his regular expenses.
>
> As recompense for his extraordinary expenses, he [Wallenstein] should be allowed to exercise the highest jurisdiction in the Empire over the territories that he occupies.
>
> The right to confiscate lands in the Empire shall be his in *absolutissima forma,* in such a way that neither the *Reichshofrat* [Imperial Council] nor the treasury nor the *Reichkammergericht* [Imperial Federal Court] at Speyer shall pretend to have any power in the matter, be it in cases of general or particular import.
>
> As in confiscation of lands so also in granting pardons, he, the Duke of Friedland, shall be allowed to act as he pleases. If anyone should obtain a safe conduct and pardon from the Imperial Court, such shall have no validity unless it is especially endorsed by the Duke of Friedland, and so shall apply in good faith and by word of mouth and not in full substance.
>
> A genuine pardon is to be only sought from, and granted by, the Duke of Friedland. For in this matter the Emperor would be too lenient and allow it to occur that anyone could be pardoned at the Imperial court, and in this way the means with which to remunerate colonels and officers as well as looking after the mercenaries as is fit, would be cut off.
>
> As it is inevitable that some time or other negotiations for peace will be started in the Empire, so let it be that the Duke of Friedland's private interests among other things concerning the Duchy of Mecklenburg shall also be included in any agreements.

If true these conditions would have reduced Ferdinand II to little more than a puppet ruler, unable to negotiate with his enemies, command in large areas of his empire or have control of his army. Neither had Wallenstein forgotten Maximilian's part in his dismissal and refused to come to Bavaria's aid when it was invaded by Gustavus Adolphus.

Wallenstein won a victory at the battle of the Alte Veste during the summer of 1632 and although he lost the battle of Lützen, this had resulted in the death of the Swedish king. He again won a decisive victory over the Swedes at Steinau in October 1633, but despite this victory he is seen to have not been pressing the Swedes hard enough especially since he had opened negotiations with Saxony and there were rumours that Wallenstein wanted the Bohemian crown. Wallenstein's enemies at the Imperial Court were only too eager to bring this to the attention of the Emperor. Ferdinand appointed

3. (Left) Assassination of Wallenstein. Original sketch by Matthäus Merian from 1634, currently in collection of National Gallery in Prague. (Michał Paradowski's archive)

three privy counsellors to look into these accusations. On 24 January they presented their findings to Ferdinand that he was guilty of treason and the evidence was such that there was no need for a trial, especially since news had probably arrived from Pilsen that on 12 January Wallenstein had made his officers sign an oath of loyalty to him rather than Ferdinand; although seven of the 49 officers present at the 'Pilsener Schluss' refused to do so.

Before deciding what to do Ferdinand sought the opinion of his confessor, the Jesuit Wilhelm Lamormaini. Upon Lamormaini's confirmation that Wallenstein was a threat to Ferdinand, the Emperor dismissed Wallenstein for a second time on 24 January and ordered the officers loyal to the Emperor to bring him to Vienna under arrest or to kill him if he refused.[3]

Lamormaini also called for prayers to be said for a peaceful outcome of this situation because many believed there was a real danger that Wallenstein and his loyal regiments might declare war on the Emperor. Therefore officers loyal to Ferdinand, who included Gallas, Aldringen, Piccolomini, and Colloredo set about securing the Imperialist Army. On 21 February Wallenstein fled to Eger with Counts Wilhelm Kinsky, Christian von Ilow, and Adam von Trcka, hoping to seek the protection of Elector John George of Saxony or Duke Bernand of Saxe-Weimar, who for many years had been his enemy. Wallenstein and his few loyal supporters were escorted by Colonel Butler's Regiment of Dragoons and Illo's Regiment of Foot under the command of Lieutenant-Colonel Gordon, Walter Butler, an Irish Catholic, and Walter Leslie and John Gordon from Scotland. It was Butler who escorted Wallenstein to Eger in February 1634, where they found Leslie and Gordon. Arriving on 24 February Wallenstein retired to bed, where he received a despatch from the Emperor dismissing him as a traitor. Those officers loyal to Wallenstein, Field Marshal Count Adam von Trcka, Wilhelm Kinsky, and Christian von Ilow, held a banquet the following day and were cut down by Butler, Gordon and Leslie with their men. Although wounded in the fray Leslie gathered together Walter Devereux with a detachment of soldiers and burst into Wallenstein's room and also killed him.

Butler, Gordon and Leslie received large rewards for their actions of about 120,000 florins each, although Butler would not live long to enjoy his reward, dying of the plague in September 1634 at Prague, where he was buried with full military honours. As well as receiving his financial reward John Gordon, who was the lieutenant-colonel of Trcka's Regiment of Foot, also took over the regiment, which he commanded until 1642 when it was reduced into Gil de Haes' Regiment. Leslie, who had brought the news of Wallenstein's death to Ferdinand,

3 Robert Bireley, *Ferdinand II, Counter-Reformation Emperor* (New York: Cambridge University Press, 2014), p.262.

was given some of Trcka's estates and made chamberlain of the Emperor's court as well as being promoted to field marshal in the Imperialist Army.[4]

There was no uprising over Wallenstein's assassination as many had feared and many saw this as God's judgement on him, but since the senior officers not only remained loyal to Ferdinand, but had conspired against Wallenstein there was no need to worry.[5]

It was not until 1636 that he was finally buried at the monastery of Gitschin. For many historians, with his death ended the interesting phases of the Thirty Years' War, but the war still had 14 years to run and would see Catholic France enter the war later in 1634. Those who were involved in the assassination of Wallenstein were reward along with his accusers who received a share of Wallenstein's estates. However, the person to benefit the most from Wallenstein's assassination was Ferdinand himself, because not only did he gain control of his army again but large parts of his empire returned to him.

In 1639, just five years after his death, a play was performed at the Globe Theatre in London about the assassination of Albrecht von Wallenstein, Duke of Friedland and Mecklenburg, which was a far cry from his origins. During the centuries that followed many books have been written about Wallenstein, and Frederich Schiller not only wrote a history of the war but also several plays which helped keep his memory alive.

4 Fritz Redlich, *The Germany Military Enterpriser and his Workforce* (Wiesbaden: Franz Steiner, 1964), p.348; Wrede, *Geschichte der K. und K. Wehrmacht*, vol. II, p.51.

5 Bireley, *Ferdinand II*, p.262.

1

Officers

As with other armies at this time the senior officers came from the nobility. In the Holy Roman Empire the nobility was formed from the *Reichsunmittelbarer Adel* or the Imperial Immediate nobility who were closest to the Emperor, and sat in the Imperial Assembly and the College of Imperial Counts and possessed vast estates. They formed the aristocracy of the Empire and were often known as 'Prince', and included the Dukes of Bavaria, Brunswick and Mecklenburg.

Then there were the *Landsadel* or *Landsassigen* or formed the territorial nobility and were subjects to the Imperial Immediate nobility. The came the *Reichsritterschaft* or Imperial Knighthood, who grouped themselves into three *Ritterkreise* or knightly circles, formed from Swabia, Franconia, and the Rhine. It would be unthinkable for families who formed these groups of nobility to begin their military career in any other rank than a colonel, which is just as well since it has been estimated that a colonel needed between 400,000 and 450,000 florins per year to maintain a regiment of foot 3,000 strong and 260,000 to 300,000 florins for a regiment of 1,200 cavalry. Fortunately for the colonels very few regiments mustered more than 500 troopers so the outlay was much smaller, but even so only the wealthiest noble could finance raising a regiment himself, because as well as the initial outlay of raising a regiment he would also need a considerable amount of capital to maintain it in the field. When Franz Albert von Saxe-Lauenburg, who came from the Imperial Immediate nobility, raised his regiment of cuirassiers in 1625, he left it to his lieutenant-colonel, Melchor von Hatzfeldt, to borrow the money from merchant company of Hetman Heffing of Cologne and Tobias and Anton Geiger of Nuremburg. The money was finally paid back in 1628 by Wallenstein's banker, Hans de Witte, using money which had been raised by the contribution system, which imposed taxation on a city or territory. It was due to this system, that by July 1628 Hatzfeldt was in credit with the Geiger brothers for the sum of 30,000 thalers, which was to be used to purchase ammunition, weapons, clothing etc. for the regiment.[1]

1 David Parrott, 'The Military Enterpriser in the Thirty Years' War', in *War, Entrepreneurs and the State in Europe and the Mediterranean, 1300–1800* (Leiden: Brill, 2014) pp. 63, 73.

4. Franz Albert von Saxe Lauenburg. Peter Drossel (1620–1667). (Michał Paradowski's archive)

Franz Albert would later change sides and was with Gustavus Adolphus at the battle of Lützen, when Gustavus was mortally wounded. Franz tried to lead him to the Swedish lines when they encountered some Imperial cavalry regiments, who not only recognised the King of Sweden: later accounts state that Franz abandoned the King to his fate, even that he had murdered the Gustavus Adolphus himself. There is no way of knowing if this is true or not, but on 4 December 1632 he entered the Elector John George of Saxony's service. It was now he became involved in the peace negotiations with Wallenstein and John George, which further led to suspicion falling upon him.[2]

However, Franz Albert was not the only one of Duke Franz II von Saxe-Lauenburg's 11 sons to raise a regiment for the Imperialist cause. Duke Julius Heinrich von Saxe-Lauenberg, was born on 19 April 1586 at Wolfenbüttel and in 1618 was commissioned to raise a regiment of foot of 10 companies. Ernst Ludwig was killed at the battle of Aschau on 15 July 1620. Despite Julius Heinrich's regiment being a harquebusier regiment and Franz Albert's a cuirassier, Julius Heinrich's Regiment was known as the Alt or Old Saxon Regiment, while Franz Albert's was known as the Neu or New Saxon Regiment.

Wallenstein also used nepotism to find his officers, including his two cousins, Berthold and Maximilian von Waldstein, both of whom were colonels. Berthold von Waldstein received a commission to raise a regiment of foot on 2 April 1629, but it was not until 1631 that it was completed when Colonel Strassikdo's Regiment was incorporated into it. When Berthold was mortally wounded at Lützen in 1632 the regiment was taken over by his brother, Maximilian, who was said to be Albrecht von Wallenstein's favourite cousin. Maximilian had been commissioned to raise his own regiment of foot on 1 September 1629, but he gave it to his lieutenant-colonel, Johan von Adelshoven, when he became the colonel of Berthold's Regiment. Maximilian rose to the rank of major-general, and despite his family connections with Wallenstein he continued to command the regiment until 1642 when it passed to Colonel Carl Friedrich Reich. However Maximilian von Waldstein would become the inhaber of another regiment of foot in 1645, which had been raised two years previously by Ladislaus Burian von Waldstein.[3]

However, family status and patronage was fine if they made a natural soldier, but the Imperialist General Federico de Savelli, who was forced into soldiering by his father, Duke Bernard de Savelli was no leader of

2 Peter H. Wilson, *Lützen*, Great Battles series (Oxford: Oxford University Press, 2018), pp.70–72.

3 Wrede, *Geschichte der K. und K. Wehrmacht*, vol. 1, p.35; vol. 2, pp.210–211, 254–256.

men. True, Federico had served in the 'Long War' against the Ottoman Empire at the turn of the seventeenth century and had been the commander of the Papal forces, but he was more fit for the life at court than that of a soldier. Despite this in 1638 he was promoted to field marshal and commanded the advance guard of the Imperialist Army at Wittenweier, where the Imperialist Army was defeated by Bernard von Saxe-Weimar on 30 July 1638. According Franz Redlich his aristocratic status prevented him from being court-martialled and instead he returned to his diplomatic career.[4]

5. Ottavio von Piccolomini. Anselm van Hulle (1601–1674). (Deutsches Historisches Museum)

Sometimes inhabers were lucky and they had another regiment incorporated into theirs, On 15 May 1629 Julius von Hardegg was commissioned to raise a regiment of foot of 10 companies, but he seems to have struggled to raise the required number of men. However, the following year five companies were transferred from Wallenstein's own regiment, which had been raised in 1621, with an additional reinforcement of a company of Colonel Perusis' Regiment in 1632. These companies would bring their own clothes and arms with them and Hardegg would not have to pay the soldiers a bounty since he did not raise them himself, but he would have to re-equip them when necessary and pay them their wages. In 1636 its lieutenant-colonel, Franz Mers, took over ownership and command of the regiment and so the burden of paying for the regiment passed to him until 1667 when he retired from the army. The regiment would eventually become the 11th Regiment of Foot and would not be finally disbanded until the 20th century.

However, Hardegg was not the only one to benefit from Wallenstein's dismissal in 1630. Octavio von Piccolomini's cavalry regiment which had been raised in 1629 was supplemented by several troops from Wallenstein's Lifeguard. When Piccolomini raised another regiment of horse in 1632 it became known as the Neu or Jung Piccolomini Regiments, whereas the one that was raised some years before was known as the Alt Piccolomini Regiment to distinguish between the two.

Piccolomini was not the only inhaber to own more than one regiment, although in the case of Guiglielmo Verdugo decided to give one of his regiments to his brother, Franz. This not only cut down the financial burden for Guiglielmo, but raised the status of Franz since he was now a colonel in the Imperialist Army. Alternatively, an inhaber might sell his regiment, as in

4 Sommeregger 'Savelli, Duke Friedrich von', in *Allgemeine Deutsche Biographie* 53 (1907), pp.720–721 <http://www.deutsche-biographie.de/pnd115775617.html?anchor=adb> (accessed November 2015); Redlich, *The Germany Military Enterpriser*, p.385.

1631 when Heinrich Holk sold his regiment of foot to Johan Philip Cratz von Scharffenstein for 6,000 thalers.[5]

Even before he became commander of the army Wallenstein had raised three regiments of horse; of course he could not command them all at once and so delegated them to their respective lieutenant-colonels. Other owners appear to have been absentee commanders having the status of a colonel while enjoying court life at Vienna. However many owners preferred to accompany their regiments on campaign, which might result in glory and riches or death being wounded or imprisonment, such as Count Ernest Montecuccoli who received a commission to raise a regiment of foot on 29 February 1632, but on 16 June 1633 he was wounded and captured at Breisach and died on 3 August, when his regiment passed to Count Orfeo Strassoldo. Montecuccoli's regiment lasted just four years, being disbanded in 1636.

However, despite all their expenditure, for one reason or another the majority of regiments lasted only two to five years. Using Alphons Freiherr von Wrede's *Geschichte der K. und K. Wehrmacht* as a guide, Fritz Redlich calculated that the lifespan of an Imperial regiment was as follows:[6]

Lifespan	Horse	Foot	Drgs.
1 year or less	10	12	1
2 to 5 years	129	116	32
6 to 10 years	42	32	5
over 10 years	31	35	4
	212	195	42

Despite Wallenstein referring to Colonel Gabriel Pechmann as 'a good fighting man', Duke Franz Albrecht von Saxe-Lauenburg described him as a 'donkey and a peasant's son', referring to his lowly birth. However, Pechmann made an advantageous marriage and when his wife died in 1619 he inherited her lands in Saxony, which ennobled him so became Gabriel Pechmann von der Schonau. In 1623 he was commissioned to raise a regiment each of foot, dragoons, and harquebusiers. Unfortunately, the cost of raising these regiments appears to have been too expensive for Pechmann, since it is not clear whether he managed to raise his dragoon regiment and his regiment of foot was disbanded the following year. He was commissioned to raise another regiment of dragoons but this was disbanded shortly after his death in 1627 in a skirmish at Friedenberg, in Pomerania.[7]

However, Pechmann's Regiment of Horse did survive his death and passed to Count Heinrich von Schlick and then to Colonel Albrecht Wengersky in 1629, who commanded it until it was reformed in 1631, but not before it had

5 Redlich, *The Germany Military Enterpriser*,pp.173, 175.

6 Redlich, *The Germany Military Enterpriser*, p.226.

7 Golo Mann, *Wallenstein, his life narrated*, transl. Charles Kessler (London: Andre Deutsch Ltd, 1976), p.302; Wrede, *Geschichte der K. und K. Wehrmacht*, vol. II, p.17 and vol. III/2 pp. 383, 419, 611.

taken part in the Battle of Breitenfield. Wallenstein described Count Heinrich von Schlick: 'If His Majesty has a good officer, then he is Count Schlick'.[8] Schlick had sided with the Bohemian rebels in 1618 and at the head of his regiment at the Battle of the White Mountain fought almost to the last. He handed his sword to the Catholic generals, Bucquoy and Tilly, and escaped the retribution of Ferdinand's officials by changing sides. He rose to the rank of field marshal in 1627.

6. Gil De Haes. Portrait from the collection of Fürstlich Waldecksche Hofbibliothek, Band 1. (Heidelberg University Library)

Pechmann was lucky in that being a commoner he had risen so far, because in 1633, only 13 out of 107 colonels within the Imperialist Army were commoners, although this number was slowly rising as the war progressed. However, this should be compared with the Army of the Catholic League, which between 1635 and 1649 out of 51 colonels, 35 were commoners.[9] Their status also meant there were some very young colonels, in fact Fritz Redlich records that of 153 colonels who served during the war and whose ages can be verified, three were under 21 when they received their commissions and the majority, 47, were between 26–30 and 41 were between 31 and 35. Twelve were 40 or over. The same can be said for the generals: out of 138 seven were under 26, although the majority, 42, were between 36 and 40.[10]

Among these 'commoners' who received a colonelcy in the Imperialist Army was Gil De Haes. Unfortunately, we know very little about his origins, except that he was a bricklayer in the Netherlands and was said to be a Jewish convert to Catholicism. At 27 he joined the Spanish Army, because according to his biographer he had been spurned by a maid. Within five years he had risen to the rank of lieutenant. However, it was not until he received the patronage of Johan von Aldringen that he quickly rose to the rank of lieutenant-colonel and after the sack of Mantua in 1630 he was able to afford to raise a regiment of Walloons for the Imperial service. Wallenstein accused him of performing badly at Lützen, but he distinguished himself at the siege of Ingoldstadt and the Battle of Nördlingen. He later became a major-general in the Bavarian Army and then in Venetian Army. He died in 1657 in Croatia.[11]

8 Wrede, *Geschichte der K und K Wehrmacht,* vol. III/2 p.419; Mann, *Wallenstein,* p.302.

9 Andreas Kraus, *Maximilian I: Bayerns Grosser Kurfürst* (Graz: Styria, 1990), p.152; Redlich, Fritz, *The Germany Military Enterpriser*, p.418.

10 Redlich, *The Germany Military Enterpriser*, pp.179–180. Of the colonels the remaining groups were 17 between 21 and 25 and 33 between 36 and 40. For the generals nine were between 26 and 30, 30 were between 31 and 40 and 21 were over 46.

11 The National Archives, Kew (henceforth TNA), SP 101/3, unfolio, Newsletters, foreign, Flanders, 1638–1667; Gregory Hanlon, *Italy 1636: Cemetery of Armies* (Oxford: Oxford University Press, 2016), p.62.

7. Matthias Gallas. Unknown artist. (Michał Paradowski's archive)

Of all the Major-Generals in Wallenstein's Army Rudolph Baron von Tieffenbach was the most senior having been commissioned on 10 March 1619, although Balthazar Maradas was commissioned on 18 June 1619, he was promoted to the more senior rank of General of cavalry on 24 October 1622, then field marshal on 24 May 1626 and lieutenant-general on 24 May 1627. Among the 30 major-generals who were appointed between 1619 and 1634, was Mathias von Gallas. Gallas was born on 16 September 1584, probably in Trent. Little is known of his early life, but like his father, Major Pancraz von Gallas, he served in Flanders and from 1616 in Italy, becoming a captain in the Catholic League on the outbreak of the Thirty Years' War and distinguished himself at the battle of Stadlohn in August 1623. On 24 March 1629 Wallenstein wrote to Collalto that Gallas had written to his friend Johan von Aldringen 'that he will certainly be with me by the end of the month [because] he does not want to stay in Bavarian service.' On 11 April 1629 Gallas was commissioned major-general in Wallenstein's Army much to the disgust of Maximilian of Bavaria. He quickly rose to lieutenant-general on 16 September 1633 and finally succeeded Wallenstein as the commander of the army in 1634, although his commission was dated 24 January 1634, several weeks before Wallenstein's death. Unfortunately, although he made a good subordinate officer Gallas was not a good supreme commander. True he had commanded the Imperialist forces at the battle of Nördlingen, where the combined Swedish Armies of Gustav Horn and Bernard of Saxe-Weimar were decisively defeated and did conquer many territories, but he later earned the nickname 'Heerverderber' or 'Army spoiler', since more men died from want of provisions and plague than through battle. He was dismissed twice by the Emperor and died in 1647.[12]

Another officer of note to join the Imperialist Cause was Count Wolfgang von Mansfeld who had commanded the Army of Saxony in 1620, but the newsletter *Advise from Augsburg* on 10 March 1628 described him as 'a man already of age and very grey yet lately turned to Popery'. He had been commissioned to raise his own army in Schwabland which was to serve against the Ottoman Empire. In June 1628 it was reported that Mansfeld was 'desirous to resign his army to Wallenstein, but Montecuccoli doth sue for that place'. Unfortunately for Montecuccoli he did not get his wish and

12 'Matthias Graf von Gallas' by Herman Hallwich in *Allgemeine Deutsch Biographie* (1878), vol. 8, pp.320–321.

Mansfeld's Army was broken up and the regiments dispersed into Poland, Holstein, and Flanders.[13]

One family to supply two field marshals were the Breuners of Styria. General Field Marshal Hans Philip von Breuner had raised a regiment of foot in 1618. Then in 1630 Hans Gottfried von Breuner raised a regiment, followed in 1632 by Philip Frederick von Breuner. To distinguish these regiments, Colonel Hans Gottfried von Breuner's was known as Colonel Breuner's Old Regiment and Colonel Philip Frederick's 'Young Breuner's' Regiment. Hans Philip was already a major-general by 1632, so his regiment was known as 'Major-General Breuner's Regiment'. All three regiments were present at the battle of Lützen, where Hans Philip was mortally wounded, while Philip Frederick von Breuner died on 25 March 1638 at Warnemunde of a 'high fever'. By now he had also been promoted to general field marshal.

According to Raimondo Montecuccoli, who served with Wallenstein and wrote a book on tactics, an officer:

> must be everywhere. Some he must exhort with hope of reward, others he must impress with fear of punishment. With everybody he must do something. He must seem to be observing all that happens so that each worthy soul will deem it an honour to meet death valorously under the eyes of his prince or general. A true leader must scorn death whenever he sees that his affairs are going badly.[14]

However, the death of an inhaber meant that their regiment would either be disbanded or passed to a new owner. However, being captured or having their regiment destroyed in a battle could ruin their investment since in the former case they could no longer look after their regiment, or in the latter they would have to bring the regiment up to strength again with all the financial burden that entailed.

Officers who had been captured could either be swapped for an officer of similar rank or pay a ransom. At first this ransom appears to have been ad hoc, but during the war a price list appears to have been agreed by both sides, with a major-general's ransom 4,000 florins and a general 8,000 florins, while a colonel was worth 1,000 thalers. However, in 1634 this was reduced to 600 florins for a cavalry colonel and 500 thalers for a colonel of a regiment of foot. If an officer was considered too valuable to be released then he might remain a prisoner for several months or even years before he was exchanged. After he was captured at the battle of Nördlingen, General Gustavus Horn was imprisoned for a staggering eight years.[15]

Another way that a colonel might lose his investment in his regiment was by being court-martialled, as happened to the officers and lesser officers of Colonel Ernst George von Sparr's and Hagen's Regiments after the battle of Lützen. As early as the 29 December 1632 edition of *Advice out of Germany*

13 TNA SP 101/29, *Advice out of Augsburg and other places* ff. 30, 93; *Advise from Diverse Parts of Germany*, 13 June 1628 f.136.

14 Thomas Barker, *The Military Intellectual and Battle; Raimondo Montecuccoli and the Thirty Years' War* (Albany: State University of New York Press, 1975), p.157.

15 Redlich, *The Germany Military Enterpriser*,pp.396–397.

8. Henrick Holk. Unknown artist. (Nationalmuseum, Stockholm)

records that 'the Duke of Friedland having cashiered and punished divers officers and soldiers that did not their duty in the last battle of Lützen.'[16] However, it was not until early the following year that the 'Blood Court' met at Prague to try those who had shown cowardice at the battle. On 2 December 1632 Nicholas Staffier, Provost General of Wallenstein's regiment, issued orders for the arrest of more than 60 officers, including Colonels Lothar Dietrich, Baron von Bonninghausen and Johan Nikolas von Hagen, and also of Lieutenant-Colonel Albrecht von Hofkirchen, who had commanded Sparr's Regiment of Horse that day since the colonel was absent. True, these officers had deserted their posts, but the other senior officers of Wallenstein's Army still believed it was against their noble status to be tried in such a way. It was only the intervention of Colonel Heinrich Holk, who had commanded the Imperialist right wing during the battle, that saved Bonninghausen from the executioner, and he would die in 1657. Unfortunately the intervention of Archbishop of Mainz on Hagen's behalf could not prevent his nephew's death. Neither could Albrecht von Hofkirchen's conversion to Catholicism during the trial could save him either, and they were among 13 officers who were beheaded by the Prague executioner on 13 February 1633. The names of 50 other officers were nailed to the gallows as a mark of dishonour. Their regiments were disbanded in disgrace and the soldiers transferred to other regiments, with the lesser officers being demoted, branded with hot irons as traitors and cashiered.

However, the men of Hagen's Regiment were luckier than those of Sparr's Regiment who were all cashiered, but not before every tenth man had been hung and the remainder flogged and branded with hot irons as traitors. Due to his status Bonninghausen received another commission to raise a new regiment, which also fled during its first battle.

For company commanders these might be a relation to the colonel, such as Ottavio Piccolomini who appointed his nephew, Silvio, as a captain in his regiment of horse in about 1629, although by 26 April 1633 he had become the regiment's lieutenant-colonel. Piccolomini was born in Florence and his regiment had been in Spanish service before entering the service of the Emperor, and the names of his 10 troop commanders appear to have been either Italian or Spanish, although his troopers appear to have more Germanic names.[17]

16 TNA SP101/30 f.97 *Advice out of Germany*, 29 December 1632.

17 Otto Elster, *Die Piccolomini-Regimenter Während des 30Jährigen Krieges* (Vienna: L.W. Seidel and Son, 1903), pp.29–30, 32–33, 40–45.

As was the case in other armies, Wallenstein relied on officers from many nations: Baron Giovanni Baptista Chiesa was Italian and lieutenant-colonel of Collalto's Regiment of Foot, later rising to the rank of colonel. As well as Italian officers, there were also those who came from England, Ireland, and Scotland, including Walter Butler, John Gordon, Walter Leslie, and Walter Devereux, who had assassinated Wallenstein and his loyal officers at Eger in 1634. Walter Leslie had joined the Dutch Army, but by the summer of 1630 had entered Imperial service. Despite Butler commanding a regiment of dragoons which had been raised in Germany, some of his company commanders appear to have come from his native Ireland.[18]

On 3 December 1629 the Venetian ambassador to the Netherlands, Vicenzo Gussoni, wrote to the Doge and Senate, that the Dutch had disbanded several of their regiments and that, 'I have hinted to some of the most experienced officers that they might go to Venice, but they do not want to abandon their men, and they hope to repair their fortunes in Sweden, Denmark or England, although they might go to Halberstadt, where Wallenstein is beating the drum and there are rumours of great levies.'[19]

How many of these officers did join Wallenstein is unknown, but they would have known that the quickest (and safest) way of obtaining advancement in rank was to join a newly raised army; especially with the expansion of the Imperialist Army in 1625, and again in 1631, many of the officers in the Catholic League resigned their commissions in order to seek employment in Wallenstein's Army. Unlike the Catholic League's army, the Imperialist Army allowed Protestants to serve both as officers and soldiers, which helped to raise such a large army. One example is the Lutheran Henrick or Heinrich Holk (Holck) who was born on 28 April 1599 at Kronborg in Zealand. He began his military career in the Danish Service being captured on July 1627 by the Imperialist Army. He returned to Copenhagen in 1628 and was sent as part of the Danish force which garrisoned Stralsund, which was besieged by Wallenstein. After King Christian IV of Denmark signed the Peace of Lübeck with the Emperor in 1629, Holk transferred to the Imperial service and became a colonel of a regiment of foot the following year. In 1632 he became colonel of a regiment of cuirassiers and was promoted to major-general and then field marshal. Unfortunately he died on 9 September 1633, possibly of the plague.

On the other hand Colonel Johann Philip Cratz was dissatisfied with the speed of his promotion in Imperial service and in 1630 joined the Bavarian service, where he rose to the rank of general. Even this did not satisfy him and he planned to betray Ingoldstadt to the Swedes, so when this plot was discovered he fled to the Swedish service, and the following year was captured at the battle of Nördlingen and beheaded for treason.

18 Gabriella Ceckova et al., *Documenta Bohemia Bellum Tricennale Illustrantia* (Prague: Academia Naklanntelstui Ceskoslovenske Akadamie, 1977), vol. 5, p.452; Albert E.J. Hollaender, 'Some English Documents on the End of Wallenstein', John Rylands Library, 1958, p.382.

19 Vinenzo Gussoni to the Doge and Senate of Venice, 3 December 1629, printed in *Calendar of State Papers Relating to English Affairs in the Archives of Venice*, vol. XXI (London: HMSO, 1916), ed. Allen B Hinds, p.246.

9. High-ranking officers, from Rudolph Meyer's series depicting soldiers of the Thirty Years' War, 1618–1638. (Rijksmuseum)

It was the lieutenant-colonel's role to command the regiment in the colonel or owner's absence, but it was the major of the regiment who looked after it, so a good major could mean the difference between the regiment performing well on campaign or not. Then there were the captains who commanded each company, the senior officers within the regiment, such as the lieutenant-colonel and major were also classed as captains since the also commanded a company, although the colonel's company often had a captain lieutenant as his company commander. The others companies had a lieutenant, who was second in command of the company, and the ensign or cornet depending on whether the regiment was a cavalry or infantry regiment. It was their duty to carry the company's or troop's colour and to protect it in battle. These positions were usually filled by the gentry who enjoyed the colonel's patronage. The captain on the agreement of the colonel would also appoint his lieutenant or ensign/cornet, which was sometimes his son or sons. If a captain left the regiment then he might recommend his replacement, but there was no guarantee that the colonel would listen, particularly if he had a candidate of his own he wished to appoint to the vacancy. Moreover it was extremely rare for a captain to take his company with him since it belonged to the colonel no matter how much capital the captain had invested in the company. Alternatively it was known for someone to be a captain in one regiment and a more senior officer in another, such as

Peter Konig von Mohr who in 1624 was a captain in Collalto's regiment of Foot and lieutenant-colonel in Colonel Lodron's Regiment.[20]

As we have seen, there are examples where common soldiers were promoted through the ranks, but those who reached the rank of colonel were the exception rather than the rule. The novelist Hans von Grimmelshausen explains this in *The Adventurous Simplicissimus*: when the hero Simple Simplicissimus asks a sergeant why the gentry are promoted rather than the more deserving common soldiers, the sergeant replies:

> Must not a general trust a gentleman more than a peasant lad that had run away from his father at the plough-tail and so done his parents no good service? For a proper gentleman rather than bring reproach upon his family by treason or desertion or the like, will sooner die with honour. And so tis right the gentles should have the first place.[21]

However, in 1639 Robert Ward complained that gentlemen:

> [Are] admitted for their wealth's sake into captainships, which neither have courage, skill nor delight in Arms themselves, nor discretion to command others … How can we hope to make our people soldiers, where they be under blind and ignorant guides; *If the blind lead the blind*. Had we but all these abuses corrected, me thinks we might make our English trained bands, parallel [to] the best soldiers in Europe.[22]

To support these officers were the lesser or inferior officers, who were composed, in order of seniority, of sergeants, corporals, and lance passidores, the latter rank being the seventeenth century equivalent of a lance corporal. Sources suggest that there should be at least three sergeants per company, but some surviving muster rolls at this time show there were just two. According to Francis Markham one of their duties was to teach the soldiers their drill and therefore should be 'valiant, expert, vigilant and diligent' and that '[a] good sergeant is an admirable benefit and if he live and execute his place well any long time, no man deserveth advancement before him'.[23]

Unfortunately some officers were reluctant to promote their sergeants especially if they covered up their incompetence.

As for a corporal, according to Francis Markham:

> [He] ought to be a man carefully chosen out, and induced with valour, virtue, diligence and experience; he ought to be of reverend and grave years, thereby to draw on respect, but withal of a sound judgement; for experience without it is but

20 Redlich, *The Germany Military Enterpriser*, p.176.

21 Hans von Grimmelshausen, *The Adventurous Simplicissimus* (Lincoln: University of Nebraska, 1962), p.36. Grimmelshausen's role in the Thirty Years' War has been debated since his novels were published. However most historians agree that due to their contents he must have served in the army.

22 Robert Ward, *Animadversions of Warre; or a Military magazine of the truest rules and ablest instructions for the managing of war…* (1639), pp.30–32. His italics.

23 Francis Markham, *Five Decades of Epistles of Warre* (London: Augustine Matthews, 1622), pp.69, 72.

> a jewel in the sea, which neither adorns itself nor others, he is to be a cherisher of virtue and a lover of concord, for he is said to be the father of his squadron and must therefore love them and provide for them as for his natural children.[24]

Markham is the only writer to suggest a corporal be of 'grave years' or elderly, while Mansfeld devoted almost four pages to the corporal's duties in his *Directions of Warre*, also referring to the corporal as the 'father' of the squadron, because it was his task to receive the men's rations and to see they were bivouacked probably. Hexham also states that the corporal should make sure that the new recruits were not bullied by the veterans and train them in the arms drill and the various positions, although Francis Markham suggests that this was one of the sergeant's duties.

In infantry companies there was the drummer whose task it was to beat out the "fall in" and the officer's other commands. According to Francis Markham, the drummer was to be:

> Every way fitting for his place, must besides the exquisiteness and skillfulness in his Art and instrument, and the rudiments of marshal discipline, be also a good linguist, and well served in foreign languages: for by the carrying of messages, he must commerce and have to do with people of sundry nations.[25]

The trumpeter performed the same duties in a troop of horse, so he not only had to be reliable, but also had to know how to play his instrument.

24 Francis Markham, *Five Decades*, pp.65–66.

25 Francis Markham, *Five Decades*, p.59.

2

Raising the Army

In theory regiments of foot mustered 3,000 men in 10 companies, but in reality they were drastically understrength. Between 24 June and 13 September 1625 Wallenstein's Army mustered as follows:[1]

Regiment of Foot	Paper strength	Actual strength	Money
Friedland	3,000	2,091	20,372 fl 30 kr
Tiefenbach	3,000	1,952	19,196 fl
Schlich	3,000	2,046	20,213 fl
Julius von Saxe-Lauenberg	1,500	1,244	11,847 fl
Colleredo	[3,000]	2,168	19,233 fl
Wratislaw	[3,000]	2,317	21,663 fl
Cerboni	[3,000]	1,823	19,235 fl
Total	19,500	13,641	131,759 fl 30 kr

The situation grew steadily worse, and at a muster on 14 April 1632 Maximilian von Waldstein's Regiment of Foot mustered 953 men in Bohemia, whereas Count Dietrichstein's Regiment numbered only 576 men and Colonel Chiesa's Regiment mustered 1,039 men in four companies.[2]

Of course the strength of a regiment could vary at various times as the muster rolls for Colonel Julius Hardegg's Regiment of Foot clearly show.

Of course the strength of a regiment could vary greatly. On 1 March 1630 Julius von Hardegg received a commission to raise a regiment of 3,000 foot, but the surviving muster returns for the regiment show a very different picture:[3]

1 Ferdinand Tadra, *Briefe Albrechts von Waldstein an Karl von Harrach* (Vienna: K Gerold's Sohn, 1879), pp.289–290. The bracketed figures are insertions of Tadra's, as the return was blank.

2 Dr B. Dudik, *Waldsteins Correspondenz* (Vienna, 1865–1866), p.214.

3 Hausmann, 'Das Regiment hochdeutscher Knechte des Grafen Julius von Hardegg', in *Der Dreissigjährige Krieg, Beiträge zu seiner Geschichte* (Vienna: Militarwissenschaftliches Institut, 1976), vol. 7, p.166.

Date	Men
26 October 1632	866
13 February 1633	999
24 October 1633	1,178
23 February 1634	1,156
6 March 1634	1,147
27 June 1634	654
29 October 1634	790
10 March 1635	1,035
4 April 1635	1,096
7 May 1635	1,114
30 October 1635	1,101
? January 1636	796
12 February 1636	774
22 August 1636	*c.*600

However, even these figures are deceptive because it was common practice for company commanders to claim 'dead pays' whereby they would collect the pay of a certain number of soldiers who did not exist and so supplement their salary.

As we saw in the previous chapter the majority of regiments lasted between two and five years, with some only lasting 12 months, if they were raised at all. During Wallenstein's two generalships the Imperialist Army mustered the following regiments of foot:[4]

Year	1625	1626	1627	1628	1629	1630	1631	1632	1633	1634
No. of regts. at beginning of yr	11	15	23	29	29	36	45	47	55	62
No. commissioned	6	8	6	5	8	12	14	23	10	9
No. disbanded	2	-	-	5	1	3	12	15	3	8
No. of regts. at end of year	15	23	29	29	36	45	47	55	62	63

The official returns for the Imperialist Army show that regiments of foot were raised in the following places:[5]

Place	1625	1626	1627	1628	1629	1630	1631	1632	1633	1634
High German1	6	14	15	14	13	9	17	25	22	18
German	3	5	4	7	9	15	14	12	8	13
Low Germany	1	2	3	5	7	13	10	6	15	13
Bohemian	4	0	0	1	2	1	4	3	0	0
Italian	0	0	0	0	0	0	1	2	4	5
Moravian	1	0	0	0	0	0	0	0	0	0
Spain	0	0	1	0	1	0	2	1	0	0
Tyrol	0	0	0	0	0	0	0	0	0	1
Walloon	0	0	3	4	3	3	4	7	5	4
Unknown	0	0	0	0	0	2	0	0	0	0
Total	15	21	26	31	35	43	52	56	54	54

4 Wrede, *Geschichte der K. und K. Wehrmacht*, vol. II, p.96.

5 Ceckova *et al.*, *Documenta Bohemia Bellum Tricennale Illustrantia*, vol. 4, pp. 421–424, 426–427, 431–433, 436–438, 441–443; vol. 5, pp.287–390, 397–400, 446–449.

The number of regiments shows some discrepancies from the data collected by Wrede, but as the returns show, apart from assistance from the Spanish Empire the Imperialist Army had no 'foreign regiments' like other armies, such as those of Sweden, Denmark, or the Dutch Republic which had regiments raised in Scotland or England. True, these were Protestant countries helping other Protestant countries, but even Catholic France for political reasons preferred to assist the Protestant Dutch rather than their co-religionists, with French regiments serving in the Dutch Army, and even the Spanish had many Irish units in its army. In fact such was the high regard the Spanish held for the Irish that their units were known as 'Tertios' rather than regiments, an honour reserved for the Spanish and Italian units. This is not to say that there were not men men from outside the two Habsburg Empires serving among the ranks of these regiment.

The lack of foreign regiments is also evident in the Imperialist cavalry, the majority of which came from the German States, as the following chart shows:[6]

Place	1625	1626	1627	1628	1629	1630	1631	1632	1633	1634
High German*	6	0	0	1	1	1	3	3	4	3
German	3	18	22	14	12	14	18	37	36	32
Low German*	1	2	3	5	5	5	4	3	7	6
Bohemian	4	0	0	1	1	1	0	2	0	0
Croatia	1	5	0	2	1	0	3	5	0	0
Italian	0	0	2	2	0	0	0	0	2	2
Lorraine	0	0	0	0	0	0	1	0	0	0
Moravia	1	0	0	0	0	0	0	0	0	0
Spain	0	1	1	2	0	2½	1½	1	1	1
Walloon	0	3	3	4	3	3½	5½	7	6	4
Unknown	0	0	0	1	0	0	0	0	0	1
Total	16	29	31	32	23	26	35	58	56	49

* Lands in southern Germany, Austria, Liechtenstein, and Switzerland are described as High German, while Low German states are those located in northern Germany.

Raised in 1629, Colonel Henricus Haraucour von Faulquemont's Regiment of Horse had mustered just five troops which had been raised in the Netherlands, however by the following year it had risen to a regiment of 10 troops with the additional five being raised in Spain. In 1635 it entered Spanish service. Piccolomini's Regiment of Horse was also divided into troops formed from Italians, Germans, and Walloons.

In theory a regiment of cavalry or 'horse' might number 500 or 1,000 depending on their commission. They were divided into five or 10 companies or troops, and like the infantry regiments seldom reached this paper strength, and also like the infantry many regiments did not last longer than five years. The following numbers of cavalry regiments were formed during Wallenstein's time:[7]

6 Ceckova *et al.*,vol. 4, pp. 423–424, 426–427, 433–436, 438–440; vol. 5, pp.387–390, 400–403, 449–452.

7 Wrede, *Geschichte der K. und K. Wehrmacht*,vol. 3, p.12.

Year	1625	1626	1627	1628	1629	1630	1631	1632	1633	1634
No. of regts. at beginning of yr	7	17	26	33	22	27	31	47	68	75
No. commissioned	13	12	11	8	6	9	23	34	12	20
No. disbanded	3	3	4	19	1	5	7	13	5	11
No. of regts. at end of year	17	26	33	22	27	31	47	68	75	84

These figures can be further broken down into the type of cavalry. For the heaviest type of cavalry, the cuirassier, who was armoured from head to knee, with boots protecting his lower legs, the number of regiments raised during this time was:

Year	1625	1626	1627	1628	1629	1630	1631	1632	1633	1634
No. of rgts. at beginning of yr	3	5	9	11	10	13	16	24	28	29
No. commissioned	3	4	3	2	3	4	10	9	3	13
No. disbanded	1	-	1	3	-	1	2	5	2	4
No. of regts. at end of year	5	9	11	10	13	16	24	28	29	38

The lighter cavalry were known as harquebusiers and the following regiments were raised:

Year	1625	1626	1627	1628	1629	1630	1631	1632	1633	1634
No. of rgts. at beginning of yr	4	9	11	16	11	13	12	13	19	20
No. commissioned	7	4	6	5	3	2	6	13	2	-
No. disbanded	2	2	1	10	1	3	5	7	1	5
No. of regts. at end of year	9	11	16	11	13	12	13	19	20	15

As in other armies there were a number of dragoon regiments in the Imperialist Army, which as the following chart shows gained popularity as the war progressed:

Year	1625	1626	1627	1628	1629	1630	1631	1632	1633	1634
No. of rgts. at beginning of yr	-	2	3	3	-	-	-	4	11	14
No. commissioned	2	-	1	-	-	1	4	7	4	3
No. disbanded	-	2	1	3	-	1	-	-	1	2
No. of regts. at end of year	2	1	3	-	-	-	4	11	14	15

Another type of cavalry not found in other Western European Armies were Croats and other light cavalry such as hussars. Their usefulness also became obvious as the war progressed which related in the following regiments being formed:

Year	1625	1626	1627	1628	1629	1630	1631	1632	1633	1634
No. of rgts. at beginning of yr	-	1	3	3	1	1	3	6	10	12
No. commissioned	1	2	1	1	-	2	3	5	3	4
No. disbanded	-	-	1	3	-	-	-	1	1	-
No. of regts. at end of year	1	3	3	1	1	3	6	10	12	16

The discrepancy between Wrede's calculations and that of the 'return' is that three regiments were disbanded in 1626.

Wherever the regiment was raised a warrant was usually issued to an officer, which was known as the *Werbepatent* (levy patent) or *Werbekontrakt* (levy contract), stating where he was to recruit his company or troop and the number of men that he was expected to raise. This patent was to be shown to the authorities within the area as proof that he had been granted the authority to raise the men.

When Wallenstein assumed command of the army, he boasted that he would raise an army of 70,000 men and issued over 100 commissions to raise his army. However, on 8 July 1625, it was said that the levies raised 'are not so great as it was reported'. If it was difficult raise the new regiments, on 6 August 1625 Aldringen wrote to Count Collalto that the seven old infantry regiments mustered just 7,283 men. The situation had still not changed two years later when in April 1627 another newsletter recalled that Wallenstein's Army was only 20,000 strong rather than the 80,000 men previously reported. At the beginning of Wallenstein's second generalship he again boasted that he would field an army on 80,000, but as a pamphlet recalled, 'it is well known there is want of both men and money'. On 29 February 1632 Anstruther wrote to Vane:

> The Duke of Friedland's [Wallenstein's] Army consists already of 24 regiments. It is meant perhaps so many colonels (which yet is much) but the question is whether or not every one of them (if he have so many) hath a regiment complete. They give out here that there are already within the Emperor's domains at Moravia and Upper and Lower Austria above 100,000 veterans and new levied soldiers.[8]

One of the problems was that there were too many armies from various nations being raised, so that someone wanting to join the army who did not care which side he fought for, could choose the army offering the best terms. When Count von Fugger was raising his regiments he could afford to pay each recruit three Thalers plus a shilling a day as soon as they accepted his service, although he had to send commissioners as far as Hungary and Poland to complete his regiment. On the other hand, in Nuremberg the soldiers being recruited for Colonel Hirchperger's Regiment quickly deserted

8 *The Continuation of our Weekly News*, 30 May 1625 no. 24 p.8; TNA SP101/28/145; SP 101/29 unfolio, Newsletters foreign, Germany 1626–1631; *Documenta Bohemica Bellum Tricennale Illustratntia*, vol. 4 p. 74; SP 80/8/167 Anstruther to Sir Henry Vane.

10. Musketeers, from Rudolph Meyer's series depicting soldiers of the Thirty Years' War, 1618–1638. (Rijksmuseum)

Imperial service due to lack of pay and so Hirchperger was unable to raise his regiment.[9]

Another problem was that towns and cities often refused to allow the recruiting party to 'beat the drum', the usual sign for raising recruits. On 10 March 1629 the burgers of the city of Nuremberg gave Captain Christopher Fontana of Wallenstein's Army permission to recruit only in the suburbs without the beat of the drum and he was not allowed to recruit any citizens of the town, only 'foreigners' and travellers. Fontana's company was also to leave Nuremberg as soon as it has been recruited and not be a burden to the city.[10]

There were many reasons why someone chose to join the army, including social deprivation or even trickery as one Swedish officer attempted in 1643: After failing to find enough recruits for his company he is reported to have thrown money into the streets of Erfurt and if an unsuspecting person

9 TNA SP101/42/169, 431, Newsletters foreign, Germany, Austria, Bohemia and Hungary, 1620–1665; TNA SP101/28/9, 28, Newsletters foreign, Germany,1620–1625, TNA SP 101/46/104, Newsletters foreign, Holland (United Provinces) 1623–1626; SP 101/30/15, 22 Newsletters foreign, Germany, 1632–1634.

10 TNA SP 81/13/174 *Advise from Swabland 13/23 August 1628.*

picked it up then he was deemed to have accepted the levy money or would face imprisonment as a deserter.

A ruler of a territory might resort to 'impressment', or conscription, such as the Duke of Brandenburg who in May 1623 decided to raise an army of 3,000 foot and 500 horse. One man in five was to be 'impressed' in the towns and cities and one in every 10 in the countryside.

All eligible men were ordered to report to a muster place, where they would hear their fate: whether they would be conscripted or not. Usually this was decided by ballot, although being a burden to the area, such as being unemployed (or masterless) men, or vagabonds, almost certainly guaranteed conscription into the army. However, as the war progressed more and more men who were valued by the parish would be enlisted, including labourers and servants.

In his *Pallas Armata* Sir James Turner, who fought in the Thirty Years' War, states:

> most captains conceive sixteen to be too young, and if so I swear sixty is too old; they need not be twenty … [but] they may pass muster of eighteen; and if they be not infirm wounded or mutilated, they may well enough continue [being] soldiers till they be fifty and upwards, though some think they should not serve after the forty six years of their age.[11]

In Sweden the minimum age of conscription was 15, and it was only in 1633 that the maximum age was to be 60. However, the following chart shows a breakdown of conscripts from Bygdeå in Sweden and shows that just three teenagers were conscripted between 1623 to 1631, but 76 were recruited between 1633 to 1639, whereas there was a steady decline in men in their 30s during this period. Although three men between 45 and 49 were conscripted, in 1637 men in their late 40s and early 50s were again being conscripted.[12]

Ages	1623	1627	1628	1629	1630	1631	1633	1637	1638	1639	Total
15–19	-	-	-	2	-	1	7	25	20	24	79
20–24	-	1	-	5	1	6	8	13	4	3	44
25–29	2	-	1	2	-	4	2	4	-	1	19
30–34	5	5	4	-	-	-	1	2	1	1	18
35–39	1	2	3	1	-	3	1	-	-	-	11
40–44	-	-	3	2	-	1	1	3	-	1	8
45–49	-	3	-	-	-	-	-	3	-	-	6
50–54	-	-	-	-	-	-	-	1	-	-	1
Total	10	11	11	12	1	15	20	51	25	30	186

It was the responsibility of the Swedish clergy to draw up lists of men eligible to serve. The men on this list were divided into a *rote*, each *rote* having to supply a certain number of conscripts. Research carried out by Jan Lindegren shows that the Swedish town of Bygdeå sent 236 conscripts to the Swedish

11 Sir James Turner, *Pallas Armata* (London, 1683), p.166.

12 Jan Lindegren, *Utskrivning och utsugning Produktion och Reproduktion I Bygdeå, 1620–1640* (Stockholm: Almqvist and Wiksell International, 1980), p.151.

11. Training of the military horse. Johann Jacobi von Wallhausen, ***Ritterkunst***, 1616. (Michał Paradowski's archive)

Army of which 215 died. One woman known by the name of Anna from the parish of Rassboo heard that her husband, Johan, had died in 1626 while serving in the Swedish Army. As the years passed Anna met Madz Persson from a nearby village and they had a child. In 1638 Anna and Madz wanted to marry, but then she discovered her husband was still alive and she was sentenced to death for adultery, although it is unlikely this sentence was carried out and she was most likely fined.[13]

During the Danish period of the war, Christian IV found it very difficult to raise recruits in north Germany since he had to compete for them with other powers. Moreover, since the Danish government saw it as a foreign war it refused to raise soldiers within Denmark itself, which forced Christian to finance the raising of 3,000 infantry himself within the country.[14]

Once selected the conscript would return home to put his affairs in order, but this gave him time to escape. Among those who decided to run away was Jöns Leinonen from Säminge, who in 1629, finding himself conscripted into the Swedish Army, ran away with his family to Kexholm. However, his *rote* still had to meet its quota of conscripts so a Mats Persson was chosen to go in Leinionen's place. Persson was sent to Germany in 1630 and was still with the army the following year, but then he disappears from history. Therefore it was in the interest of the other members of a conscript's *rote* to prevent him running away; in 1638 the province of Nyland appears to have shaved the

13 Michael Roberts, *Gustavus Adolphus, a History of Sweden 1611–1632* (London: Longmans, Green and Co., 1958), vol. 2, p.208; Mary Elizabeth Ailes, *Courage and Grief, Women and Sweden's Thirty Years' War* (Lincoln: University of Nebraska, 2018), pp. 66–67, 80.

14 Paul Lockhart, *Denmark in the Thirty Years' War, 1618–1648: King Christian IV and the Decline of the Oldenburg State* (Selinsgrove: Susquehanna University Press, 1996), p.136.

heads of the conscripts to mark them out from the rest of the community. Some conscripts appeared to prefer mutilating themselves to avoid military service. Possibly one of these was Lars Josefsson from Alavieska in Sweden, who in 1629 was conscripted into the Swedish Army, but broke his leg; whether deliberately it is not known, but probably as an example to the rest of the settlements, instead of replacing him the authorities allowed him to recover before sending him to the army in Germany. He died at Wismar during the autumn of 1631.[15]

A person who had been conscripted could also hire a substitute, but this would depend on whether he could afford to pay for someone to go in his place. If this substitute deserted en route then the original person had to take his place. In 1627 Gustavus Adolphus forbade the hiring of substitutes except at the muster place or if they were peasants on a noble's estate. In 1630 he prohibited all peasants to hire substitutes, but this was relaxed the following year, but only when the conscripts were being mustered.[16]

Although conscription was a cheaper option of raising an army, rather than hiring mercenaries, heads of state had a low opinion of them. Writing during the Kalmar War of 1611–1613 King Christian IV of Denmark described his conscripts as 'worse than beasts', whereas Maximilian of Bavaria wrote on 10 December 1632 that, 'experience has proved that conscription of subjects is of no use whatsoever, and that any expenditure on them is nearly futile and a waste.'[17]

12. Army on parade. Jacques Callot, 1628. (Rijksmuseum)

How many conscripts served in Wallenstein's Army is not known. Unlike Maximilian of Bavaria's Catholic League Army, Wallenstein allowed Protestants within his army, but on 28 April 1626 a letter printed in a news sheet recorded that:

> The Circle of Lower Saxony hath commanded by a public proclamation all subjects that serve their enemy, to come home under pain of confiscation of their goods. Adding that all those as profess themselves Protestant and yet notwithstanding do fight against the same religion should be put to death, wheresoever they were taken. This is said to diminish much the forces of Wallenstein.[18]

One way of obtaining a large number of well-trained soldiers was offering prisoners of war the option of changing sides. The Protestant, but mutinous, garrison of Cassel during the summer of 1627 is said have been bribed by Wallenstein in to not only giving up to the town to him but, 'almost all the soldiers, allured by some ready money of Wallenstein were received into his army.' However, soldiers did not necessarily have to change sides: when Wallenstein was raising his army, many of Tilly's soldiers deserted to enlist under Wallenstein, knowing that newly raised regiments would have better resources available to them.[19]

Once raised, the recruits, whether mercenaries or conscripts, were assembled at an appointed *Laufplatz* within their town or village. It was here that they would receive a sum of money, or *werbgeld*, which was also known as *Handgeld*. The amount would depend on how much demand there was for recruits at the time, but it marked the recruit's process from a civilian life into that of a soldier. They would then be sent to the rendezvous or *Sammelplatz* (assembly place) in the district, before being marching to the *Musterplatz* (muster place) of the regiment.

The recruit would receive an allowance, or *laufgeld*, which would cover his travelling expenses to the muster place, which was between eight and 13 thalers a day. Sometimes the recruits appear to have made their own way to the muster place, which had been common practice in the sixteenth century, but it was also an opportunity for them to desert. It was not unknown for a

13. Recruitment of the troops. Jacques Callot, 1629-1633. (Rijksmuseum)

14. Cavalry charge. Jan Martszen de Jonge, 1629. (Rijksmuseum)

recruit to desert and then re-enlist in another regiment and so claim a further bounty, although if he was caught then he would be severely punished.[20]

In January 1625 Ferdinand's instructions to Wallenstein stated that the muster place was to remain for '15 days and no longer'. Maximilian in 1611 had specified that the recruits had six days to arrive at the muster place, where they would be drilled and then on the ninth day they would be inspected by their officers. During this time recruits would also swear an oath of allegiance to the Emperor and their officers. There is also some evidence from surviving colour poles that the recruit may have hammered a nail into the staff of their company's colour so reinforcing their commitment to the company.[21]

According to the *Keiserliche Kriegssverfassung* (Imperial Quartering in Wartime) which was issued to the Imperialist Army in 1626, the commissioner were to keep a register of all the recruits which recorded his name, any previous service, the date of enlistment, his age, father's and mother's name and any distinguishing marks. Sometimes the recruit's profession was also recorded.[22]

20 Redlich, Fritz, *The German Military Enterpriser* vol. 1, pp.272–273.

21 'Kaiserliche Instruktion fur Wallenstein' printed in Gottfried Lorenz, *Quellen zur Geschichte Wallensteins* (Darmstadt, 1987), pp.93–94.

22 Anon., *Keiserliche Kriegssverfassung oder Articles Brief: Darauff der Romischen Keiserliche zu Hungarn und Boheimb Koniglichen Mayestat zu Soldatesca so wol zu Ross als zu Fuss bei Auffrichtung eines jeden Regiments gelobt und geschworen* (1626), p.6 paragraph xi.

15. Imperial or Spanish infantry in 1634. Pieter Snayers (Nationalmuseum, Stockholm)

The muster place had to be chosen carefully because sometimes the enemy on hearing that a regiment was mustering at a certain town would sent a detachment to break up the formation of the regiment. If this did not happen then such was the disruption that some towns and cities paid a ransom to stop it being used as a muster place, such as Nuremberg in 1625 whose inhabitants paid 100,000 florins to stop it being used as a muster place or having a garrison imposed on it. However, if Nuremberg thought this was an end to the matter it was sadly mistaken, as in 1627 a further 60,000 florins were paid, including 16,500 to Hans George Margrave of Brandenburg, a further 900 to Duke Julius Heinrich von Saxe-Lauenburg, and 183 florins to his lieutenant-colonel, not to use the city as a muster place. The following year Nuremberg paid another 100,000 florins. Other payments were made to officers to make their troops move on quickly, or if they were forced to quarter within the city then the officers were to guarantee their men's good behaviour.[23]

Nuremberg probably hoped that with the defeat of Christian IV of Denmark this financial burden would cease, but between 1629 and 1630 the city had to pay the largest amount to date, 180,000 florins, which was followed from June 1630 to June 1631 by a staggering 240,000 florins.[24]

23 TNA SP 101/46/104, Redlich, *The Germany Military Enterpriser*, pp.339–341.

24 Redlich, 'Contributions in the Thirty Years' War', p.249.

Despite payments like those of Nuremberg, Wallenstein was not finding it easy to raise his army. According to the newssheet *Advise from Bonn* on 5 August 1628:

> Divers troops of the Imperialists (in the circle of Swabland) are daily cashiered without pay so that they should make any head amongst them they might make some new trouble … Wallenstein [is] to borrow in Italy 2 million for the Emperor's promising interest of 12 for 100 and offering withall for warrant such an Imperial town as the creditors will choose. Assuring that Wallenstein is able to cause any Imperialist town to be bound to him.[25]

Even before the defeat of the Danish Army there were calls to reduce his army's size, since the Catholic rulers feared Ferdinand and Wallenstein was becoming too powerful as the newssheet *Advice from Schwabland* for 21 June 1628 records:

> It is general reported that the Emperor's forces are … either to make a general reformation of religion or else upon some design to weaken the princes and Lords that have any power yet others of the opinion that the Emperor regards no more the Electors and that he means to make himself absolute and to make the empire hereditary.

The princes complained to Ferdinand 'not to put too much trust in Wallenstein'.[26]

Therefore when Wallenstein defeated King Christian IV's Danish Army at the battle of Wolgast in 1628, the political pressure on Ferdinand became too much and according to the *Advise from Bonn* for 26 September 1628, it was decided that 'Wallenstein's Army shall be reduced unto some 50 companies of horse and about thirty thousand foot'; although in a later edition the *Advise from Bonn* doubted if he would obey. It was not until 13 August 1630 that the Catholic rulers finally got their way and Wallenstein was dismissed. The regiments of his army now came under Johan von Tilly, the general of the Catholic League's forces.[27]

However, in December 1631 Wallenstein was reappointed commander-in-chief of the Imperialist Army after Gustavus Adolphus of Sweden's entry into the war and his defeat of General Tilly at the battle of Breitenfeld on 17 September 1631. Wallenstein set about increasing the strength of the Imperialist Army once more, and according to *Advise from Divers Parts of Germany* on 21 January 1632 he boasted that he would have 80,000 men in the field by Easter, 'but it is well known that there is a great want both of men and money.' A letter from Rome dated January 1632 records:

> Wallenstein shall return into the field with 100,000 foot and 60,000 horse but this cannot be done without great sums of money and because they cannot have it

25 TNA SP 101/29/167 *Advise from Bonn,* 5 August 1628.

26 TNA SP 101/73/173, *Advice from Schwabland* 21 June 1628.

27 TNA SP 101/29/200, 205, *Advise from Bonn,* 26 September 1628, 29 September 1628.

> elsewhere it is necessary then the Churches of Spain should assist for the defence of the Catholic Religion ... since the rest of the Catholics [of Europe] ... will not assist.[28]

In another newssheet, dated 13 May 1632, Wallenstein is said to have just '20,000 men ... ill armed and unwilling to fight. And Wallenstein himself desires to have three months pay before he [will] march.'[29]

Regiments during their existence might march thousands of miles over the years, such as Berthold von Waldstein's Regiment of Foot, which was raised on 2 April 1629. It first campaigned in Mecklenburg between 1629 and 1630, then the following year it was sent to Landsberg. In 1632 it campaigned in Bohemia and then Saxony and was present at Nuremberg (Alte Veste) and Lützen, where the colonel was mortally wounded. Under his brother, Maximilian, the regiment appears to have served in Bohemia again between 1633 until 1637, when it moved to the Upper Rhine and was present at the battle of Wittenweier, before serving in Upper Germany. In 1642 under a new colonel, Carl Friedrich Reich, it was present at the second battle of Leipzig and at the end of that year was incorporated into Archduke Leopold's Lifeguard. Whereas Colonel Conrad Bohm's Regiment, which was commissioned to be raised on 9 May 1631, remained in Silesia until 1634 when it also appears to have been incorporated into another regiment.[30]

28 TNA SP101/30/15, *Advise from Divers Parts of Germany* on 21 January 1632; SP 101/74 f.3, 94 Anonymous letter from Rome, 23 January 1632.

29 TNA SP101/30/212, *Advise from Nuremberg*, 13 May 1632.

30 Wrede, *Geschichte der K. und K. Wehrmacht*, vol. II pp.35, 43.

3

Clothing

It is usually said that Wallenstein was one of the first commanders to issue clothing to his soldiers. However this is not so: soldiers' uniforms are known to have existed in the sixteenth century and probably long before that, and a news sheet dated 4 October 1622 reported that the Marquis de Montenegro's soldiers:

> returning from Hungary, Moravia and Silesia were so tattered, torn and in a manner of countenance, when they came to civil places that he was compelled to take order for the new arming and apparelling [of them], dispersing great sums among them for their further satisfaction.[1]

On 20 October 1621 Colonel Collalto received 8,000 florins for 'livery' and armaments for 1,500 men of his regiment. Unfortunately the colour of this livery is not recorded, although in 1630 his regiment was known to have worn blue coats. Other warrants do not record any livery, such as the order granted to Jiriho Seldra of Prague, dated 4 October 1622, who was supplying suits of clothing, stockings and shoes to the Imperialist Army. Another merchant was George Ayermann of Nuremburg, who in 1625 was ordered to supply 2,400 musketeer's coats to Colonel Wolfgang von Mansfeld's Regiment of Musketeers.[2]

Unfortunately the colour of the clothing supplied by Seldra or Ayermann is not recorded, but this is not to say they were not of one colour, because when making out a receipt the number of coats etc. received was more important to the clerks rather than their colour. Johan von Wallhausen recommends that the colour of the coats should be 'blue, red, yellow etc (and other colours except black).' Whereas Edward Davies in 1619 suggests that they be made of 'cloth of [a] fresh colour … red, murrey, tawney and scarlet makes a gallant show in the field.'[3]

1 *A True Relation of the Affairs of Europe*, 4 October 1622.

2 Anton Ernstberger, *Hans de Witte, Finanzmann Wallensteins* (Wiesbaden: Franz Steiner, 1954) p.242; V. Liva, *Prameny k Dejinam Tricetilete Valky, 1618–1625*, vol. 3 (Prague, 1951), pp. 206, 363.

3 Edward Davies, *The Art of War and English Training* (1619), p.24. OED Murray = mulberry, or purple red colour.

In 1630 Collalto's Regiment of Foot wore blue coats, whereas Schaffenburg's Regiment are known to have worn yellow coats. George Gush has also suggested that Maximilian von Waldstein's Regiment wore yellow coats and that his brother Berthold's wore green coats since they were the colours of their ensigns. Unfortunately, neither George Gush or Francis Watson, who also mentions the colours of their ensigns, gives a source for this information, and I have found evidence for neither coat nor ensigns for these two regiments.[4]

It is also possible that a regiment changed the colour of its coats when new clothing was issue to the regiment, (see below) although it would not be until 1708 that the Imperial Council of War adopted pearl grey uniforms for the Austrian infantry soldiers. On the 30 September 1632 36,000 Ells or 1,200 pieces of grey or silver coloured cloth were ordered for clothing which was probably for 6,000 suits which were ordered for the soldiers, which gives an average of six ells.[5]

In 1645 Count Mathias Gallas' sent samples of grey cloth to make coats, breeches, stockings and shirts. Gallas' notes and sample still survive and are held by the Army Museum in Vienna. These show that he intended to clothe his regiment of foot in three sizes using five, six and seven ells of great cloth. The shirts were to be of white linen.[6] In 1646 the Bavarian Army also made their coats in three sizes, which were made from either two, two and three quarter or even three ells of cloth, presumably depending on the size of the soldier, and their breeches were made from two ells of cloth, which are somewhat smaller to those ordered by Gallas, so may be of different styles. Unfortunately, accounts for other armies only list the number of coats supplied and the cost of making them, rather than any sizes, so other armies might also have supplied their men in three sizes.[7] A soldier was meant to receive a new set of clothes each year, usually before the onset of winter. No shoes are mentioned mention in Gallas' order, but shoes and stockings are more common since they wore out more quickly than the other items of clothing.

The type of coat supplied by George Ayermann is described as a *schutzenrock*, which is just one of numerous styles mentioned in the contracts for clothing, which include cassocks, which may have been another name for the *schutzenrocks* since both were loose-fitting so that the musketeers could hide their muskets, match, and gunpowder under their coats when it was raining. They could also keep the soldier warm at night. The *Kaiserliche Kriegssverfassung* which was printed in 1626 recorded that each recruit

4 George Gush, *Renaissance Armies, 1480–1650* (Cambridge: Patrick Stephens, 1975) p.76; Watson, Francis *Wallenstein, Soldier under Saturn,* (London, Chatto and Windus, 1938) p.366. For other coat colours see Appendix 1.

5 Ernstberger, *Wallenstein als Volkswirt in Herzogtum Friedland* (Reichenberg i.B.: Sudetendeutscher Verlag Franz Kraus, 1929), pp.78, 81 quoting National Archives of Prague reference F67/1/5 Hauptbuch 30 September 1632 and 10 October 1632. Unfortunately, since Dr Ernstberger wrote this book the archives have been renumbered and this 30 September 1632 letter can no longer be found.

6 Display in the Thirty Years' War Gallery of the Army Museum at Vienna.

7 Bavarian Main Archives, Kurbayern Ausseres ms 2883.

should receive an 'overcoat or coat' to keep him warm and keep him dry when it rained.[8]

There are also references to coats and 'Hungarian coats', the latter of which seem to have been popular with the Imperialist and Swedish Armies. Hungarian coats appear to have been tight fitting. One tight-fitting coat dating from about 1600 was in a Berlin Armoury before the outbreak of the Second World War. Unfortunately this coat now only appears to survive in a black and white photograph, but appears to have had about 16 buttons down the front, large 'wings' or pieces of cloth at the top of the sleeve, and a stand-up collar which seems to have been fastened possibly by hooks and eyes. The edges of the coat, and the bottom of the collar were laced. The wings were also laced with about 10 thin strips of lace running from edge to edge. Judging from the photograph the buttons seem to be the same colour as the lace, which suggests they might have been cloth-covered buttons.

An order for coats and breeches for Guard of the Elector of Brandenburg in 1620, the items were to be made of five ells of a 'good blue' cloth, plus five ells of an unspecified colour for the lining and 12 ells of white, black and red stiff ribbon. The coats and breeches were to have six dozen bows and three dozen iron buttons, plus a hat. An ell of thread was used to trim the cassock. Whereas in June 1626 the 1,100 horse and 2,000 foot of the Brandenburg militia had red, yellow and blue and light grey clothing, although his field army is known to have worn blue coats with different coloured facings. Later illustrations of soldiers show lace bows on the shoulders and waist of their coats.[9]

In the grave of two soldiers killed at the siege of Stralsund in 1628, were found the remnants of a jacket or doublet. It had 28 hemispherical lead buttons about 1 cm wide, with iron, copper, or nickel eyes to fasten the button to the coat. Eight buttons fastened in a row in the front of the coat, along with three buttons in two rows at the waist of the coat and a further seven buttons were on each forearm of the sleeve. Eleven similar buttons were found in a mass grave on the battlefield of Wittstock, along with six pairs of hooks and eyes of various sizes.[10] Lead buttons were handy for musketeers, because at the battle of Zablat on 10 June 1619 Count Ernest von Mansfeld records that, 'having spent all their bullets as also the buttons of their doublets, and their powder', his infantry surrendered.[11] No buttons appear to have been found near the second skeleton in the Stralsund grave; if he was wearing a coat then

8 Anon., *Keyserliche Kriegssverfassung oder ArticulsBrieff: Darauff der Römischen Keyserliche, auch zu Hungarn und Böheimb Königlichen Mayestät, etc. zu Soldatesca so wol zu Ross als zu Fuss bei Auffrichtung eines jeden Regiments gelobt und geschworen* (1626), p.27 paragraph v.

9 A.C. von der Oelsnitz, *Geschichte des Königlich Preussischen Ersten Infanterie-Regiments* (Berlin: E.S. Mittler and Son, 1855) pp.18, 20.

10 Konze et al., 'Der the siege Laufgraben von 1628 – Verschüttette Söldner und Waffen in sit. Festungsbau im Süden der Hansestadt (Quartier Frankenhof) im Spiegel archäologischer Befunde und historischer Quellen', in *Forschungen zur Archaologie im Land Brandenburg* (2014) vol. 15, pp.208–209; Sabrine Eickhoff, and Franz Schopper, *1636 Ihre Letze Schlacht* (Archäologisches Landesmuseum Brandenburg, 2012), pp.174–175.

11 Count Ernst von Mansfeld, *The Appollogie of the illustrious Prince Ernestus, Earle of Mansfeld etc. ... Translated out of the French copie*, by SW (Heidelberg, 1622), p.13.

16. (left, top): Musketeer and officer/NCO, from Rudolph Meyer's series depicting soldiers of the Thirty Years' War, 1618–1638. (Rijksmuseum)

17. (left, below): Pikeman and officer/NCO, from Rudolph Meyer's series depicting soldiers of the Thirty Years' War, 1618–1638. (Rijksmuseum)

the buttons either have not survived for example if they were made of cloth, or the coat was fastened in a different way.

Certainly cloth buttons or buttons covered with cloth are also known to have been sewn to soldiers coats, or it might have been like the soldier's coat which is preserved at The Hermitage in St Petersburg. It is a loose-fitting garment with baggy sleeves and made of red woollen cloth with white lining. A large white Burgundian cross is sewn to the front and back of the coat as well as the sleeves. It does not have any buttons, but is sewn together with a V-neck, so that the soldier could pull it over his head. Although it is said to date from the late sixteenth century, paintings of the battle of the White Mountain (8 November 1620) which are preserved in the Maria della Victoria Church in Rome show similar coats but blue with the white Burgundian cross. How long this style lasted is not known, but as one would expect styles changed greatly during the war. Originally only musketeers were issued with coats.

Among the many towns in the Holy Roman Empire to produce cloth was Reichenberg. In 1621 there were about 35 cloth mills at Reichenberg, but when Wallenstein became the town's owner he established 76 new cloth mills between 1622 and 1634. After his death these mills passed to Gallas and they continued to supply cloth to the Imperialist war effort. Under Gallas the number of clothiers appears to have increased by another 20 between 1635 and 1637 and a further 28 between 1638 and 1645. In 1628 these mills were producing blue, red, black, and grey cloth in two widths, two and two and a half ells. Blue cloth appears to have been the most popular colour for the Reichenberg merchants. Cologne and Aachen are also known to have supplied clothing to the Imperialists as well as other armies.[12]

This cloth would be purchased by merchants like Jiriho Seldra and George Ayermann who would have their own team of tailors and seamstresses, such as Robert Swann of England who employed 300 to 400 men and women to make shirts for the Duke of Buckingham's Army.[13] Tailors would usually cut out the various parts of the coats etc., to be sewn by lesser skilled workers. In theory outer garments were made by male tailors who had served a seven-year apprenticeship, whereas shirts etc. were mostly made by women. However to save money some merchants hired 'foreigners', who did not belong to a guild and were therefore considered unskilled labour, and who were much cheaper than their professional counterparts but produced

12 Joseph Grunzel, 'Die Reichenberger Tuchindustrie', in *Vereines Für Geschichte der Deutschen in Bohemia* (Prague, 1893), no. 5, pp.54, 56, 59.

13 TNA SP 16/34/112, Petition of Robert Swann, ?August 1626, AO1/299/1135 Roll, Sir William St Leger Colonel and land forces in the Expedition to Cadiz, 4 July to 31 October 1625.

poor quality clothing. Clothing made by this unskilled labour was likely to split or fall apart when worn. Another trick of the merchants was to make the clothing from cloth which had not been soaked to make it shrink, or to stretch the cloth so that it would make more clothes. Unfortunately, this meant when it did rain the clothing would shrink and be too small for the soldier. To prevent these abuses the clothing was meant to be brought to an arsenal to be inspected to see if the clothing was suitable to be issued to the soldiers. Unfortunately for the merchants, paying for the clothing was not high on the government's agenda and so many merchants would sometimes have to wait for years before they were paid.

There is some evidence to suggest that special clothing factories were established to make the clothing centrally and so increase production. Gustavus Adolphus planned to set up a magazine or factory, which was to employ between 40 and 50 tailors to make army uniforms. Unfortunately, the Swedish state papers for this period do not survive so we do not know if it was established or organised, but in a letter dated 18 June 1632, concerning clothing eight regiments of foot and 3,000 horse, Gustavus does refer to 'clothes makers or factories' and also to a 'clothing store'. During the English Civil War King Charles I is also known to have set up a similar factory in the Music School and the Astronomy School at Oxford University and possibly another one in Reading, since all the tailors from the surrounding area were ordered to come to the town to produce clothing for the main Royalist Army. So these types of factories were known at this time. Anthony Wood, who was a schoolboy in Oxford during the war, recorded that in the factory:

> [There] were a great many tailors, as well as foreigners as townsmen, set on work to cut out these coats, to the number [of] 4,000 or 5,000) as I was told which presently afterwards put forth to the tailors here, [the] inhabitants and to strangers within ten miles who were called into Oxford to be made up and finished.[14]

There is also some evidence to suggest that the clothing may have been made according to a relevant pattern, certainly that issued to English troops in the 1620s was to be copied from patterns in the Royal Wardrobe, and there is a hat said to be the pattern worn by Queen Christina's infantry during the latter part of the war.

To prevent corruption by the merchants who supplied the clothing, two people were meant to inspect the clothes to make sure that they were suitable to be issued to the soldiers. As one 1606 clothing contract put it, once the order had been completed it was to be:

> Brought to such convenient place or places … to be viewed and there shall suffer and permit the persons that shall be appointed... for viewing of the said apparel

14 Erik Bellander, *Dräkt och Uniform: den Svenska Arméns beklädnad från 1500-talets början fram till åara dagar* (Stockholm: Norstedt och Söners, 1973), p.588; Letter No. 460 'Bref fran Konungen till Riks-Radet Claes Fleming, 18 June 1632', printed in Upland, H.K.H. Prins Gustaf, Duke of, *Arkiv till upplysning om Svenska Krigens och Krigsinrättningarnes historia* (Stockholm, 1854), pp.634–635; David and Hillary Hopkins, *The Tale of a Soldier's Coat* (Stuart Press, 2000), p.5.

> to see, visit and survey every part and parcel thereof. To the end that they find the same apparel agreeable with the patterns may give their allowance of the transportation thereof, or disallow and reject such part of the same as they shall see to be defective and not answerable to the patterns.[15]

It was believed that there should be at least two examiners because it was feared that the merchant might try to bribe a single examiner, although nobody seems to have thought of the possibility that both examiners might have been bribed.

Once the examiners were satisfied that all the clothing was correct it was to be:

> Put in several packs … The pack to be sealed with the particular seal of the said persons or some other common seal to be agreed upon by them which packs so sealed shall without restraint of any officers of the Customs House [to be] immediately transported and not opened either here or beyond seas until they arrive at the garrison or place … Whereunto the same shall be consigned and there seen by the commissary of the muster being now the deliverer of the apparel … The same to be opened and the apparel immediately distributed to every company.[16]

During the English Civil War these packs or 'dry fats' as they are also known, contained about 500 coats and were numbered and loaded onto carts to be transported to the army. Unfortunately it is not known whether the clothing within each bundle of clothing was the same colour, although presumably a numbered dry fat was allocated to a particular regiment. However, there are examples of some of this clothing becoming rotten due to getting wet during transportation due to foul weather; or even being stolen.

If an army overran the enemy's territory then it might be lucky enough to capture supplies of clothes, such as when the Swedish Army occupied Munich in 1632: they found between 8,000 and 10,000 soldiers' clothes under the floor of the arsenal, which according to *Theatrum Europaeum*, were 'newly made soldiers' coats of yellow, blue, and green colour which were distributed to some regiments under the Swedish Army.' Not only did this mean Gustavus Adolphus could resupply his own army, but also he could deprive the Bavarian Army of their next issue of clothing. The Swedish were lucky again in 1642 when they captured an 'abundance of soldiers' coats and other provisions' from Piccolomini.[17]

---

15 TNA E351/170, U. Babington and R. Bromley Contract for Clothing 30 September 1602 to 1 April 1606.

16 TNA E351/170, U. Babington and R Bromley Contract for Clothing 30 September 1602 to 1 April 1606.

17 Dr Adolf Danner, 'Der Kommierzienrat in Bayern im 17 Jahrundert' part 1 Under Maximilian I', *Oberbayerisches Archiv fur Vaterländische Geschichte* (München, 1910), p.277; Erik Bellander, *Dräkt och Uniform*, p.590; Monro part II, p.125; *Theatrum Europaeum*, vol. 2, p.645; Franz Christoph Khevenhüller, *Annales Ferdinandi* (Leipzig, 1727), vol. 12, p.142; British Library Thomason Tracts E 107/7, *News from Foreign parts July 1642*.

18. (left): pikeman, 19. (below and bottom left): musketeers.
Jacob de Gheyn, ***De Wapenhandelinghe van Roers, Musketten ende Spiesen, 1607*** (Rijksmuseum)

A number of letters survive which show that Wallenstein was interested in clothing his men. The first was written on the 13 June 1626 by Wallenstein to his cousin Maximilian von Waldstein requesting 4,000 suits of soldiers' clothing: jackets, to be made of cloth with lined with linen, and cloth breeches and stockings. This clothing was to be well made and delivered into the camp by the end of August. On 6 August 1627 Wallenstein wrote to Taxis that the Kriegszahlmeister or the Army Pay Master must pay 13,000 Reichsthalers for shoes and stockings and on 9 August a further 40,000 thalers were to be paid for soldiers' clothing in Gitschin. There was also an order for 4,605 suits for the same year, but whether this in addition to the other coats is not clear. Certainly Wallenstein's Army mustered more than 4,000 at this time because he also ordered 10,000 pairs of shoes.[18]

On 10 October 1632 Wallenstein requested a further 6,000 suits including stockings for his army, the coats to be 'Hungarian Jackets, lined with linen, a pair of cloth breeches and a cloth pair of stockings.' This clothing had to be of good quality and the merchants were given seven weeks to complete this order, although 3,000 suits were to be delivered within three weeks. It may be for this order of clothing that on 30 September 1632 36,000 ells or 1,200 pieces of grey or silver-coloured cloth were to be supplied.[19] Which regiments these clothes were allocated to is not recorded. Neither did the supply of clothing dry up after Wallenstein's assassination in February 1634. On 13 January 1637 2,021 coats of 'coarse cloth' and lined, 3,018 pairs of shoes and 3,000 pairs of stockings were delivered to Adjutant General Count Ernest von Konigsneck and on 19 January 1642 Count Rudolf Colleredo wrote to Hatzfeldt asking that clothing be sent to Cologne for his men.

However, this clothing came nowhere near the clothing the entire army and there is evidence that regiments tried to obtain their own clothing. Why this is so is not known, but for at least some regiments it meant that colonels and their company commanders were always on the lookout for new sources of clothing for their men. In 1628 or 1629 Wallenstein received 1,000 ells of light blue cloth, 300 ells of carmine red and 100 red pairs of stockings from England via Amsterdam probably to clothe his own regiment of foot since red and blue were his livery colours. On 25 February 1629 Wallenstein wrote to Walter de Hertoge that the cloth and stockings must be of good quality otherwise it was of 'little use' and that he would not accept it.[20]

The archives of Colonel Julius von Hardegg's Regiment record that in May 1632 Tobias Verlohrn from Schweidnitz supplied 130 ells of blue and 67 ells of red cloth for the colonel's company, which were also the colours of Julius von Hardegg's coat of arms. The red cloth was to be used for the coat's lining and on 25 July 1632 a payment was made to Paul von Addsdorff, the captain lieutenant

18 Dr Friedrich Forster, *Wallenstein, Herzog zu Mecklenburg, Friedland und Sagan* (Potsdam: Ferdinand Riegel, 1834), p.53; Sombart, Werner *Studien zur Entwicklungsgeschichte des Modernen Kapitalism* (Munich and Leipzig, 1913), p.169.

19 Ernstberger, *Wallenstein als Volkswirt in Herzogtum Friedland*, pp. 78, 81 quoting National Archives of Prague reference F67/1/5 Hauptbuch 30 September 1632 and 10 October 1632.

20 Ernstberger, *Hans de Witte, Finanzmann*, p.287; Auguste Hanauer, *Trente Guerre Ans a Haguenau* (Colmar: H. Hufel, 1907), pp.138, 138, 175; Geoffrey Parker, *The Thirty Years' War* (London: Rouledge and Kegan Paul, 1987), p.192.

20. Cavalry skirmish. Johann Wilhelm Baur, 1636. (Rijksmuseum)

of Hardegg's Regiment, for 2,095 ells of linen thread, and yellow and blue lace from Reichenbach.[21] An account dated 9 September 1632 also mentions a payment of '15,000 fl' to Julius von Hardegg for the purchase of cloth.

In February 1633 Lieutenant-Colonel Mers wrote to Hardegg for money 'in order to buy clothes' for the soldiers because the colonel may get 'a bad reputation' otherwise.[22] While some regiments do appear to have tried to keep the same colour coats throughout their existence, others probably used whatever colour cloth they could find, therefore in 1634 Hardegg's Regiment appears to have been issued with red coats faced blue, which although still his livery colours, was the reverse of what they had been two years previously.

On 17 March 1635 when Hardegg's Regiment was in still in winter quarters around Jugbunzlau, when Ensign Johan Streusser of colonel's company wrote to Hardegg suggesting he had found a source of red material which was cheaper and of better quality than the 'livery cloth' used the year before. Not having received a reply from his colonel, Streusser again wrote to Julius von Hardegg, but this time he also sent some samples of the cloth. These samples have survived, one being double-width cloth and textured like Loden and cost 28 Reichsthalers for 21 Vienna ells long, and another was single width and was also similar to the first sample only a little more hairy and cost 13 Reichsthalers for 26 Vienna ells long. Streusser also sourced some blue lining material which cost 45 kreuzer per yard. On 24 June Streusser reported that he had obtained the cloth, but had no money to pay for it,

21 Hausmann, 'Das Regiment hochdeutscher Knechte des Grafen Julius von Hardegg' in *Der Dreissigjährige Krieg: Beiträge zu seiner Geschichte* (Vienna: Militarwissenschaftliches Institut, 1976), vol. 7, p.159, note 406.

22 Hausmann, 'Das Regiment hochdeutscher Knechte des Grafen Julius von Hardegg', p.131.

despite Hardegg having ordered the Principality of Troppau to pay for it on 14 April. However, by now the regiment had taken the field once more and so the cloth had to be sent to the regiment, which meant that the regiment had begun the campaign in their old 1634 clothes.[23]

In an undated warrant for 22 recruits to Hardegg's Regiment were ordered to have coats of an unspecified colour, but with red facings and 'silver coloured' or light grey cloth for the lining. In addition the coats were to have silk ribbons and buttons. Each recruit was also to be issued with a pair of breeches, a shirt, stockings and a hat for a total cost of 141 gulden and two kreuzers.[24]

Boots and shoes were also needed in great quantities since they quickly wore out. In February 1626 Wallenstein wrote to his administrator, Gerhard von Taxis:

21. Harquebusier, Johann Jacobi von Wallhausen, Ritterkunst, 1616. (Michał Paradowski's archive)

> Also have 10,000 pairs of shoes made for the infantry so that later I can divide them out among the regiments. Have them made in my towns and markets and pay a fair price for them in cash. See especially that the shoes are always carefully bound pair by pair, so that one will know which belong together. At the same time have leather prepared for I shall shortly order a further few thousand boots to be made. Have cloth ready also for it may be that clothes will be required.[25]

The city of Cologne supplied Colonels Pappenheim and Comargo with 20,000 pairs of shoes and 3,000 boots.[26] The towns of Schweidnitz and Reichenbach did not only supply cloth to the armies, but also shoes and in July 1632 six Schweidnitz shoemakers supplied 461 pairs of shoes to Hardegg's Regiment at a cost of 36 kreuzers each. A further 200 pairs of shoes were supplied by Reichenbach shoemakers to the same regiment shortly after for 36 kreuzer a pair. In November 1635 the town of Zabern supplied 66 pairs of shoes, which were distributed to those who needed them within Hardegg's Regiment, but now they cost one gulden and four kreuzers per pair. The town also seems to have supplied breeches and stockings for the regiment, but no coats are mentioned.[27]

When it comes to the cavalry there are fewer sources available. True the cuirassiers would have three-quarter armour, and the harquebusiers may have been issued with buffcoats, whether with sleeves or without. Certainly

23 Hausmann, 'Das Regiment hochdeutscher Knechte des Grafen Julius von Hardegg', pp.133–134..

24 Hausmann, 'Das Regiment hochdeutscher Knechte des Grafen Julius von Hardegg', p.132.

25 Quoted in Francis Watson, *Wallenstein, Soldier under Saturn* (London: Chatto and Windus, 1938), pp.177–178.

26 Johann Heilmann, *Kriegsgeschichte von Bayern, Franken, Pfalz und Schwaben von 1506 bis 1651* (München, 1868), vol. 2, pp.242, 910.

27 Hausmann, 'Das Regiment hochdeutscher Knechte des Grafen Julius von Hardegg', p.132.

22. Cavalry fighting infantry. Johann Wilhelm Baur, 1636. (Rijksmuseum)

surviving examples show that the sleeves could either be of cloth or leather. However, they would still need to be issued with breeches, shirts, stockings etc.

Wallenstein's Lifeguard had four troops, one of lancers, another of harquebusiers, a third of dragoons and a fourth of Croats, each mustering between 100 and 150 troopers. Later a fifth troop of dragoons was raised. In a letter dated 28 October 1626 the troop of lancers is described as wearing the full cuirassier armour, the lancers also had cassocks with black facings and red silk trimmings and large buttons. Their lances had yellow pennants. The 14 officers had gold trim for their cassocks and ornate buttons, the sleeves were armed with carmine red silk, while the trumpeters' coats had Turkish red silk lace.

The harquebusiers were similarly uniformed, except without armour apart from a helmet, and were armed with a carbine and red bandoliers, the officers and trumpeters were uniformed as those of the troop of lancers. The dragoons and Croats wore a similar uniform to the harquebusiers, but the Croats had a red fur hat. These troops were raised by Piccolomini and as one eyewitness who saw this regiment recalled, 'He brought with him all the way from Milan to the Baltic such beautifully adorned troops that the Duke [Wallenstein] mindful of his great endeavour, immediately provided him another regiment as compensation.' In another account, this time by Gualdo-Priorato, Piccolomini is said to have 'soon armed the latter extremely well and clothed them in a magnificent livery. So luxurious was their garb that the Duke refused to view them other than in the form of an artist's sketch.'[28]

However, since there was no standard uniformity within the armies to prevent a regiment attacking a friendly unit field signs were adopted, which could be a sprig of greenery in the hat or a piece of paper. The soldiers might also adopt a field word, such as 'Santa Maria' or 'Gott Mitt Uns'. The officer would wear a scarf either around their waist or over their shoulder. In 1626 Wallenstein wrote to Lieutenant-Colonel St Julien stating that the Emperor had instructed the Imperialists to wear red taffeta scarves to distinguish them from the enemy. Other nationalities' scarves were as follows:

Bohemia	Blue
Bavaria	Light blue or blue & white, although from 1635 red
Saxony	Red (1620–1624, after 1635) Yellow (other years)
Catholic League	Black, white scarves, white golden, red Yellow and after 1635 red scarves
Protestant States	Green scarves
France	White scarves
Sweden	Green or blue scarves
Hanseatic States	Black scarves
Dutch	Orange scarves
Spain	Red scarves
Baden	?Yellow-red scarves
Bohemia	Red-white scarves
Brunswick	Yellow-red scarves
Denmark	White scarves
Hesse	Blue or sky blue
Mansfeld (1620–1622)	Red-white or black and white
Weimar	Green, green golden, and in French service, white
England (1622)	Dark blue

28 Elster, *Die Piccolomini-Regimenter Während des 30jährigen Krieges*, pp.21–22; Thomas M. Barker, *Army, Aristocracy, Monarchy: Essays on War, Society and Government in Austria, 1618–1780* (New York: Columbia University Press, 1982), p.76.

4

Arms and Armour

In 1615 Johan Jacob von Wallhausen wrote, 'if you have a company of 300 men, consisting of 100 pikemen, 160 musketeers, 20 halberdiers and 20 with shield, or pikemen instead of halberdiers, making 120 pikemen, 160 musketeers and 20 with shield, as I consider the ones with shield more useful than halberdiers.'[1] However, Wallhausen was writing of his experiences at the beginning of the seventeenth century, by the time of the outbreak of the Thirty Years' War, very few soldiers with shields and bucklers appeared on the battlefield, and the days of those carrying a halberd were also numbered.

However, officers continued to carry a shield into the 1620s at least and sergeants carried halberds into at least the 1640s. Wallhausen also suggests that there was roughly a one to one ratio of pike to musket, but during the 1620s the ratio was much greater for musketeers, with some regiments being formed entirely of musketeers, especially if they were raised to form part of garrison a town or city.

In theory pikemen wore a back- and breastplate and tassets to protect the thighs and in the latter part of the sixteenth century, and possibly at the beginning of the seventeenth century, pauldrons which protected the arms. During the latter half of the 1620s some armourers also seem to have experimented with a type of metal 'skirt' at the front instead of the breastplate instead of tassets, but this does not appear to have been a success and tassets were reintroduced in the 1630s. In 1622 Francis Markham wrote a treatise on soldiers and their arms and recommended that pikemen should wear:

> Spanish morions well lined within which a quilted cap of strong housewives linen; for Buckram which is the usual lining is too course and galleth the soldier's head, as also is too stiff and unplyable by which means it will not quilt like the other. The ear plates shall be lined also.

There are several surviving examples of helmets having cotton lining, including two at the Wallace Collection in London. One is a red woollen and

1 Johan Jacob von Wallhausen, *L'Art Militaire pour l'infantie* (Uldrick Balck, 1615), p.71.

linen cap filled with raw cotton wadding, although this was designed for a burgonet helmet. The other is made of canvas and linen padded with bast.[2]

An undated document probably written in about 1614 records that pikeman's armour weighted as follows:

A headpiece	4 pounds
Gorget	2 pounds
Fore part [breastplate]	7 pounds
Back [plate]	4 pounds
Tassets	3 pounds
	20 pounds[3]

Surviving examples of the pike, which has been described as 'the Queen of the battlefield' have a varnished or 'well oiled' pole with various shaped pike heads. However, in November 1624 an order for '657 long pikes' for the English Army in Ireland were to be painted yellow. These were to be '16 feet long with a board head [in the] Spanish fashion'. Originally pikes were 22 feet long, but by the seventeenth century they had been reduced to between 15 and 18 feet.[4] They were made of ash about 1¾ inches thick. At the end of a pike was a steel head with two metal strips, about two feet long, running down the shaft of the pike, 'well riveted' to its side to prevent the head being cut off. It has been suggested that pikemen used to cut down their pikes to a more manageable size, but in the Dutch Army at least, this was forbidden since it would put him at a disadvantage when it came to battle and make a weakness in the formation.

Examples of Infantry carrying firearms date back to the Hundred Years War, but it was not until the early sixteenth century that they were carried in large numbers. However, their introduction was seen as unsoldierlike: Blasie de Monluc, who fought in the Italian Wars of 1521–1544, wrote that they were, 'the devil's invention to make us murder one another'., whereas Francois de la Noue wrote that, 'To be brief, the harquebus without pikes are as arms and legs without bodies.'[5] Slowly the harquebusier, which was a lighter form of musket but less powerful, would become an essential part of warfare and by the early part of the Thirty Years' War. Early muskets were heavy and so needed a rest for the musketeers to steady them when aiming, but as the war progressed muskets became lighter, although the rests were slowly discarded.

The muskets issued to regiments were usually smoothbore, i.e. they did not have a great deal of accuracy at long range, but rifled muskets or 'fouling

2 Francis Markham, *Five Decades of Epistles of Warre*, p.39; A.V.B. Norman Wallace *Wallace Collection Catalogue, European arms and armour supplement.*

3 TNA SP 9/202/1 unfolio 'The lengths and bigness of the musket as is used'.

4 TNA SP63/238/2/176

5 Blaise de Monluc, *The Valois-Habsburg Wars and the French Wars of Religion* (London: Longman Group Ltd, 1971), ed. Ian Roy, p.41; Francois de La Noue, *The Politicke and Militarie Discourses of the Lord de La Noue, whereunto are adjoined certain observations of the same author, of things happened during the three late Civil Wars of France ... Translated out of the French by EA* (London, printed for Thomas Cadman and Edward Aggas by Thomas Orwin, 1588), p.176.

pieces' were known. These were usually used for hunting but their military value was not lost on the commanders of the day. Scotsman Robert Monro records that he was shot at by a sniper during the Battle of the Alte Veste during the summer of 1632. The armoury at Graz has several rifles which were manufactured in Styria Nuremberg and Ausgburg, which have calibres between 11 mm and 16.5 mm.[6] How widely used these rifles were is not known, but at the end of the Thirty Years' War Maximilian of Bavaria is said to have raised a regiment of cavalry armed entirely with rifles.

Once delivered into an armoury muskets would often be tested or 'proofed' to see that they were safe for the musketeer to use. An undated document also records that:

> The barrel of the musket be four foot long shooting a bullet of 10 in the pound upon the proof and in ordinary shooting a bullet of 12 in the pound that may easily roll down the piece. The weight of them with stock and all the iron work weights 13–14–15 pounds. The barrel alone weights 9½–10½–11½ pounds all the stocks with the plate behind doth weight 3½ pounds. To proof a musket there must be just as much powder as the bullet weights and in ordinary shooting there must be but half as much powder as the bullet weights all new pieces doth recoil more than an old piece. A bandolier doth weight 2½ pounds and a rest 1½ pounds so there must be a pound of bullets, a pound of powder, with a pound of match which is six fathoms every fathom is 72 inches … So the whole weight that a musketeer doth carry is 25 pounds besides his bread and other necessaries.
>
> Every 24 hours 144 inches of match, so that 2 pounds will serve 6 days and night to burn … continually.
>
> To every pound of powder there is allowed two pounds of match which is 12 fathoms and a pound of bullets a pound of powder is 16 charges which is the two parts of bullets of 12 in the pound.[7]

To save match musketeers could extinguish their match, leaving just the file leader's match still alight, but this could lead to a desperate scramble for the other musketeers to light theirs if the enemy was spotted. On the other hand match could be improvised by using bed cord which was soaked in saltpetre.

According to Francis Markham:

> About their bodies baldrickwise from the left shoulder under the right arm, he shall carry bandoliers of broad leather … and to this bandolier shall be fastened by long double stings (at least a quarter of a yard in length a piece, that they may with more ease be brought to the mouth of the musket) one large priming charge … and at least twelve other charges of wood, all made of some tough light wood or else of horn, and covered with leather.[8]

6 Andre Schurger, 'The Archaeology of the Battle of Lützen: an examination of 17th Century military material culture' (University of Glasgow, Ph.d Thesis, 2015), p.86.

7 TNA SP 9/202/1 unfolio 'The lengths and bigness of the musket as is used'.

8 Francis Markham, *Five Decades of Epistles of Warre*, p.34.

23. Musketeers, from Rudolph Meyer's series depicting soldiers of the Thirty Years' War, 1618–1638. (Rijksmuseum)

24. Pikeman and officer, from Rudolph Meyer's series depicting soldiers of the Thirty Years' War, 1618–1638. (Rijksmuseum)

25. Halberdier and armoured pikeman, from Rudolph Meyer's series depicting soldiers of the Thirty Years' War, 1618–1638. (Rijksmuseum)

These bandoliers have erroneously been referred to as the '12 Apostles' since they had 12 small flasks or 'charges' which contained enough gunpowder to fire a musket. However, there is no evidence to suggest that they were ever called this. In fact Edward Davies writing in 1619 suggests that musketeers carry a bandolier of '16 or 18 charges or mates, at the least, hanged thereunto with strong laces, with a priming charger or mate and also a bullet bag.' Whereas Gervase Markham, Francis' brother, suggested 12 or 13 charges which 'must contain powder according to the bore and bigness of the piece by due measure.' Two surviving early seventeenth century examples said to have come from Austria and sold at an auction in New York in 1926, only had eight charges, and there was no evidence that they were missing any of their flasks. The powder carried in these charges were poured down the musket barrel, and 'a charge greater than the rest ... for pan powder.' Sometimes a musketeer would be equipped with a separate triangular-shaped flask.[9]

An order for bandoliers to be used by the New Model Army stated that they were to be, 'of wood with whole bottoms, to be turned within and not bored, the heads to be of wood, and to be laid in oil (viz), three times over, and to be coloured blue with blue and white strings with thread twist and with good belts.'[10]

Fortunately for the Emperor's cause, when the Imperial-Catholic League Army captured Prague after the battle of the White Mountain on 8 November 1620 the city's large arsenal was able to supply arms to the Catholic regiments, for example on 19 October 1621 Hans de Witte, Wallenstein's financier, was issued with 496 muskets, 490 bandoliers and 498 musket rest. A number of warrants from the Prague arsenal have survived, including one dated 28 March 1626 for Oldrich Kalt to issue Lieutenant Ferdinand von Nagoroller 200 muskets with bandoliers and rests, 50 pikes and 50 halberds, plus 100 moulds for musket balls. On 18 June 1626 a further 200 pikes, 200 muskets, 200 sets of armour and 50 halberds were ordered to be issued Colonel Hans Philip von Breuner's Regiment of Foot. Another warrant this time dated 4 October 1627 was to delivered to Lieutenant Alexander Playlebenoni, 60 muskets, 30 halberds, 40 sets of armour for the use of Wallenstein's Army.[11]

However, the Prague arsenal was not large enough to supply all the Imperialist regiments, so other armourers had to be found. The largest producer of arms was Nuremburg, which was situated near the Elbe and Rhine and so could easily transport its arms throughout Europe, including Denmark, Sweden, and Russia. As well as the armourer's mark, the city's examiners would stamp the city's coat of arms on the weapons and armour as proof of its quality.

---

9 Edward Davies, *The Art of War and England's Trayning* (1619); Gervase Markham, *The Souldiers Accidence* (London: printed by John Dawson for John Ballamie, 1625), p.3; Anon., *European Arms and Armour, mainly XVI and XVII Centuries* (New York: American Art Association Inc, 1926), p.64 and Plate XXI.

10 Gerald Mungeam, 'Contracts for the Supply of equipment to the New Model Army', *The Journal of the Arms and Armour Society*, 1968, pp.88, 90.

11 V. Liva, *Prameny k Dejinam Tricetilete Valky, 1618–1625* vol. 3 (Prague, 1951) pp. 64, 66, 206, 229.

On 11 June 1625 an order was placed by on the merchants of Nuremberg by Wallenstein's Financier, Hans de Witte, to furnish seven complete regiments of Wallenstein's Army, including armour for pikemen at 5½ florins each, muskets at 2½ Reichsthaler and for small arms at 70 kroner. Among its merchants was Ulrich Loser, in 1631 is known to have supplied hundreds of back and breastplates, pikes and muskets to the Imperialist Army. On 12 August 1625 David Heidler a gunsmith of Nuremberg agreed to supply 500 muskets and on the 16–17 August 1625 the Nuremberg merchants were to provide enough arms and armour for a further three regiments. What regiments these arms were destined for is not recorded, but in 1629 Orazio del Monte wrote to Octavio Piccolomini about an order for muskets. It was not just muskets that the city produced: in July 1626 George Ayermann, also of Nuremberg, was to supply 500 back- and breastplates to Colonel Hieronymus Count von Colloredo's Regiment of Foot. On 5 January 1632 Nuremberg supplied 1,000 pistols and carbines to Wallenstein's Army, but later that year the city declared for Gustavus Adolphus' cause and so the city's arms factories were cut off from the Imperialist cause. However, by March 1638 the city supplied a further 3,000 muskets, 2,000 pairs of pistols and 2,000 pikes to the Imperialist Army. In 1640 Martin Volckhamer of Nuremberg was supplying Ottavio Piccolomini's Regiment with 500 pistols and holsters.[12]

Liège would become one of the greatest firearm producing towns in Europe, its arms industry dating back to the sixteenth Century. Since it was situated in Northern Europe it usually supplied arms to the Dutch and French armies, but in 1621 the merchants received 50,000 florins to arm Count Ernest von Mansfeld's and the Duke of Brunswick's Armies.[13] Whereas the town of Suhl appears to have been one of the main suppliers for the Imperialist Armies, although it is also known to have also supplied arms to the Protestant general Prince Bernard of Saxe-Weimar. The town's arms trade dates back to 1535 and its specialised in good quality weapons for common soldiers. To uphold this quality a proof mark 'SVL' was hammered into the barrel, whereas Nuremberg had the 'N' above the city's arms as its mark.[14] There is also evidence to suggest that musketeers also carved their initials into their musket. At an excavation at Stralsund in July 2010 three muskets from the siege of that city were discovered, one had 'WN' engraved on the musket butt and another had 'NO'. The third musket had 'C', with possibly another letter which is now lost. All three initials were on the right hand side. Their rough appearance rules out any makers' or

12 Ernstberger, *Wallenstein als Volkswirt in Herzogten Friedland*, pp.137–140; Ernstberger, *Hans de Witte, Finanzmann Wallensteins*, pp.241–242; Peter Krenn and Walter J. Karcheski, *Imperial Austria, Treasurers of Art, Arms and Armour from the State of Styria* (Art Exhibitions Australia Ltd, 1998), p.43; SOA Zamrsk RA Piccolomini Nachod, 16549; Orazio del Monte wrote to Ottavio Piccolomini, 1629 and SOA Zamrsk RA Piccolomini Nachod, 21407, Martin Volckhamer to Piccolomini, 1640.

13 Jaroslav Lugs, *Firearms Past and Present: a complete review of firearm systems and their histories* (London: Greville, 1973), vol. 1, pp.450–453.

14 Nuremburg's coat of arms was half an Imperial eagle on the left side and red and white stripes on the right side.

Guild mark, so we will probably never know the musketeers' full names or the regiment they belonged to.[15]

Unfortunately, the archives of the Suhler gun makers have not survived so we do not know the exact number of muskets supplied to both sides during the Thirty Years' War. However, between 1619 and 1632 it is known to have supplied at least 61,000 muskets at a cost of between 2 and 3 Reichsthalers per musket. In 1622 just one Suhler gunsmith, Simon Stohr, received an order for 4,000 muskets for the Imperialist Army and in 1631 Wallenstein placed orders with six Suhler gunsmiths to equip his army with 28,950 muskets. Suhler muskets were 140 cm long and the barrel was 102 cm and weighed between 4.5 and 4.7 kg, which was shorter than the muskets being produced by Sweden at this time, which were 156 cm long, with a barrel length of 115 to 118 cm. The lightness of these muskets meant that the musketeers were able to discard their musket rests, although the older heavier muskets continued to be used.

Unfortunately in 1634 Isolani's Croats burnt down the town, thus robbing both causes of a valuable supplier.[16] However by 1639 the gunsmiths of Suhl were producing arms once more and during the summer of 1639 the Jung family were ordered to deliver 4,000 muskets to Vienna. In 1643 another order was placed, this time for 20,000 muskets, 4,500 pistols, 400 carbines and 1,000 pistol holsters and in 1645 Nicholas Jung received another order from Vienna for 8,000 muskets, 1,000 carbines and 4,000 pistols. The Jung family were not the only arms manufacturers to receive such orders Valentine Schneider also received an order in 1639 for 4,000 muskets and 2,000 pistols, so the Suhler gunsmiths had clearly recovered from Isolani's raid.[17]

However, the city did not just make firearms, but also armour and other weapons as well, as the following order, dated 2 November 1625 shows:[18]

6,000 muskets with accessories, each at 2½ Reichsthaler	22,500 Gulden
2,278 pikes at 36 Kreuzer	1,366 Gulden, 48 kr
715 common halberds at 1 gulden	715 Gulden
30 halberds at 1 gulden	30 Gulden
27 partizans at 1 Reichsthaler 30 kr	30 Gulden
74 bandoliers at ¼ Reichsthaler	27 Gulden 45 kr
146 musket rests at 9 kr	21 Gulden 54 kr

Essen and Hamburg also supplied arms to both sides. Among the armourers of the latter town were Albert Balzer Bearne and Leonard Mercellus, who on 16 April 1639 supplied the English government with 3,000 muskets, 700 cuirassier arms, 700 pairs of holsters and 1,500 pikemen's armour, all 'according to the patterns already delivered', which were to be supplied in just eight to 10 days. Probably, like shipments from other cities,

15 Konze et al., 'Der Stralsund Laufgraben von 1628...', p.212.

16 Ernstberger, *Wallenstein als Volkswirt in Herzogten Friedland*, pp.137–140.

17 H. Ebner et al., *Festschrift Othmar Pickl zum 60 Geburtstag* (Leykam Verlag, 1987), p.685.

18 Ernstberger, *Hans de Witte, Finanzmann Wallensteins*, p.241.

26. (above and right): dismounted harquebusiers or dragoons, Spanish siege of Breda 1624–1625. Jacques Callot, 1628. (Rijksmuseum)

27. (left): pikeman, and 28. (below), musketeer. Jacob de Gheyn, ***De Wapenhandelinghe van Roers, Musketten ende Spiesen***, 1607 (Rijksmuseum)

29. (left and below): weapons and equipment of the cuirassier. Johann Jacobi von Wallhausen, ***Kriegskunst zu Fuss***, 1616 (Michał Paradowski's archive)

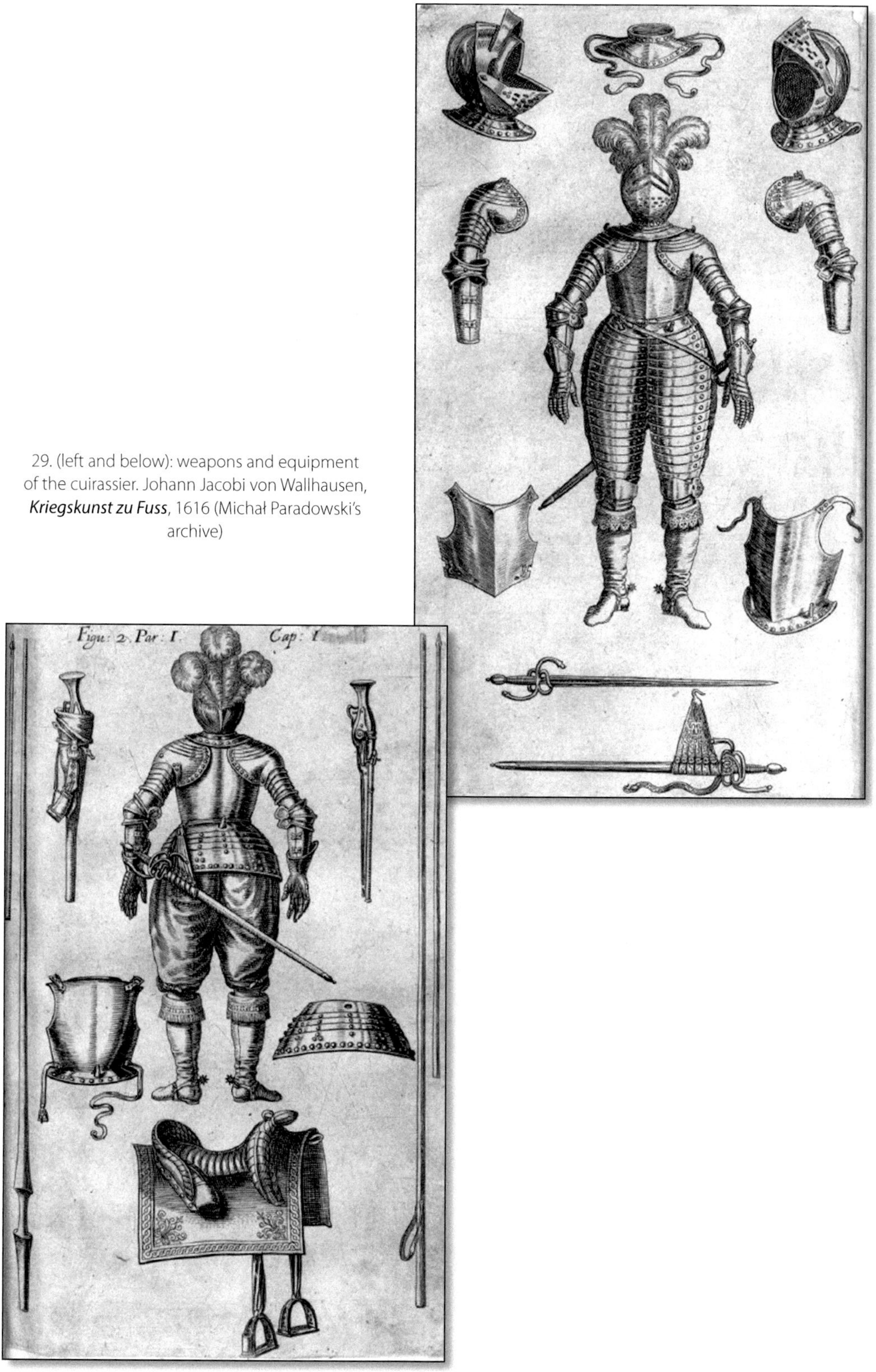

30. Pikemen. Friedrich Jungermann, ***Paraten Schlachtordnunn***, 1617–1625. (Biblioteka Cyfrowa Uniwersytetu Wrocławskiego)

these muskets etc. were packed in cases while the accoutrements, such as the bandoliers, spanners and flints would be packed in 'dry fats' which were numbered, so that they could be easily distributed to a regiment. The English government seems to have been lucky and the arms were delivered on time, but such was the demand for firearms that orders outstripped production, so there was sometimes a long delay in completing these orders.[19]

The Dutch arms trade was one of the largest, if not the largest, in Europe because not only did it supply its own armed forces, but in 1621 the

19 TNA SP 81/46 ff.214, 220, 243, Arms from Hamburg, 13, 16 and 28 April 1639.

merchants in Amsterdam supplied 300 harquebusiers, 400 carbines, 1,000 muskets with rests and bandoliers, 1,000 suits of armour, 1,000 pikes, 30 halberds, 16 drums, and 1,000 pounds of lead, match, and gunpowder to the Protestant Union. The following year as well as supplying arms to the Danish and Swedish armies, the Dutch also supplied 3,000 muskets, 3,000 suits of pikemen's armour, 3,000 pikes, 1,000 back- and breastplates, and 1,000 harquebusiers with bandoliers, to Christian of Brunswick's army. This was in addition to 10,000 pounds of gunpowder, 20,000 pounds of match and 10,000 pounds of lead shot for his army.

During the 'Danish period' of the war Christian IV purchased 33,000 muskets, 15,000 pikes and 20,000 sets of armour, in addition to 400,000 pounds of gunpowder and 1.7 million pounds of match.[20]

Unfortunately, receiving arms from different cities and even armourers had its drawbacks, in that the calibres for the various firearms differed, with musket calibres ranging from 17.5mm to 19.7mm, or in the case of those from Holland, 21.6mm and in England between 19.0 and 22.6mm. The calibres for pistols also varied between 10.0 and 14.9mm. This made it difficult to supply the appropriate musket shot with the number of musket balls varying from eight to 15 balls to the pound. There are accounts of the shot having to be melted down and recast or even the musketeers having to gnaw the musket balls down to make them fit into the barrel. Calibres also changed during the war. Nuremberg supplied muskets with 18.3mm calibre or 14 balls to the pound in 1631, but in 1634 the city was supplying muskets with a 17.5mm calibre or 16 balls to the pound. Even when the same gunsmith was supplying muskets or pistols they could vary in weight due to the design of the stock.[21]

The benefits of the arms trade being apparent, new centres for manufacturing arms and armour were established during the war, such as Munich, Graz, Dresden, and Vienna, and the bell founders of Nuremberg and Regensburg converted their foundries into making cannon. Pieces of artillery could also be bought from Nuremberg, Frankfurt, Augsburg, Strasbourg, Ulm and Essen. Essen's gun foundries dated back to the fifteenth century, and so was one of the earliest gun foundries established. Under the guidence of Louis de Geer arms factories were also established in Sweden.[22]

31. Musketeer. Friedrich Jungermann, ***Paraten Schlachtordnunn***, 1617–1625. (Biblioteka Cyfrowa Uniwersytetu Wrocławskiego)

20 Hans Vogel, 'Arms Production and exports in the Dutch Republic, 1600–1650' in M Van Der Hoeven, *Exercise of Arms*, pp.201, 207.

21 Peter Engerisser, 'Matchlock Musket, Suhl approx, 1630' <http://www.engerisser.de/Bewaffnung/weapons/Matchlockmusket.html> (accessed 8 May 2015)

22 E.W. Dahlgren, *Louis de Geer, 1587–1652: Hans Lif und Verk* (Uppsala: Almqvist och Wicksell, 1923) vol. 1 p.106

32. Exercises with a cannon. Jacques Callot, 1635. (Rijksmuseum)

Despite these centres for arms they were not enough to meet the needs of the Imperialist War effort, therefore in April 1632 Wallenstein, who is often credited with supplying his army from his own estates, suggested measures be implemented to centralise war production. On 16 April 1632 a document was presented to the War Council and the Court Chamber by Von Muhlheim after a conference with Count Walzenhoven the previous day on Wallenstein's opinion of the state of the arms industry in the Holy Roman Empire. Wallenstein suggested that he be given the right to purchase materials within the Empire to make arms and armour at a cheaper rate and that suitable buildings should be purchased where forges could be established to make these arms. The armourers etc. were to be 'strictly bound to their work' in producing arms only for the Imperialist Army, 'under the threat of severe punishment'. A person was also to be appointed to 'submit any problems for quick decisions in order that such transactions would not have to be presented to the pertinent authorities or commissions thereby losing time'. The War Council and the Court Chamber unanimously agreed with these proposals and that they should be presented to Ferdinand, except for the proposal of the single appointed person, since both the War Council and the Court Chamber were unwillingly to give up their 'custom and practice with Your Majesty to handle such matters'. However, they did admit that the Emperor's monetary 'credit is lacking' so that a third person dealing with these arms factories might have more financial success.[23]

Archaeological evidence from the battlefield of Lützen suggests that 75 percent of the muskets carried by both sides were manufactured either in Amsterdam and Suhl, with a smaller percentage of regiments in the Imperial Army being supplied with muskets from Augsburg and Nuremberg. Moreover there is no evidence to suggest that the Swedish Army carried lighter muskets compared to their Imperialist counterparts.[24]

In theory the cuirassier was armoured from head to knee and rode a horse of about 16 hands (1 hand is about 8.86cm). The armour was usually blackened to prevent it from rust, but also gave it a sinister look. Each cuirassier was allowed a boy who would help him on with his armour in the morning and take it off when not on duty.

According to the Royalist officer Sir Edmund Verney, who recorded his experience of wearing cuirassier armour, 'It would kill a man to serve in a whole cuirass. I am resolved to use nothing but back, breast and gauntlet.' The Parliamentarian, Edmund Ludlow, records after falling from his horse, 'I could not without difficulty recover on horseback being loaded with cuirassiers arms.' As well as it being impractical to wear cuirassier armour, horses able to carry their weight were even more difficult to find, as General George Monck records in his *Military and Political Affairs*: 'I have omitted here to speak anything of the armour of the cuirassier, because there are not many countries that do afford horses fit for the service of cuirassiers.'[25]

The following muster of General Octavio Piccolomini's cuirassier regiment taken in December 1633 shows that Monk was correct:

23 Ernstberger, *Wallenstein als Volkswirt im Herzogtum Friedland*, pp.134–136.

24 Schurger, *The Archaeology of the Battle of Lützen*, p.157.

25 John Heath, *Observations upon military and Political Affairs written by the Most Honourable George, Duke of Albemarle* (London: Henry Mortlocke, 1671), p.25; Quoted in David Blackmore, *Arms and Armour of the English Civil Wars* (Royal Armouries, 1990) pp.8–9; John Cruso, *Militarie Instructions for the Cavalrie*, ed. Brigadier Peter Young (Kineton: The Roundwood Press, 1972), pp.28–29, 31.

Troop	Mounted	Dismounted	Total
Colonel's troop	120	8	128
Lieutenant colonel's	85	11	96
Major's troop	90	14	104
Captain Baron Matthei	70	36	106
Captain de Creaspu	85	14	99
Captain Saracini	80	8	88
Captain Graf Avogrado	80	8	88
Captain Loson	95	8	103
Captain Ordlingher	85	10	95
Captain Berger	85	13	98
	875 troopers	130 troopers	1,005 troopers

Obtaining horses for the cavalry etc., was an ongoing problem throughout the war, but, having dismounted cavalry did not necessarily mean they could not take part in the fighting since they were often used instead of the infantry when storming towns. *The Work of the Famous Nicholas Machiavelli*, records at Carmignuola against Swiss troops, that Machiavelli:

> caused all his cuirassiers to dismount, and at the head of his foot, fall on upon the Swizzers, who were not able to resist them. For the cuirassiers being completely armed, forced their way into the body of the Swizzers without any loss so as their whole Army was defeated and cut off.[26]

In 1641 it was found that of 727 troopers in Piccolomini's Regiment, just 127 were still wearing full cuirassier armour. No doubt the troopers of Piccolomini's Regiment were not the only ones to discharge their armour. Later the Imperial General Montecuccoli wrote to the Duke of Modena suggesting that '[the] cuirassier should be equipped with breast and back harness, storm hat [helmet] together with two pistols and a sword. This is the way the Swedish cuirassiers are armed.' By the 1670s this is how a 'cuirassier' was described.[27]

How many armourers would be employed in making this armour is not recorded, but the European cuirassier armour preserved in the Wallace Collection in London weighed as follows:[28]

26 Niccolo Machiavelli, *The work of the famous Nicholas Machiavelli, citizen and secretary of Florence written originally in Italian and from thence newly and faithfully translated into English* (Henry Neville).

27 Thomas Barker, *The Military Intellectual in Battle*, p.110.

28 Sir James Mann, *Wallace Collection Catalogue, European Arms and Armour* (London: William Clowes and Son Ltd, 1962), vol. 1, pp.83–90.

Pieces of armour	Savoy, *c.*1620–1635	Augsburg, *c.*1620	French, *c.*1640
Helmet	2.11 kg	2.11 kg	5.7 kg
Gorget	0.652 kg	0.974 kg	1 kg 4½ g
Breastplate	3.51 kg	5.2 kg	3 kg 8½ g
Backplate	4.05 kg	2.488 kg	3 kg 11½ g
Tassets			
Left	1.88 kg	3 kg 3½ g	Not mentioned
Right	1.585 kg	1.74 kg	Not mentioned
Garde rein	1.92 kg	0.510 kg	Not mentioned
Pauldrons and arms			
Left	2.54 kg	5 kg 9¾ g	8.0 kg
Right	2.46 kg	4 kg 10½ g	8 kg 4½ g
Gauntlets (pair)	6.12 kg	2 kg 1½ g	2 kg 5½ g

Making cuirassier armour, or 'arms' was a slow process. On 20 January 1640 a certificate of the armourers of the citizens of London, stated that 'we are able to make 35 cuirassier arms a month and 210 harquebusier arms per month … [but by] not making any other sort in a month we are able to furnish 70 cuirassier arms and 500 harquebusier arms and 700 foot arms.'[29]

There are many surviving examples around the world of cuirassier armour dating from the early seventeenth century, the design of the body armour is basically the same, but there are marked differences when it comes to the design of the helmet. One type of helmet from Germany had a visor which could be raised giving the cavalrymen a wider view. Then there is the 'close burgonet', which had a peak and one or more vertical bars to protect the cavalryman's face. The front piece was fixed to the helmet by hooks and eyes so that it could easily be removed. Examples of this form of helmet can be found in the Bavarian Army Museum, and the Royal Armouries in Leeds. Then there are close burgonets which have a type of 'face'. What these helmets were originally called is not known, but it was not until the latter part of the nineteenth century they became known as the 'Savoyard' helmet, since a large number were captured from the Duke of Savoy's soldiers when they tried to storm Geneva in December 1602. These helmets are now preserved by the Museum of Art and History in Geneva and some have personalities with different types of 'faces', with large holes to see through and a slit for a mouth, and which can be either with or without a nose. Early Savoyard helmets appear to have oval eye holes, whereas some dated believed to be dated about 1635 still have oval eyeholes, but also a gap down each side of the nose no doubt to improve visibility. There is also a more rounded Savoyard helmet which is also known as 'totenkopf' or 'death's head'.

Despite being considered as of Italian origin, examples of cuirassier armour with this type of helmet can be found in the Austrian Army Museum in Vienna and the Zeughaus at Graz in Austria, so were probably worn by at least some of Wallenstein's cuirassier regiments. However, this is not to say that the cuirassiers of the Catholic League wore one type of helmet and the

29 TNA SP16/442 f173, A certificate of the armourers of the citizens of London, 20 January 1640.

Imperial cuirassiers another, because the Graz Armoury also has cuirassier armour with the close burgonet with one or more bars.[30]

In some museums around Europe some cuirassier armour is displayed with a *Zischagge* type helmet which had its origins in Eastern Europe, but by the seventeenth century it was made by German armourers. This had a single facial bar, and articulated neck guard which weighed about four pounds. However, most contemporary illustrations show cuirassiers with a closed burgonet or a visored helmet.

It was more prestigious to command a regiment of cuirassiers, but some inhabers preferred to raise a regiment with a combination of cuirassier and harquebusiers, while others just raised a harquebusier regiment, which was a cheaper option. Harquebusiers wore buff coats which could either be sleeveless or have cloth or leather sleeves. An account dated October 1632 records that hides from two elks were bought to make Gustavus Adolphus' buff coat, while another buff coat weighted about 3.35 kg, although it was embroidered. Troopers' buff coats varied in weight, the 33 belonging to the Littlecote Collection, which are now stored at the Royal Armouries at Leeds in England are between 1.9 kg to 3.1 kg. They are made of four pieces of leather for the body panels and four panels for the sleeves stitched together with linen thread. The sleeves are lined with linen, while the main body of the coat was lined with coarse canvas. The Littlecote buff coats are bright yellow, but underneath the linings they are natural leather, like other surviving buff coats, suggesting they were stained sometime after they were made, possibly before they were displayed at Littlecote House in Wiltshire. These coats were fastened by either cord or leather thong down the front, although several buff coats preserved at the Army Museum in Paris are fastened by hooks and eyes down the left side.[31]

The various military manuals also suggest that the harquebusier should wear back- and breastplates. The collection of harquebusier armour preserved in the Royal Armouries in Leeds, made between 1625 and 1630, weighed 6,245 g for a breastplate and 4,905 g for a backplate. However by 1651 the weight had been reduced to between 2,865 g and 4,600 g for a breastplate and 1,190 g to 1,530 g for a backplate. Straps were attached to the shoulders of the backplate which were attached to the breastplate with two small pommels on the chest and sometimes locked into place by a catch. Two small belts were also attached to the waist to fasten it at the front by a buckle. These plates could either be lined with leather, which made it more expensive, or had no lining at all. In addition a harquebusier might also have a helmet, usually like the *Zischagge* and those could weigh between 1.4 and 1.8 kg. True, these

30 Thomas Hoft, et al., *Shiny Shapes, Arms and armour from the Zeughaus of Graz* (Vienna: Springer, n.d.), pp.104–105; Blackmore, *Arms and Armour of the English Civil War*, pp.12–13; Stuart W. Pyhrr, *European Helmets, 1450–1650, Treasures from the Reserve Collection* (The Metropolitan Museum of Art, 2000), p.39.

31 Seventeenth century war weaponry and politics 10th Swedish conference, p.191; Thom Richardson and Graeme Rimer, *Littlecote, The English Civil War Armoury* (Leeds: Royal Armouries, 2012), pp.132–161.

relate to English harquebusier armour, but there is no reason to suggest those produced on the Continent varied greatly in weight.[32]

However, returns of harquebusiers raised in London in 1642 show that a trooper either wore a back- and breastplate and a helmet or a buff coat and a hat, not both. However, later in the Civil War both sides seem to have preferred their cavalry to wear back- and breastplate and there are few examples of buff coats being issued. After the battle of Lützen, Wallenstein sent a letter to all his colonels of his cavalry complaining that his cuirassiers were not fully armoured as they should have been. In fact by the latter part of the seventeenth century a cuirassier was clad in the traditional harquebusier attire rather than the three-quarter armour as prescribed in the military manuals.

Originally dragoons were armed with pikes and muskets, but since the pike was so unwieldy while on horseback it was soon discarded. In theory the dragoons carried a flintlock musket, but matchlock muskets were known to have been used and sometimes musketeers would be temporarily mounted for manoeuvrability on campaign. According to Cruso a dragoon '[was] to expedite his march, alighting to do his service', therefore his horse was often the cheapest that money could buy.

The lightest cavalry were known as Croats, or 'Crabats', although this was a term usually given to all light horseman no matter what their origin. It was these 'Croats' who were often blamed for the worst atrocities committed during the war, and were even said to have eaten children such was their reputation for barbarity. They were usually armed with a harquebus, sword, which was rumoured to be poisoned, a dagger and pistols. As well as having complete regiments of Croats, there were also troops attached to regiments of horse, such as the regiment which belonged to Colonel Otto Fugger.

In theory armour should be bullet proof, with a small dent in it to show that it had been 'proofed' by firing a pistol at close range at it. However, unscrupulous armourers would often make the dent with a hammer instead. Also some armourers would send obsolete armour which was found to be unserviceable.

Another trick was used by at least one manufacturer of gunpowder in the Lower Saxony circle. In 1634 John Kip mixed his gunpowder with large quantities of salt rather than saltpetre, making the powder useless. This deceit was only discovered when the barrels it was stored in were opened. Gunpowder was essential for any army and was in constant demand since the musketeers and troopers needed it to shoot their firearms and the gunners needed large quantities to fire their artillery pieces. On 23 September 1625 Nuremburg was ordered to supply 200 cwt of gunpowder and four days later an order was placed with the city to supply 200–300 cwt of match, whereas the powder mills of Southern German were to supply 1,000 cwt of powder on 14 March 1625 and a further 1,000 cwt of powder and match on 7 June 1625. Between 1625 and 1633 further orders for powder and match were supplied from Cologne, Lausitz, Nördlingen, Muhlhausen, Nordhausen,

32 Richardson and Rimer. *Littlecote, The English Civil War Armoury*, pp.2–69.

33. Artillery at the siege of Magdeburg. Peeter Meulener, 1650. (Nationalmuseum, Stockholm)

Salzburg, Ulm, Hamburg, Aachen and the Southern German states, while large quantities were also imported from Italy and Poland.[33]

This gunpowder varied in quality insomuch that on 29 July 1634 while at the siege of Forchheim Count Cratz von Scharfenstein wrote to the council of Nuremberg complaining that his musketeers were barely able to fire 80 metres using the gunpowder his regiment had been supplied with and even then they had to use double the quantity usually needed.[34] English gunpowder was considered the best, but there is no evidence to show that it was imported for the Imperial Army.

The badge of the soldier was the sword, since it marked him out from the civilian population. The town of Solingen was famous for its sword makers. Fifty-one sword makers can be identified by their makers' marks during the early seventeenth century, including Peter Munich whose workshop manufactured sword between 1595 and 1660, Then there was the Tesche family who worked at Solingen from about 1518 to 1700. Such was the high quality of Solingen's swords that these sword makers were greatly sought after to set up sword factories in other towns and countries, such as Johannes Hoppe or Happe, who later moved to the Royal Armouries at Greenwich, near London.[35] Most illustrations of soldiers, whether from a print in a manual on tactics or in paintings by such artists as Peter Snayer or Philip Wouvermans, show them wearing rapiers which had long blades. However, there are many surviving swords of this period with short blades, either curved or straight, which must have been more practical during a melee and must have been produced in their tens of thousands.

No army would be complete without its artillery, although some modern writers often refer to it as being ineffective in battle. Robert Monro records at the battle of Wolgast, Wallenstein 'did plant fourteen pieces of Ordnance, and played on the king [of Denmark's] battle till his Majesty perceiving the danger, not being bastant to resist the enemy, retired confusedly in great haste to Wolgast; and having lost without fighting the greatest part of his army.'[36] In 1632 Gustavus Adolphus would also use massed artillery to defeat Count von Tilly at the battle of the Lech. Moreover there are several examples of soldiers seeing a file of soldiers without heads, they having been ripped off by an artillery shot.

Charles V had introduced the several types of artillery pieces, the Karthaune or in Dutch 'Cartow', and there are references to these artillery pieces being used at various battles, including Lützen.[37] The English name for them was 'cannon', although Wallenstein appears to have used them in a battery at Lützen. Charles V also referred to culverins and falconets which were used in battle and then there were mortars, which were also used in sieges.

---

33 Ernstberger, *Wallenstein als Volkswirt in Herzogten Friedland*, pp.141–145; TNA SP 81/42 f.83.

34 Schurger, *The Archaeology of the Battle of Lützen*, p.76; Peter Engerisser, *Von Lützen nach Nördlingen* (Weissenstadt: Spathling, 2007), p.553.

35 Dudley Hawley-Grynsell, *Armourers' Marks* (London: Thorsons Publishing Ltd, 1959), pp.37–46.

36 Robert Monro, *Monro, His Expedition with the Worthy Scots Regiment (called Mac-Keyes Regiment) levied in August 1626* (London: William Jones, 1637), part I, pp.61–62.

37 These are described as whole Karthaune, ¾ Karthaune, half Karthaune, ¼ Karthaune and 1/8 Karthaune.

The ranges could vary greatly depending on the quality of the powder.

Type	Weight of shot (pounds)	Length of barrel after calibre*	Range in paces	No. crew	No. helpers	No. horses req. to pull the piece
Whole Karthaune	48	17–19	1,000	4	12–16	24
Half Karthaune	24	19–21	900	3	10–12	16
1/4 Karthaune	12	22–23	700	2	6–8	8–10
1/8 Karthaune	6	16–19	700	1	4	6
1/16 Karthaune	3	14–19	650	1	2–4	4–6
1/32 Karthaune	1½	14–19	570	1	2–4	4
1/44 Karthaune	3/4	14–19	320	1	1	1–2
Culverin	24	28½–30	-	3	9–10	14
Ordinary Culverin	18	30–31½	1,200	3	-	?
Demi Culverin	12	30–32½	900	2	6	6
1/4 Culverin	6	33–33½	570	1	4	4–6
1/8 Culverin	3	30–34	320	1	4	4

* 'Length of barrel after calibre' is measured by the number of shot that can be loaded into the barrel, i.e. 17–19 shot can be fitted into the barrel of a 'whole Karthaune'.

This chart should be compared to the chart below on English artillery. The weights and measures varydepending on the authority writing the manual on artillery, although Ward in his *Animadversions of War* gives the following dimensions:

Type	Shot weight (pounds)	Diameter of shot	Range in paces	Powder weight (pounds)	No. horses needed to pull piece
Cannon	64	7¾	300–1500	40	16
Cannon Serpentine	52	6¾	340–1600	25¼	14
French cannon	46¾	7	360–1740	25	12
Demi Cannon eldest	36¼	6½	370–1,800	20¾	11
Demi Cannon ordinary	32	6¼	350–1700	20	10
					9
Demi Cannon	24½	5¾	340–1600	18	8
Whole Culverin	19	5¼	420–2,100	16	8
Culverin	16¼	5	400–2,000	15	7
Demi Culverin	11¾	4½	380–1,800	9	6
Demi Culverin Lesse	9	4	320–1600	8	5
Saker	5½	3¼	300–1500	5½	4
Minion	5	3	280–1,400	5	3
Falcon	2½	2½	260–1,200	2½	2
Falconette	1½	2	220–1,000	1½	2
Rabinet	¾	1¼	150–700	¾	2
Base	½	1	100–560	¼	2

The mortars were divided as follows:

Type	Bomb diameter	Shot weight (pounds)
Whole Mortar	12"	400
3/4 Mortar	12"	300
2/3 Mortar	9"	266
1/2 Mortar	8"	200
1/3 Mortar	7"	133
1/4 Mortar	7"	100
1/8 Mortar	5"	50
1/16 Mortar	4"	25
1/32 Mortar	3"	12½

There were also a large number of artisans, such as blacksmiths, saddlers, coopers, carpenters, wheelwrights, tanners, and painters, who supplied the saddles and harnesses for the horses, the blacksmiths made horseshoes, nails and other tools and wheelwrights made the wheels for the artillery and carts, which carried supplies for the army. Without these artisans the army would not have been able to take the field.

5

Regimental Colours

The honour of the each company or troop of a regiment was in the colours it carried, whether they were ensigns for the foot, cornets for a cavalry troop, or a guidon for a dragoon company. There is evidence to suggest that when a soldier joined a company or troop they would hammer a nail into the colour's staff. Dragoon guidons usually had a swallowtail and sometimes a fringe. A cavalry troop's trumpets also had a banner with either the captain's coat of arms in the centre with a similar field of the troop's cornet or, if the commander did not have a coat of arms then it might be identical to the troop's cornet. The drums of a company also appear to have borne the same system.

The regimental colours varied greatly in size, 295–414 cm wide by 315–362 cm high for ensigns and 53–67 cm wide by 53–60 cm high for cavalry standards. The colour poles also varied from 315 to 400 cm for ensigns 209–250 cm for cornets. They were usually made of silk, damask or taffeta with either device either being painted or appliquéd on.

According to Gervase Markham, the cornet:

> [Shall] carry on his right thigh his Captain's Cornet, which (being a private captain) should be compounded of colour and metal, that is the one half colour and metal impaled. The substance of the cornet should be of Damask, and the form must be almost square, (only a little longer from the staff then on the staff.) and fringed about suitably. The staff shall be small like a foot ensign, and not so long as an ordinary lance; it must be headed with steel and either guilt or silvered, with fair tassels suitable to the cornet. If the cornet belong to a great officer, it shall then be of one entire colour, of less quantity and full square; And in this cornet, the captain may carry device and word, or else none, at his own pleasure.[1]

To help a commander choose the right device or motto on his colours, books were published on emblems and their meaning such as Henry Estienne, Lord of Fossez whose book *The Art of Making Devices* was translated into English in 1646 by Thomas Blount. He argued that symbols should be 'of three kinds, moral, natural and theological'. Whereas an emblem should be,

1 Gervase Markham, *The Souldiers Accidence*, p.44.

'a sweet and moral symbol, which consists of pictures and words ... Emblems are reduced to three principal kinds, viz. of manners, of nature of history and fable.' When it came to the motto it was recommended that they should be 'concise or brief'. and usually in Latin.[2]

Some regiments were known by the colour of their ensigns, originally there were just four 'coloured' regiments in the Swedish Army, Yellow, Blue, Red and Green. These were later joined by the Orange, Brown and White Regiments and in 1629 there were three Black Regiments, although the last one was disbanded in 1634. A 'New Blue Regiment' was also raised so the original regiment became the 'Old Blue Regiment'. It was not just the Swedish Army that adopted 'coloured' regiments: the Danish Army had a Red Regiment, and Duke Bernard von Saxe-Weimar's Army in French service is known to have had a Black, a Yellow and a Red Regiment. In England probably the most famous coloured regiments are the London Trained Bands, with the White, Yellow, Red etc. during the English Civil War.[3]

Coloured regiments are usually associated with infantry regiments, but the Duke of Brunswick's small army also had a Red and a Blue Regiment of Horse, as well as a Red, Blue and a Yellow Regiment of Foot. In August 1631 the *Leipzig Chronicle* records that the army of the Elector of Saxony appears to be unique in that some of its regiments were known by two colours, such as the Red and Black Regiment (Field Marshal Arnim's Regiment); the Yellow and Black Regiment (Starschaldel's); the Blue and White Regiment (unknown) and the Red and White Life Regiment (Schaumburg's). These four regiments had been raised earlier in the year as part of the massive expansion of the Elector of Saxony's Army. Saxony sometimes published newssheets describing a regiment's colours, such as Starschaldel although it referred to the regiment by the name of its colonel rather than the Yellow and Black Regiment.[4]

Why these regiments should be known by the colour of their ensigns rather than their colonel's or owner's name is not known. Certainly some are known to have the same coloured coats, but other regiments also had the same coat and ensign colour but were not known by a 'colour'. While other contemporary sources refer to a colonel's regiment have red, blue etc. colours. Moreover, neither Wallenstein's Army, the Army of the Catholic League or that of Catholic France had regiments known by their colour, apart from the three mentioned above which were part of Bernard von Saxe-Weimar's Army, but these had been part of his army in Swedish service. Therefore coloured regiments appear to be wholly a Protestant occurrence.

2 Henry Estienne, Lord of Fossez, *The Art of Making Devices treating of Hieroglyphicks, Symboles, Emblemes, Aenigma's, Sentences, parables, reverses of medalls, Arms Blazons, Cimiers, Cyphres and Rebus* (London 1646), translated by Thomas Blount, pp.5, 7, 21.

3 Richard Brzezinski and Richard Hook, *The Army of Gustavus Adolphus,1 Infantry* (London: Osprey, 1991), p.14; Jean Le Laboureur, *Histoire du Mareschal de Guébriant* (Paris, 1676), pp.158,165, 169.

4 Tobias Heidenreich, *Leipzigische Chronicke: Nebst der Continuation* (Leipzig, 1635), pp.455, 457. The Regiments of London Trained Bands were also known as the 1st or White Regiment, etc.

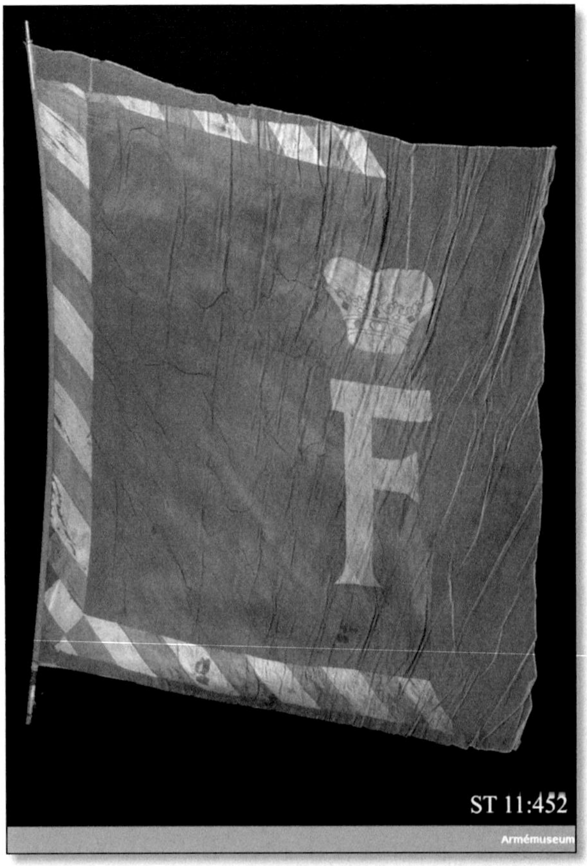

34. (left): Imperial infantry standard. Partially visible is Emperor Ferdinand II's monogram. (Armémuseum, Stockholm)

35. (below): Imperial infantry standard. (Armémuseum, Stockholm)

Facing page:

36. (top): Imperial infantry standard with Emperor Ferdinand II's monogram – 17th century, Olof Hoffman's drawing from the original. (Armémuseum, Stockholm)

37. (centre, below): Imperial infantry standards with ***Reichsadler*** (double-headed black eagle) symbol. (Armémuseum, Stockholm)

ST 11:364

TOT
INVICTA
ST 11:364

38. Imperial infantry standards.
(Armémuseum, Stockholm)

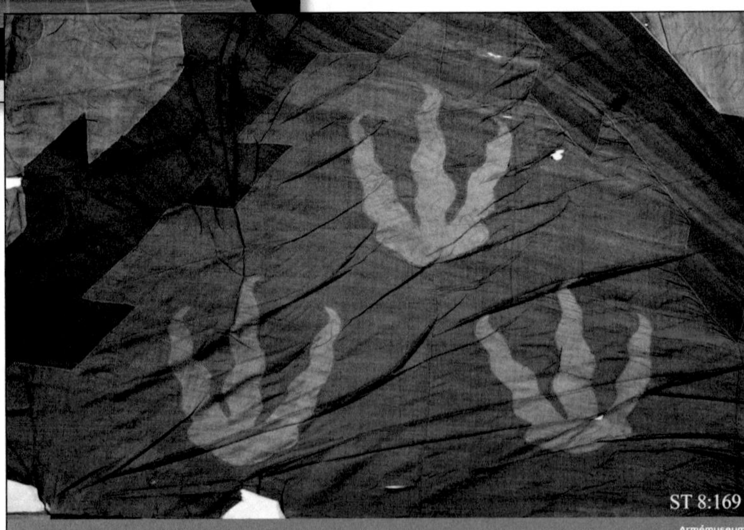

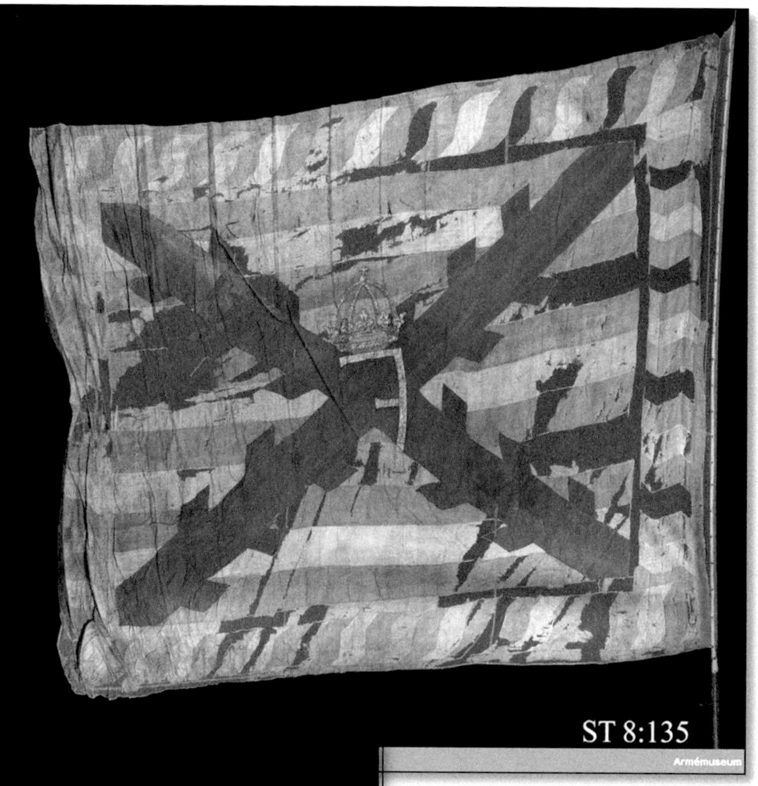

39. Imperial infantry standards with Emperor Ferdinand II's monogram. (Armémuseum, Stockholm)

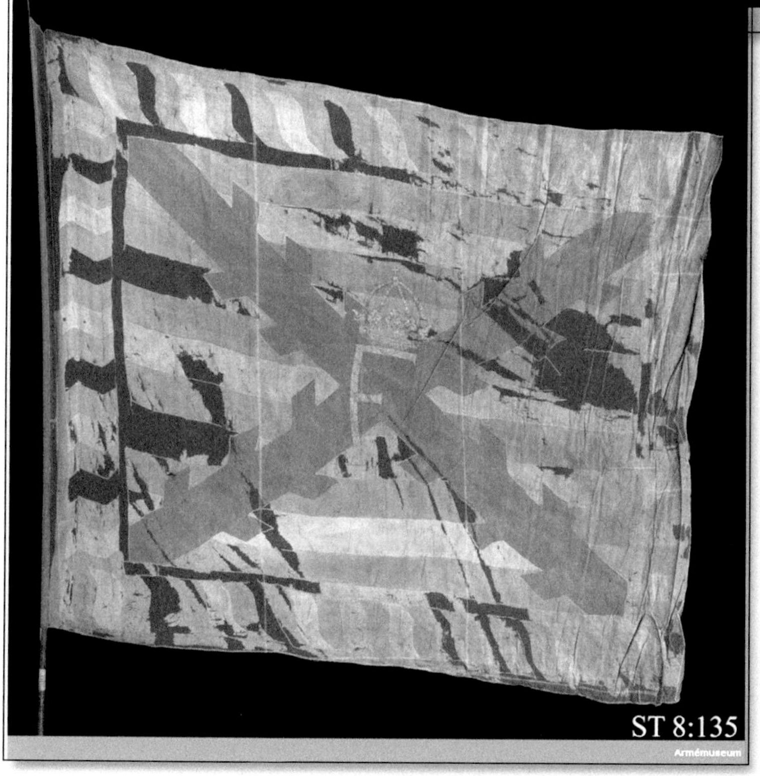

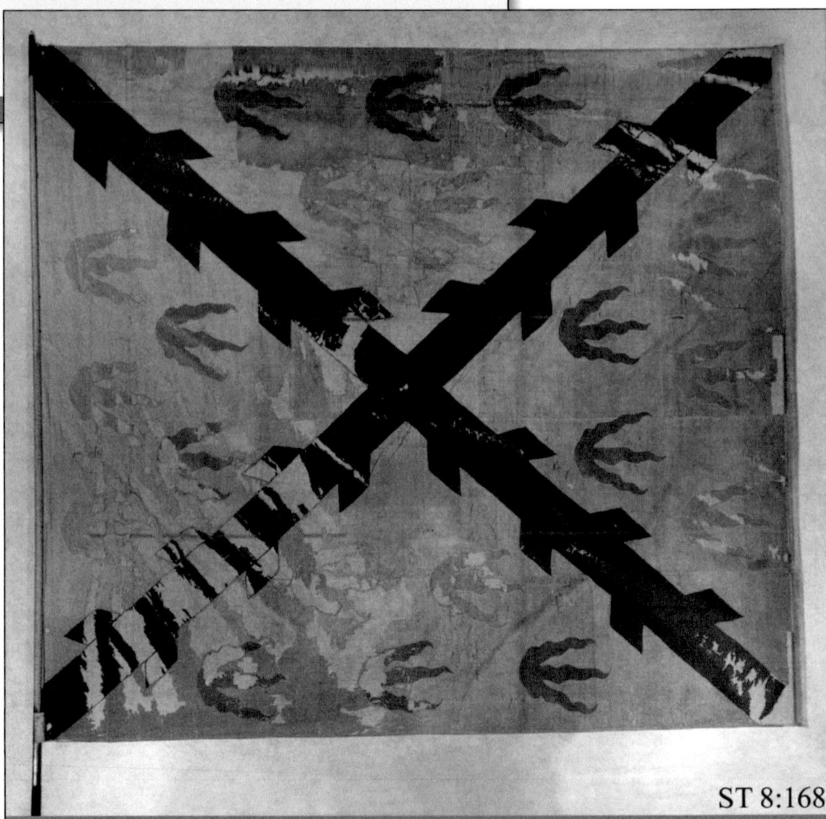

40. Imperial infantry standards (Armémuseum, Stockholm)

Some regiments appear to have carried different coloured ensigns. An eyewitness at Wittenberg observed the Swedish Army on 3 September 1631 and recorded a regiment with eight ensigns, 'two yellow and six white'. Then there was also a body of '730 infantry in 16 ensigns, among them, four red and white, seven red and one white', which may have been at least two regiments brigaded together. Other regiments carried ensigns described as 'old [and] torn'. Unfortunately, the eyewitness do not identify which regiments these colours belonged to, or for the most part the devices on these colours.[5]

Sometimes contemporary sources also mention regimental colours such as Colonel Johan von Wangler's Regiment of Foot which in *Theatrum Europaeum* carried red ensigns in 1631. The *Leipzig Chronicle* also mentions a Duke von Altenburg who commanded a body of cavalry during the summer of 1631 which included four troops of cuirassiers with orange standards, four troops of harquebusiers also with orange standards and five troops of harquebusiers with steel green standards. Also Colonel von Bindauf's Regiment, had four troops of cuirassiers with white cornets and five troops of harquebusiers with green cornets.[6]

However, sometimes these sources should be taken with care. Despite the eyewitness at Wittenberg recording that many of the Swedish colours were in a poor state, an account of the battle of Breitenfeld states that the Swedish infantry 'were divided into six battalions each of them consisting of 1,500 foot ... these companies were under 72 ensigns of various and lovely colours, upon the which was set the King's Arms and upon that a great crown the motto, was, *Gustavus Adolphus Rex Fedei Evangelica defensor*'. This statement seems simple enough, but Count Galleazzo Priorato admits that he relied on secondary sources and was not even present to see these colours at Breitenfeld.[7]

Despite this German historians such as K.A. Wilkie and Dr G. Sollner have depicted the Swedish infantry colours with the motto 'GARS' (Gustavus Adolphus King of Sweden) in their illustrations for their articles which were printed in the model soldier magazine, Zinnfiguren. Wilkie even went so far as to claim that they were based on images he had seen in the 'Anderson' manuscript, but Wilkie did not record where this manuscript was, and it is now believed that he made the whole thing up. Unfortunately, their illustrations have been copied since their articles first appeared. When writing his biography on Gustavus Adolphus during the eighteenth century Walter Harte boasted that he had seen a manuscript showing all different types of colours, and 'what surprised me was, that those belonging to the

5 Upland, H.K.H. Prins Gustaf, Duke of, *Arkiv till upplysing om Svrnska Kriegens och Krigsinrattningarnes Historia* (Stockholm, 1861) tredje Bandet no. 910 pp.80–81. See Appendix 2 for full list.

6 Johan Philip Abelin, *Theatrum Europaeum* (Frankfurt, 1643), vol. 2, p.436; Tobias Heidenreich, *Leipzigische Chronicke: Nebst der Contination* (Leipzig, 1635) p.457.

7 Count Galleazzo Priorato, *An History of the Late Warres and other State Affairs of the Best Part of Christendom beginning with the King of Swetlands entrance into Germany and continuing in the yeare 1640*, translated by Henry Carey (W. Wilson, 1648), author's note and book 2. p.42; Francis Watson, *Wallenstein, Soldier under Saturn* (London: Chatto and Windus, 1938), p.366.

Croatians were the best imagined of any.'[8] Unfortunately, he did not have a pen to take any notes, nor did he say where he had seen the manuscript.

However, this is not to say that there are no surviving manuscripts showing regimental colours carried by armies during the Thirty Years' War. Two manuscripts are held by the Saxon State Archives in Dresden and were composed by Balthasar Böhme between 1632 and 1633. The first volume contains 92 illustrations and the second 160 illustrations of the colours carried by the Army of Saxony. There also appears to a manuscript of several colours belonging to Mansfeld's Army in 1620, which is held at the Museum of the Thirty Years' War at Wittstock.[9]

For Swedish colours there is the manuscript compiled by Reginald Mohner a Benedict Friar of St Ulrich and Afra in Augsburg which dates from April 1632 to April 1635 and shows several Swedish regimental colours did have the inscription, 'GARS', which includes Gustavus' Red Regiment of Horse, which also included a device, such as three golden crowns, two lions supporting a crown, and two blue volcanos erupting. However, the majority have other devices, such as arrows, the moon and stars, animals, heraldic devices or a simple two-colour ensign without any device or inscription. Unfortunately, none of these colours still exist, although in August 1632 when Reginald Mohner is believed to have compiled his manuscript many are shown still in poor condition.

However, the same cannot be said of Imperialist colours, which are now preserved at the Armémuseum in Stockholm. In 1685 a survey of all the colours captured by Sweden was held and it found that there were 1,821, including 261 cornets, 48 dragoon guidons and 621 ensigns which had been captured during the Thirty Years' War. Unfortunately they were not very well protected and in 1907 when another survey was held of the colours, which by now had been supplemented by those captured in other wars, it was found that the collection now consisted of 1,291 infantry colours; 385 staves with fragments of infantry colours; 382 cavalry and dragoon standards; 202 staves with remnants of cavalry and dragoon standards and there were 280 staves without any colours on them at all. However, an Olaf Hoffman had drawn many of these colours at the end of the seventeenth century thus preserving the appearance of many of these lost colours.[10]

Unfortunately, those captured by the French during the Thirty Years' War were burnt in March 1814 to prevent them falling into enemy hands, just before the surrender of the French capital. If this was not bad enough these

8 Walter Harte, *The History of the Life of Gustavus Adolphus* (London: G. Hawkins, 1759), vol. 1, p.28.

9 Hans-Christian Huf, *Mit Gottes Segen in die Hölle: Der Dreissigjährige Krieg* (List Taschenbuch, n.d.), pp.239, 383.

10 Fred Sandstedt and Lena Sandstedt, 'Proud Symbols of Victory and mute witnesses of bygone Glories', in *Hoc Signo Vinces* (Helmstand: National Swedish Museums, 2006), pp.78–88; T.J. Petrelli and E.S. Liljedahl, 'Standar och dragonfanor' in *Antiqvarisk Tidskrift for Sverige Vol. 14* nr 3, p.4; Shakespeare Birthplace Trust Library Reference no. DR762/332.

trophies may have included standards from other states which had been sent to Paris when Napoleon's Armies captured an enemy's capital.[11]

A study of the surviving examples of Imperialist colours show there are several patterns of ensigns and standards. Like the Swedish colours some are just a plain ensign of one or two colours, while others have a Burgundian or plain cross with the monogram 'FII' or more rarely, 'F2' for Ferdinand II. Some had just an 'F' under a crown, while others had an 'FII'. Sometime the 'F' is reversed suggests that the colour was only a single thickness, while others have the same image either side suggesting a double thickness. Some cavalry standards had different images on either side of their cornet.[12]

In 1637 when Ferdinand II was succeeded by his son, also known as Ferdinard, the ensigns had the Imperial monogram of 'FIII' Other ensigns had the Imperial double-headed eagle, while others the Burgundian cross or just a plain St Andrew's Cross, with or without the Imperial monogram.

Examining Olaf Hoffman's manuscripts the Burgundian cross appears to have been one of the most popular device, sometime they have the Imperial monogram or the Virgin Mary. Another common device was a laurel wreath with an image inside, again with the Imperial monogram, an anchor or an elaborate scene.

Unfortunately, which regiments these belonged to is unknown, but sometimes it is possible to identify the ensigns that belonged to an unknown regiment since they have the same border, but a different device in the centre, while others have the same device in the centre, but different borders.

Among the captured colours are five yellow ensigns with a black Imperial eagle and a yellow and black border, each border having a different shapes. Unfortunately, it is not known to which regiment these belonged, although it has been suggested that they were either Colonel De Suys' or Berthold von Waldstein's Regiment of Foot. This is based on the assumption that black and yellow were the colours of their coats of arms. In this fashion Eva Turek believed she could identify Adolf von Holstein's Regiment of Foot as having a white field with a green laurel wreath encircling a crowned 'F' with a red and white zigzag border; and possibly Merode's Regiment which had blue and white bars with a red Burgundian cross. In the centre was a golden Imperial monogram under a crown. The border was blue and white.[13]

Wilkie also tried to identify several colours, including two blue ensigns as belonging to Colonel Lobl's Regiment of Foot which have a black Burgundian cross and a gold crown over the Imperial monogram at the top. The border was white and black teeth around its four sides. On one the black teeth were on the outside, and on the other the inside. A white ensign with an Imperial eagle in the centre identified by Wilkie as belonging to Savelli's Regiment of

11 Bibliothèque Nationale, *Drapeaux et Etendant pris depuis le commencement du regne de Louis 14 jusqu'en 1688*, FR14166 unnumbered page. Certainly Frederick the Great's sword was sent to Paris when Napoleon occupied Berlin.

12 Unless otherwise stated the descriptions of Imperialist colours come from Olaf Hoffman's manuscript preserved at the Armémuseum, Stockholm.

13 Correspondence between Eva Turek of the Swedish Army Museum and myself, during the late 1980s early 1990s.

Anti-clockwise from top:

41. Three Imperial cavalry cornets with Reichsadler symbol – seventeeenth century Olof Hoffman's drawing from the original. (Armémuseum, Stockholm)

42. Imperial cavalry or dragoon cornet with Emperor Ferdinand II's monogram – seventeenth century. Olof Hoffman's drawing from the original. (Armémuseum, Stockholm)

Foot. The eagle has a shield on its chest with the Austrian colours of red and white and its border was is repeating green, red and yellow all around the ensign except for the four corners which are white with a gold cross. Wilkie is said to have identified other regiments, such as Verdugo's and Breuner's, but he does not record his reasoning behind why he attributed these ensigns to these respective colonels. In fact the ensigns reportedly belonging to Lobl and Verdugo do not appear among the Swedish Army Museum's trophies.

Certainly provenances of the regimental colours can change, such as the ensigns which were believed to be carried by Wallenstein's own regiment of foot. These had a white field with a border of different shapes and colours and a Burgundian cross in each corner. In the centre was a green wreath within which were various scenes depicting the misfortunes of Frederick V of Bohemia. A study by Eva Turek examined these colours and came to the conclusion that they belonged to the regiments of Karl von Liechtenstein.

An invoice dated the September 1621 from Stefan Birckman, a tailor from the Old Town in Prague, records that Liechtenstein ordered 15 white ensigns at 100 florins each. These were made from about 11 metres, with red silk taffeta for the Burgundian crosses. He also commanded a regiment of horse, each troop having a different coloured standard; the white cornet cost 11 florins, the red one cost nine florins and green, yellow and blue cornets at 6 florin each. He also ordered two red damask kettledrum banners and three trumpet banners in red, blue, green and yellow which cost 120 florins. On 18 October 1621 Daniel Schmidt, the court painter, was paid 100 florins, possibly to paint the devices on these colours.

On 8 January 1624 Ferdinand II ordered that Liechtenstein's Regiment be reduced from 15 companies to 10 and that it should be placed under the command of Colonel Jan Philip von Cratz von Scharfenstein who as early as 4 November 1623 had ordered 10 new ensigns and 10 standards from Stefan Birckman. This research means that the design of the ensigns of Wallenstein's own regiments are unknown, but are believed to have been blue and gold.[14]

One regiment whose colours we can be assured of is Colonel Julius von Hardegg's Regiment, since their designs and descriptions can be found in the regimental archives. The colonel's ensign was blue with a large white Burgundian cross and in the centre was an 'F' for Ferdinand, under a crown. The edges of the ensign were bordered by red and blue flames and in each corner was a small white Burgundian cross. In the middle of the four sides of the border was a shield with the Austrian coat of arms.

The regiment's second colour, which belonged to Lieutenant-Colonel Mers' company, was also blue and had a red sun in the centre with a border similiar to the colonel's colour, but without the coats of arms and the Burgundian crosses.

Captain Concin's Company carried a colour similiar to Lieutenant-Colonel Mers' company, only with the figure of Fortuna standing on a globe, which had wings, and above her the motto TEMPORA, TEMPORE TEMPERA ('guide the passage of time through time') in red letters. Whereas Captain Zeck's colour

14 Eva Turek, *Under False Colours* (Stockholm: Armémuseum, 1996), pp.31, 33, 38, 46.

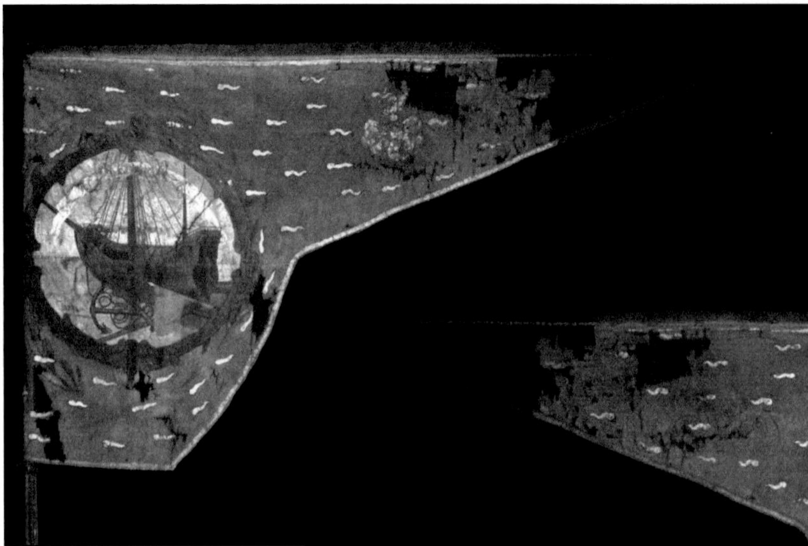

43. (left, below): Guidon of Stefana Draghi's Croat regiment. (Armémuseum, Stockholm)

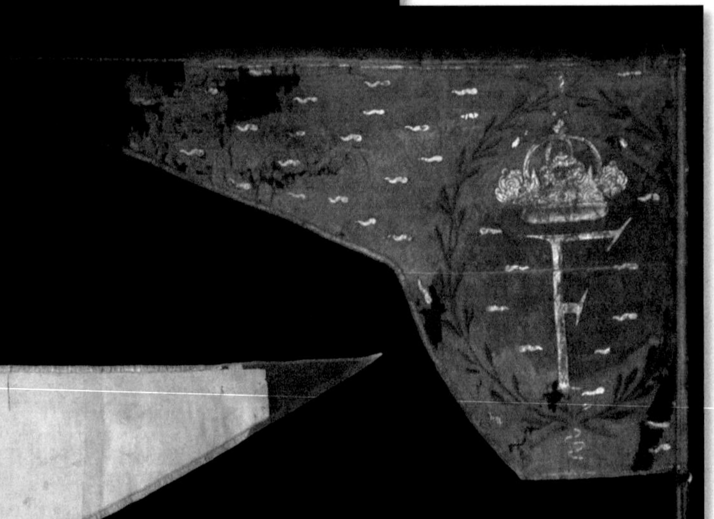

44. (left, below): Guidon of unidentified Croat regiment. (Armémuseum, Stockholm)

had a green rosary in a leaf and the motto LEGITIME CERTANTIBUS ('for the rightful combatants') in red letters. Captain Fragstein's company had a red eagle and the initial 'F' in the centre. The ensign carried by Captain Cannaert's company was similiar to that of the colonel's company, but with the Austrian coat of arms instead of Ferdinand's initial.

The cost of making these six colours came to 249 florins and 18 kreuzers. As one would expect, the colonel's ensign cost the most with the crowns costing nine gulden 13 kreuzers and the other decorations 24 kreuzers. The colour staff cost 18 kreuzers and the flag band one gulden eight kreuzers, and in addition to the silk this ensign cost 46 gulden 30 kreuzers. Moreover these colours were made in two places and cost seven gulden 12 kreuzers for those made in Breslau and 9 gulden 36 kreuzers for those made in Schweidnitz.

Whether the design of the ensigns of the regiment's other four companies were similar to these colours is not known, nor when they were presented. However, on 21 April 1632 the colours of the six companies which were then in Silesia were blessed and presented to the officers and non-commissioned officers and corporals of the regiment. It may have been these soldiers who nailed the ensign to the colour pole. After the service Hardegg's company spent seven guilders 46 kreuzers on food and drink to celebrate the occasion; what the other companies spent on their celebrations is not known. Five days later (26 April) these ensigns were presented to the regiment, with the soldiers swearing to their company's ensign and paying 12 guilders 30 kreuzers as 'worship'.

Unfortunately for Hardegg's Regiment on 16 June 1634 when it surrendered at Glogau to the Army of Saxony, it had to give up its 10 colours, which were sent to Dresden as trophies, but their subsequent fate is unknown. The regiment retreated to Habelschwerdt and Glatz, where Hardegg set about replacing these colours, which cost 17 guilders 48 kreuzer per ensign. An undated estimate for the new ensign was to be composed of nine sheets of Viennese cubits, which measured 312 cm by 390 cm per sheet of blue silk, or 45 yards of silk in all, plus 11 cubits of white silk, which was to be used to form a large Burgundian cross. Another quotation for the regiment's colours, dated 15 July 1634, was for nine blue ensigns with a white Burgundian cross, but the colonel's company was to have a white colour with a blue Burgundian cross, again each colour would cost 17 guilders 48 cruisers. There is no reference to any borders on these colours, nor any distinguishing devices of how each company colour was to be recognised.[15]

Cavalry standards could be plain, while others would not look out of place in an art gallery. Some cornets bore the Burgundian cross, such as the six identical green cornets with black Burgundian cross which were captured by the Swedish Army at some point during the war. There is no doubt that they came from the same regiment since the design is too similar and none have a fringe, which usually appears on cavalry standards. How each troop identified their own standard is not known, certainly the staves of these cornets appear to have been the same colour. Sometimes colours had the

15 Hausmann, 'Das Regiment hochdeutscher Knechte des Grafen Julius von Hardegg', pp.126–129.

date of when a regiment or troop was issued making it easier to narrow down which regiment it might be.

In 1625 when Piccolomini was raising Wallenstein's Lifeguard the cornets were to be:

> The sun casting its rays on a crescent moon, with the motto MUTUANDO SPENDOREM STELLI SPENDIDOR.
> A defiant lion escaping from other animals and the motto, OMNIA VIVINCIT or OMNIA CEDANT.
>
> A lion with a paw placed on a wheel or a ball, with the motto, MEA HAUD LUDITUR UNGUIA.
>
> A depiction of Ancas who from the burning debris of Troy rescues his father, Anchises, with the motto, PER TELA PER IGNES.
>
> The fifth troop's cornet shows a ship full of soldiers sailing towards a star above a mountain. No motto is recorded.
>
> These cornets also were to have the monogram, 'AFD' or 'AVDF' (Albertus Friedlandt Dux or Albertus Vallestain Duca Friedlandt), plus the Imperial monogram 'FS' (Ferdinand Seconda). Unfortunately, what colour these cornets were to be is not recorded.[16]

Chequerboard designs were also common, either made up of a square design or diamond shapes, or the cornet was just divided into quarters with each quarter being a different colour such as black and white. Then there were cornets with more elaborate designs, such as having images of the Virgin Mary and the baby Jesus; St George and the dragon; the various Saints; or an altar. A common device was an arm, often holding a sword, emerging from a cloud. A variation of this devices includes two hands emerging from clouds holding two water jugs trying to put out a fire or even a hand holding a stick and about to beat a beehive. Usually these designs were within a wreath. The Roman God of fortune, Fortuna, appears on some of the cornets, although she could bring good luck as well as bad.

One regiment of horse known to have had Fortuna for one of its devices was Colonel Heinrich Holk's Regiment of Horse, which is known to have had red cornets with a red fringe. This cornet had the motto, VNVER SAGI. Another cornet belonging to Holk's Regiment had a snake intertwined with a sword and the motto, HIS DVCIRVI.

One regiment with yellow standards had two troops of cavalry facing each other, with the motto, INMAUS DOMINI SORTE SMFA. The nest cornet shows the left had troop having been defeated with dead men and horses on the ground, while the other troop is still in good order. Its motto is, DEUS NOBIS HECOT IA FACOT above. On another troop's cornet was a

16 Elster, *Die Piccolomini-Regimenter Während Des 30jährigen*, pp.25–26.

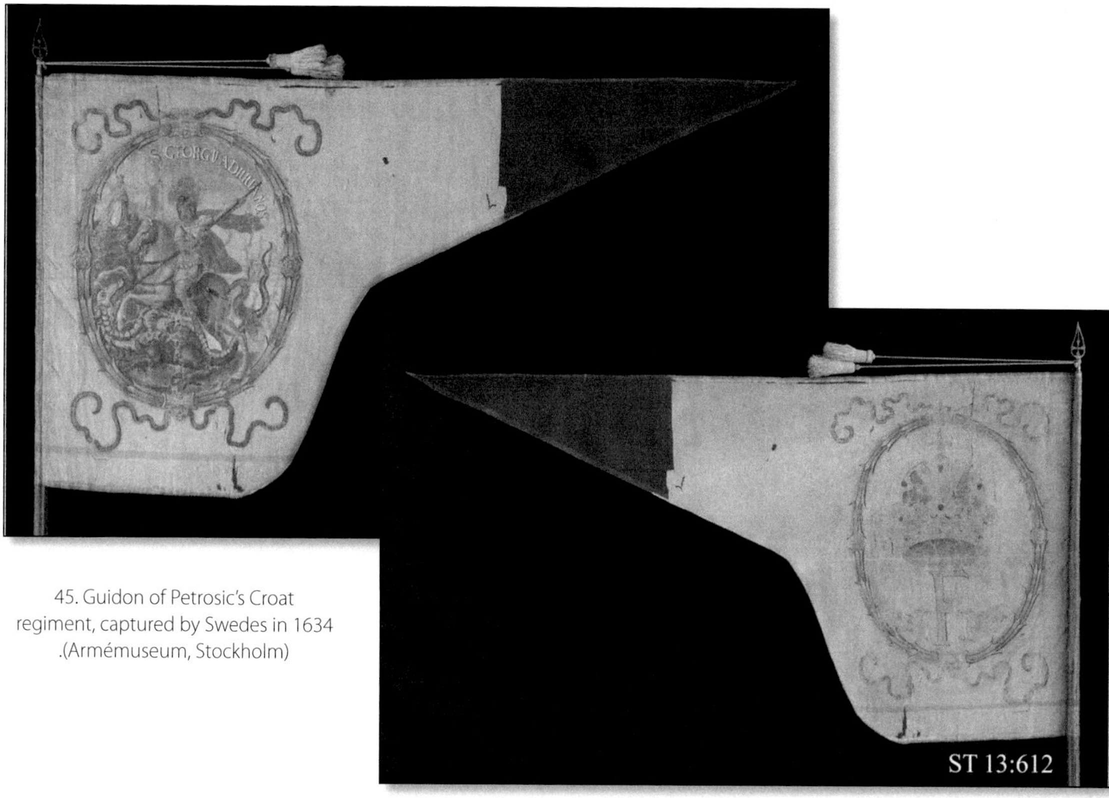

45. Guidon of Petrosic's Croat regiment, captured by Swedes in 1634 .(Armémuseum, Stockholm)

cavalryman in classical dress holding a shield and sword white riding a white horse over some red flames. Its motto was SPERMIT PERICUL AVIRIUS. A third cornet had a phoenix rising from the flames with the motto CONCVSSVS RESVRGO. The fourth cornet had swords, helmets muskets, crowns and an orb being cast on a fire, with the motto, SIC TRANSIT GLORIA MUNDI. All these devices were in a white wreath with the Imperial eagle on the other side of the corner with a black and yellow fringe. Unfortunately, which regiment these cornets belonged to is not known, but since painting the devices must have cost a fortune, they probably belonged to a very rich nobleman.

Then there are the comical standards, such as one showing a cat trying to catch 20 or so rats, unfortunately the motto was lost by the time Hoffman drew it. Then there is Colonel Dietrich von Taube's Regiment of Dragoons which was raised in 1632 and formed part of the Army of Saxony, which had 10 blue guidons with small gold flames; the devices of which included a monk giving a woman an enema, a brown bear raiding a beehive and a wolf in priest's vestments preaching to some chickens.

Both the 'Mohner Chronik; and Hoffman's drawings show that some of the colours were obviously in a poor state and still being carried by the regiment, with just fragments of the seven ensigns either tied or nailed to the pole. Others had about a third of the cornet attached to the pole, not always the right way up. According to the *Swedish Intelligencer*, at the battle of the Alte Veste, 'three cornets were then obtained and 2 ensigns; as for the rest, the ancients [ensigns] had slipped them of their flag staves and then run away with them.'[17] However, when the colour was nailed to the staff it was not so easy to save and so had to be ripped from the pole so tearing it in the process. There are several poles at the Armémuseum which show this, while other colours appear to have been reattached probably to a different pole and were captured at a later date. Ths in theory would mean that the Swedish forces captured the pole and a fragment of the colours and so could claim that they were a trophy, whereas the regiment they belonged to could also claim that they had saved their colours.

Depending on how long a regiment existed, it might also have more than one issue of standards, such as the Alt Piccolomini's Regiment of Horse, although they were always blue and had gold and blue devices. Six cornets presented to the regiment in 1629 were captured at the Second Battle of Breitenfeld on 23 October 1642, where the Imperialist Army is said to have lost 69 standards and 121 ensigns. In 1643 the regiment received new colours, one white colour for the colonel's troop and six blue with the devices painted in gold, but these were captured at the battle of Jankow on 24 February 1645. Whether the regiment was presented with new standards after this is not known, but the next recorded issue was in 1656 the year after Piccolomini's death, when the new colonel, Ludovico Caprara, continued the tradition of blue cornets that his uncle had introduced.[18]

The design of 1633 issue of Piccolomini's cornets varied, the colonel's troop had the Imperial eagle and on its chest the arms of Austria surrounded by a gold chain, and above the shield a golden crown. Other troops had a white riderless horse, Fortuna, a man kneeling at the foot of the crucified Jesus; a cuirassier on a brown horse stabbing an unidentified figure with a sword, and a king in classical dress holding a sword and sceptre.

Several Croat colours have survived in the Swedish Army Museum, which include one with a green field with St George and the dragon inside a green wreath looked upon by a Queen on a hill, and the motto S. GEORGIJ ADIUUANOS. Another Croatian cornet is red with yellow flames and a gold Imperial monogram under a gold crown within a green laurel wreath. On the reverse is a stranded sailing ship with a red flag and anchor lying on the shore, with natural colours for the sky, sea and shore which is framed within a white wreath and the motto SPPS MEA INDO EST. There are three blue cornets with a gold Imperial monogram under a red and gold crown with a pot of flames each side of the 'F'.

The capture of standards in battle was greatly sought after, because the greater the number of standards captured the greater the victory, but also those who captured them were likely to get a financial reward, as the following chart shows for standards captured by Wallenstein's Army at the battle of Lützen:[19]

17 William Watts, *The Swedish Intelligencer, the third part* (London: Nathaniel Butter and Nicholas Bourne, 1633), p.22.

18 Arne Danielsson, 'Det Kejserliga kyrassiarregementet Alt Piccolomini trofeer I Statens Trofesamling', in *Meddelande* vol. 49 (Stockholm: Armemuseum, 1989) ed. Jan von Konow. pp.103–110.

19 Henrich Holk, 6 December 1632 in Herman Hallwich, *Briefe und Akten zur geschichte Wallensteins (1630–1634)* (Vienna: Hölder, 1912), vol. 3, pp.577–578.

46. An Imperial standard from the painting depicting the siege of Magdeburg. Peeter Meulener, 1650. (Nationalmuseum, Stockholm)

Regiment	No. of standards captured	Financial reward
Comargo	10 ensigns, 1 cornet	550f
Pappenheim's Lifeguard	1 cornet	50
Keraus	4 ensigns	200f
Lamboy	1 cornet	50f
Young Breuner	2 ensigns	100f
Old Breuner	2 ensigns	100f
Major-General Breuner	3 ensigns	150f
Baden	2 ensigns	100f
Holk	1 ensign 1 cornet	100f
Piccolomini	1 ensign, 1 cornet	100f
Corpes	1 ensign	50f
Isolani	1 ensign	50f
Merodes	1 cornet	50f
Polcken	1 cornet	50f
Total	27 ensigns and 7 cornets	

On the other hand losing a standard could have dire consequences for a regiment. After the battle of Lützen Wallenstein disbanded two regiments of horse which had performed badly. Colonels Sparr and Johan Nicholas von Hagen's Regiments were disbanded but not before the monogram of the Emperor and his arms had been cut from the standards and then they were torn from the colour poles and publicly burnt by the executioner of Prague. The executioner also beheaded Hagen, Lieutenant Waltenburg and Cornet John Kaschering who were seen as responsible for losing the 'Mainz Colonel's cornet' since it had belonged to the Archbishop of Mainz. The cornet was made of white damask with a white fringe and measured 0.53 m by 0.6 m and on the top of the colour pole was a six-spoked wheel with three prongs. On one side it bore the scene of the Crucifixion with Mary and

St John in blue and red robes and a gold halo on either side of the cross, and the motto SPES MEA CHRISTUS above Christ. At the bottom of the cross was a skull. The colour was double thickness so on the reverse side was an armoured arm emerging from a cloud; unfortunately part of the cornet is missing so the arm is probably holding a sword, which was a typical device for a cavalry cornet, although a sceptre is another possibility.

6

Rations and Pay

Rations

In 1607 Wilhelm Dillich in his Kriegsbuch suggest a soldier's diet should be divided into 30 days, 16 of which should be meat days, six fish days and eight cheese days. On each of these days bread and beer was also to be issued.[1] Whereas John Glanville suggested that the soldiers' rations were to be divided into a 28 day month or a seven day circle, "for the first three days ... bread and cheese, and for the latter four days bread and beef, and the drink for the whole time [was to be] beer or beverage [cider]." It was laid down the Catholic Church, that no flesh should be eaten on Wednesdays, Fridays and Saturdays, plus Advent and during Lent and certain Saints Day so this almost certainly influenced the rations that the soldiers received.[2]

The daily ration for a private soldier appears to have varied between 1626 and 1634 as the following chart shows:[3]

Date	Provisions
16 November 1626	2 pounds of bread, 2 pounds of meat and 2 measures of beer.
5 November 1627	2 pounds of bread, 2 pounds of meat and 2 measures of beer.
5 December 1627	3 pounds of bread, 2 pounds of meat and 3 measures of beer.
1628	2 pounds of bread, 2 pounds of meat and 2 measures of beer.
5 January 1632	2 pounds of bread, 1 pound of meat and 2 measures of beer.
1 August 1633	2 pounds of bread, 1½ pounds of meat and 1½ measures of beer.
13 March 1634	2 pounds of bread, 1½ pounds of meat and 2 measures of beer.

1 Wilhelm Dilich, *Kriegsbuch darin die Alte und neu Militia eigentlich beschrieben un alle Krigssneulinge, Bau und Büchsenmeistern zu nutz und guter anleitung in Druck geben und verfertigt* (Cassel: Wilhelm Wessell, 1607), p.217.

2 John Glanville, *The Voyage to Cadiz* (London: Camden Society, 1883), p.52.

3 Dr Victor Loewe, *Die Organisation und Verwaltung die Wallensteinschen Heere* (Freiburg i.B.: J.C.B. Mohr, 1895), pp.69–70.

47. Field butchery in a military camp. Spanish siege of Breda 1624–1625. Jacques Callot, 1628. (Rijksmuseum)

The daily ration for officers and lesser officers were greater, six portions for a captain, five for his lieutenant and four for the ensign or cornet. A colonel would receive a staggering 24 measures of beer, 15 measures of wine, and 18.16 kg of bread and meat per day.

Dilich suggests that the meat was to be bacon, veal or mutton, which could either be fresh or salted to stop it going bad. During the Napoleonic Wars it was estimated that 900 g of salt was enough to preserve 3.6 kg of meat and so it often had to be soaked in water to make it edible. If the meat was salted then the army would need horses and carts to transport it, in which case the horses and carter would also have to be fed. On the other hand if the army was to have fresh meat then this would mean providing fodder and water for the animals before they were slaughtered, and the meat would have to be eaten quickly to stop it going off. Father Fitzsimon, who accompanied the Catholic League's Army in November 1620, records that, 'our food was meat killed on the spot, and spoiled by the smoke of fir trees.'[4] The meat would be weighed on a pair of scales; the remains of a pair were found on the Tudor battleship, the Mary Rose. These scales have a centre bar with a wooden handle and two large wooden plates which were probably attached by cords. However, when weighing the meat no consideration was taken of any bone or fat within it, so if the men were unlucky then their meat ration for that day would be mostly bone or gristle. Cheese would probably be sourced locally and so would be of various varieties.

The staple diet for both soldier and civilian was bread. The recipe for the bread seems to have varied from army to army and region to region, but was a mixture of rye, oats, or flour and water, and since no yeast was involved in making it, it would be similar to sour bread, which is available today. When an army could not rely on the local bakers then brick ovens were built. G. Perje estimates that it would take about 500 bricks to build an oven, which was big enough to bake between 599.85 and 1,125 kg of bread per day. Therefore an army of 10,000 men would need between eight to 15 ovens or 4,000 to 7,500 bricks,

4 'Father Fitzsimon's Diary of the Bohemian War of 1620', in *Words of Comfort to persecuted Catholics* (Dublin; M.H. Gill, 1881), p.94.

48. Soldiers pillaging a village. Jan Martszen de Jonge, 1609–1647. (Rijksmuseum)

which would have to be transported along with the firewood to heat the ovens, as well as the ingredients to make the bread, and the bread itself once baked. Where possibly these ovens would continue to bake the bread for a number of days while the army was stationary.[5] The bread was measured in the same way as the meat, but many bakers under-baked their bread to make it heavier. In September 1620 Father Drexel records that he bought a loaf of bread from a soldier which was 'black and a wet mass' which he could push his finger through like 'dough'. On the other hand, out of the 70 loaves that were given to Colonel Schmidt's Regiment only 10 were edible, the rest were too mouldy to eat.[6]

A substitute for bread was 'biscuit bread', but it was almost certainly not like the biscuit bread described by Gervase Markham in *The English Housewife,* which was first published in 1615. According to Markham it was a dessert made from flour, sugar, and eggs and served with 'a little cream'.[7] The 'biscuit bread' issued to the soldiers was more like the hardtack biscuit issued to later generations of soldiers, which lasted much longer than bread and was supplied by the bag. Writing after the American Civil War, John

5 G. Perjes, 'Army provisioning, logistics and strategy in the second half of the 17th Century', in *Acta Historica Academiae Scientiarum Hungaricae*, vol. 16 (1970), pp.8–9.

6 Father Drexel's diary, in Sigmund Riezler, *Kriegstagebücher Aus Dem Ligitischen Hauptquartier 1620* (München: G Frans'chen, 1908), p.161.

7 Gervase Markham (ed. Michael R. Best), *The English Housewife* (Quebec: McGill-Queen's University Press, 2003), pp.112–113.

D. Billings dedicated at least seven pages of his 600 page memoirs to this humble biscuit. He recalls:

> What was hardtack? It was a plain flour and water biscuit … [measuring] one-eighth by to and seven-eighths of inches, and are nearly half an inch thick … While hardtack was nutritious, yet a hungry man could eat his ten [the daily ration] in a short time and still be hungry.

Unfortunately, we do not know the size of these biscuits or how many were issued, but there are accounts of hardtack biscuits being returned to storage if they were not used. Billings continues:

> When they they were poor and fit objects for the soldiers' wrath, it was due to one of three conditions: First, they may have been so hard that they could not be bitten: it then required a very strongblow of the fist to break them. The cause of this hardness it would be difficult for one not an expert to determine. This variety certainly well deserved their name. They could not be *soaked* soft, but after a time took on the elasticity of gutta-percha.[8]
>
> The second condition was when there were mouldy or wet as sometimes happened and should not have been given to the soldiers. I think this was often due to their having been boxed up too soon after baking. It certainly was frequently due to exposure to the weather…
>
> The third condition was when from storage they had become infested with maggots and weevils. These weevils were, in my experience, more abundant than the maggots. They were a little slim, brown bug an eighth of an inch in length, and were great *borers* on a small scale, having the ability to completely riddle the hardtack. I believe they never interfered with the hardest variety … [but] eaten in the dark no one could tell the difference between it and hardtack that was untenanted … If a soldier cared to do so, he could expel the weevils by heating the bread at the fire. The maggots did not budge in this way.[9]

Fortunately the American Civil War soldier had coffee in which he could soak the 'biscuit bread', but all the seventeenth century soldier had was beer. The alcohol content of the beer would have been low, and which in England was known as 'small beer'. It was probably issued to the soldiers using a measuring jug, although there is no evidence to suggest that soldiers were issued with containers to store the beer in. Neither is there any evidence that they were issued with drinking vessels, but some soldiers' accounts refer to them using their own hats for drinking.

A soldier might have plenty to eat one day and nothing the next. In December 1623 Montenegro's Imperialist Army was said to have 'endured so great a want as they had no bread during the space of three or four weeks and were constrained

8 A rubbery substance produced by tropical trees, and formerly used in electrical insulation and golf balls.

9 John D. Billings, *Hardtack and Coffee or the unwritten Story of Army Life* (Boston: George M. Smith & Co, 1887), pp.113–116.

to eat dead horses and dogs.'[10] Therefore it was important to find provisions to keep up the army's morale. War contributions are usually associated with a monetary payment, but clothing and food could also be demanded from the local population. On 29 August 1631 the *Leipzig Chronicle* records that the city was ordered to supply Tilly's Army – Tilly at this point commanding both the Imperialist as well as the Catholic League's Army – 80,000 pounds of bread daily and on 15 November 1631 the Swedish Army demanded from Leipzig 45,000 pounds of bread, 40,000 pounds of meat, 40,000 jugs of beer and 3,000 bushels of unspecified cereal, such as oats, barley etc.[11]

On the other hand foraging parties might be sent out in enemy as well as friendly territory to round up all the provisions they could find. In 1635 158 Malted cereals (wheat, rye and barley), 127 cows, 241 sheep and 30 pigs were captured by Imperialist forces in a village in Upper Franconia, which was said to be enough to feed a regiment of five companies.[12] Foraging could be used to desolate the enemy's lands so that they could prevent it supporting their army, as happened when Swedish troops occupied large areas of Bavaria in 1632.

A soldier carried his provisions in a knapsack, which was a cylindrical bag fastened at both ends with a cord or a strap, which was long enough for the soldier to sling it over his shoulder. Documentary evidence suggest that they were mainly made from leather but canvas ones are known. Illustrations suggest that they were only large enough to carry a day or two's rations, plus any personal items the soldiers might have. As mentioned above there is no evidence to suggest the existence of drinking bottles, although leather and pottery bottles are known to have existed. These were usually rectangular in shape with a hole where a person could fill the bottle and drink from it, plus two loops where a piece of cord or thong could be threaded through so that the person could carry it over their shoulder.

If a soldier was quartered in a town or city then they would receive the same food as the occupants of the house where they were quartered. In theory a householder would be repaid for the soldier's bed and board, but this was paid in arrears, if at all, and would almost certainly cause the inhabitants hardship.

Horses whether to mount the cavalry or hitched to a wagon also needed to be fed, likewise any cattle used for meat to feed the officers and soldiers. It has been estimate that a horse doing a moderate day's works needs about 25,000 calories per day and 10 gallons of water. Therefore a regiment of horse about 500 strong needs 3,400-4,500 kg of fodder and 5,000 gallons of water per day. Therefore if a commander valued his cavalry the he would not only have to plan a campaign for strategic gain, but also how best he could feed his horses. As for cattle it has been estimated that justone head of cattle consumes about 11kg of hay per day, plus water.[13]

10 TNA SP 101/46 f.249, *News from the Hague,* 28 December 1623

11 Heidenreich, *Leipzigische Chronicke*, pp.460, 547.

12 Statni Oblastni Archive in Zamrsku RA Piccolomini Nachod 17556, list of provisions captured, 1635.

13 Robin Higham, 'Some Thoughts on the Thirty Years' War', in *Bellum Tricannale* (Prague, 1997), p.340, and on horse feeding on <http://ecoquine.wordpress.com> (accessed December 2015).

Pay

As well as being issued with their daily rations a soldier could supplement his rations by buying extra food from the many sutlers which accompanied the army. Unfortunately for the soldier they were rarely paid on time if at all. Usually the soldiers' pay was calculated by the month, although in the Spanish service a financial 'month' could be between six and eight weeks long. Moreover the exchange rate within the Empire varied greatly, with a gulden or florin which was often shown as 'fl' equalling 60 kreuzer and a Reichstaler was worth 1½ fl or 90 kreuzer, whereas 2 fl equalled an English pound. This exchange rate does not include the early 1620s when hyper inflation was rife throughout the Empire due to the coinage being debased through the edges of the coin being clipped for its silver.[14]

In theory the pay was the same throughout Wallenstein's Army, but there seems to have been marked differences between regiments serving with the main army and those in quieter war zones. The following chart shows the quarterly salary of the staff for a regiment of horse:[15]
The pay of the officers within a troop of cavalry also varied:

Rank	10 Nov 1625*	21 Nov 1627†	5 Dec 1627‡	1628§	10 Nov 1629	9 Nov 1630	4 Oct 1634¶
Colonel	500 fl	300 fl	300 fl	300 fl	300 fl	240 fl	150 fl
Lt Colonel	150 fl	150 fl	120 fl	120 fl	120 fl	60 fl	37½ fl
Major	125 fl	75 fl	90 fl	90 fl	-	20 fl	-
Quartermaster	20 fl	30 fl	20 fl	18 fl	18 fl	20 fl	12½ fl
Secretary	20 fl	20 fl	-	18 fl	-	20 fl	7½ fl
Provost	35 fl	30 fl	30 fl	30 fl	-	24 fl	7½ fl
Commissary	8 fl	12 fl	10 fl	9 fl	9	16 fl	12½ fl
Chaplain	8 fl	15 fl	10 fl	-	-	12 fl	7½ fl
Wagonmaster	6 fl	7½ fl	6 fl	6 fl	-	12 fl	7½ fl
Judge	-	30 fl	-	-	-	-	7½ fl

The pay for those in *Brandenburg, †Silesia, ‡the Empire, §Winter quarters in Brandenburg, ¶under Gallas in the Empire.

Rank	11 Nov 1625	5 Dec 1627	1628	10 Dec 1629
Captain	100 fl	75 fl	75 fl	75 fl
Lieutenant	40 fl	30 fl	30 fl	30 fl
Cornet	26½ fl	20 fl	22½ fl	22½ fl
Quartermaster	21 fl	12 fl	7½ fl	12 fl
Corporal	6½ fl	6 fl	7½ fl	6 fl
Farrier	6½ fl	8 fl	? fl	7½ fl
Trumpeter	5 11/30 fl	4½ fl	2½ fl	3¾ fl

14 Frederick Boas (ed.), *The Diary of Thomas Crosfield* (Oxford: Oxford University Press, 1935), p.67.
15 Loewe, *Die Organisation und Verwaltung die Wallensteinschen*, p.63.

A. Dress of a Senior Officer; B. Reconstruction of a trooper of Wallenstein's Lifeguard by K.A. Wilke; C. Cuirassier, taken from Johann J. Von Wallhausen's *Kriegskunst zu Pferdt*, of 1616

(Illustration by Mark Allen, © Helion & Company)

See Colour Plate Commentaries for further information.

A. Dragoon pikeman; B. Harquebusier, medium cavalry

(Illustration by Mark Allen, © Helion & Company)

See Colour Plate Commentaries for further information.

A. Various figures from Pieter Snayers' battle paintings; C. Overhose, casaque and breeches; D. Pikeman in half armour

(Illustration by Mark Allen, © Helion & Company)

See Colour Plate Commentaries for further information.

Plate Four

A. Sergeant of musket or pike; B. An update of the 'de Gheyn' musketeer of 1607; C. Musketeer; D. Decorated ropills; E. Marching musketeer; F. Soldier wearing ruff

(Illustration by Mark Allen, © Helion & Company)

See Colour Plate Commentaries for further information.

A. Colours of infantry regiment Savelli; B. Breuner regiment colours; C. Colonel's colour of Adolf Von Schleswig Holstein Gottorf; D. Three unidentified Imperial colours

(Illustration by Mark Allen, © Helion & Company)

See Colour Plate Commentaries for further information.

A. Unknown Imperial Infantry colour; B. Colour from Johann Graf Von Aldringer; C. Colours associated with Aldringer's; D. Three of a set of four extant Imperial colours

(Illustration by Mark Allen, © Helion & Company)

See Colour Plate Commentaries for further information.

A. Two of four flags of Graf Hardegg's regiment; B. Two colours from an unknown regiment; C. Reconstructed colours of Graf Heinrich Von Holk

(Illustration by Mark Allen, © Helion & Company)

See Colour Plate Commentaries for further information.

A. Holk's cavalry cornet; B., C., unknown cavalry cornets of white damask; D., E., unidentified dragoon guidons

(Illustration by Mark Allen, © Helion & Company)

See Colour Plate Commentaries for further information.

The pay of the staff of an infantry regiment was as follows:[16]

Rank	Oct 1625	Nov 1625	Jul 1627	Nov 1627	Dec 1627	1628	Nov 1629	Nov 1630	Oct 1634
Colonel	500 fl	500 fl	300 fl	300 fl	300 fl	300 fl	300 fl	125 fl	125 fl
Lt Col	200 fl	150 fl	120 fl	120 fl	120 fl	120 fl	120 fl	30 fl	30 fl
Major	50 fl	120 fl	30 fl	90 fl	90 fl	90 fl	90 fl	10 fl	10 fl
Q'master	8 fl	20 fl	15 fl	15 fl	20 fl	15 fl	15 fl	10 fl	10 fl
Provost6	-	35 fl	10½ fl	21½ fl	30 fl	30 fl	30 fl	7½ fl	15 fl
Secretary	-	20 fl	15 fl	15 fl	20 fl	15 fl	15 fl	6 fl	15 fl
Judge	50 fl	25 fl	15 fl	30 fl	20 fl	15 fl	15 fl	10 fl	10 fl
Commissary	-	8 fl	6 fl	6 fl	10 fl	6 fl	6 fl	10 fl	-
Chaplain	-	8 fl	6 fl	6 fl	10 fl	9 fl	9 fl	6 fl	6 fl
Wagonmaster	-	8 fl	6 fl	6 fl	6 fl	6 fl	6 fl	6 fl	6 fl

The pay for officers of an infantry company was as follows:[17]

Rank	Nov 1625	Apr 1626	July 1627	Nov 1627	Dec 1627	1628	Dec 1629	Nov 1630	Oct 1634
Captain	100 fl	100 fl	60 fl	75 fl	75 fl	75 fl	75 fl	64 fl	40 fl
Lieutenant	50 fl	35 fl	21½	30 fl	25 fl	22½	22½ fl	24 fl	15 fl
Ensign	30 fl	25 fl	15¾	22½ fl	18 fl	15 fl	15 fl	20 fl	12½ fl
Sergeant	8 fl	7 fl	6 fl	12 fl	8 fl	7½ fl	7½ fl	8 2/5 fl	5¼ fl
Clerk	8 fl	7 fl	3¾ fl	4½ fl	7 fl	-	5¼ fl	3 fl	3 fl
Surgeon	6 fl	5¼ fl	3 fl	4½ fl	-	3¾ fl	4¾ fl	3 fl	3 fl
Leader	6 fl	5¼ fl	3¾ fl	-	4 fl	3¾ fl	4¼ fl	3 fl	-
Q'master	6 fl	5¼ fl	3¾ fl	6 fl	4 fl		4¼ fl	3 fl	-
Corporal	-	3½ fl	3 fl	3 fl	3 fl	-	3 fl	4 4/5 fl	3 fl
Drummer	-	2 fl	-	2 fl	2 fl	2¾ fl	3¼ fl	2 fl	-

The pay for a soldier in Wallenstein's Army also varied:[18]

Date	Infantry	Cavalry
10 November 1625	2 fl 48 kr	-
18 July 1627	2 fl	-
5 December 1627	1¼ fl	3 fl
1628	2¼ fl	3 fl
9 November 1630	1¼ fl	3¾ fl (cuirassier) 3 fl (Harquebusier)
4 October 1634	1 fl 60 kr	3 fl (Harquebusier)

There was another problem with not paying the soldiers, in that it bred poor discipline. True, there were military laws preventing plundering, rape, and murder, but these appear to have been largely ignored since officers felt unable to impose the harsh punishments these laws prescribed while their men were in arrears, since without money they could not buy food or other essentials and the only way to obtain them was to steal them.

On the other hand crimes which endangered the army were strictly enforced, such as hitting an officer, giving the password to the enemy or

16 Loewe, *Die Organisation und Verwaltung die Wallensteinschen Heere*, p.67.
17 Loewe, *Die Organisation und Verwaltung die Wallensteinschen Heere*, p.68.
18 Loewe, *Die Organisation und Verwaltung die Wallensteinschen Heere*, p.68.

Israel ex. cum Priuil. Reg.

Israel excud. cum Priuil. Reg.

Facing page:
49. (top, centre): Execution in a military camp. Spanish siege of Breda 1624–1625. Jacques Callot, 1628. (Rijksmuseum)

50. (bottom): Military discipline. Jacques Callot, 1633. (Rijksmuseum)

falling asleep while on guard duty. For this a soldier would expect to be hanged. If there was more than one soldier involved then they might cast lots, which could either be in the form of throwing a dice and the one with the lowest score being executed, or drawing tickets from a hat and the soldier who drew the piece of paper with a gallows on it being hanged. Officers would expect to be shot or beheaded.

For minor crimes a soldier might be made to 'ride the wooden horse', whereby the soldier had his hands tied behind his back and sit on the edge of two wooden planks for a given amount of time. Weights might also be tied to his feet to make the punishment more severe. Then there was the 'strappado', whereby a soldier would have his hands tied behind his back and hoisted up by the hands or thumbs so that they could barely touch the ground. Sometimes they might even be hoisted off the ground before being dropped, but they would be stopped before they hit the ground which often dislocated their arms. It was said that the very sight of a strappado, 'will do good in a wicked mind'. In his *Miseries of War* Jacques Callot shows a soldier undergoing this punishment having been raised high above his comrades. The caption reads, 'It is not without cause that great captains have well advisedly invented these punishments for idlers, blasphemers, traitors to duty, quarrelers and liars, whose actions, blinded by vice, make those of others slack and irregular.'[19]

Imprisonment was also used if a soldier blasphemed for the first time or was 'seen without his sword', or if he left his garrison or lodging without a pass, struck a fellow soldier or was insolent to an officer, did not keep his arms clean or even sold or pawned them. Selling his arms could lead to the death of the soldier. For a second offence 'blasphemers' and 'common swearers' could expect to have their tongue bored with a red hot iron. How often this punishment was carried out is not known.

However, soldiers in Wallenstein's Army could also expect a bonus. After the action at the Alte Veste in September 1632 Wallenstein awarded 400 gulden to the colonels who had been wounded, 300 guldens to any wounded captains, 40 guldens to corporals or 10 gulden to any wounded soldier.[20] Soldiers would also be rewarded for bravery in battle by capturing an enemy standard, or as in Piccolomini's Regiment of Horse selected troopers were awarded 15, 18 or 30 Thalers for the part they had played at the battle of Lützen, while corporals could expect 70 thalers and cornets 150 thalers.

19 Howard Daniel (ed.), *Callot's Etchings* (New York: Dover Publications, 1974), sketch no. 274.
20 Mann, *Wallenstein, his life narrated*, p.635.

7

Quartering

One thinks of armies clashing in battle, but for the majority of soldiers their service would be as part of a garrison of a town or city and they might never see a skirmish let alone a battle. However when called into the field or were part of a field army they had three types of accommodation: being quartered on the local population, sleeping in a hut or tent, or – if they arrived too late at their rendezvous or there was not enough material to construct a hut – then they would have no choice but to sleep under the stars.

As one would expect, an army quartering in a territory would be unpopular to the inhabitants, therefore generals of armies would do their best to keep quartering in an allied country to the minimum. However, Wallenstein is known to have quartered his army in the lands of friend and foe alike, but when it came to his own lands in Bohemia, and later the Duchies of Friedland and Mecklenburg, quartering was kept to a minimum. As one can imagine, this selective quartering meant that Ferdinand II received a great number of complaints from his allies, insomuch that Maximilian of Bavaria ordered the Army of the Catholic League not to work with the Imperial Army and this tension would be one of the reasons why Wallenstein was dismissed in 1630.

Billeting in Towns or Cities

The soldiers probably preferred being quartered on the inhabitants of a town or village, especially during the winter, and especially if they were treated as Edward Davies prescribed:

> A soldier in garrison being furried [quartered] in a house, is allowed the best bed and chamber save one, fair sheets, board clothes, plates, napkins, towels, dressing of his meat, service at the table, oil, vinegar, salt, mustard, candlelight, fire etc.[1]

Davies also suggested that in the soldier's room a candle or fire should always be lit so that he could find his arms in an emergency and if he was a

1 Davies, *The Art of War and England's Training*, p.18.

musketeer light his match for his musket. However, not many civilians could afford candles since they were expensive, and the poorest inhabitants they usually had to rely on reeds or rushes soaked in animal fat, which gave very little light.

Johan von Wallhausen recommended that, 'in friendly country I will never counsel any Lord or Potentate to lodge a regiment of soldiers in villages, except that great necessity requires it, as time of frost [or] cold weather.' His reasons include that the householders could not afford to keep the soldiers, who might behave badly, and so cause ill feeling between their subjects. Wallhausen also warned that, being quartered in towns and villages, they did not have the proper protection of a fortified military encampment and so might have their quarters 'beaten up' by the enemy.[2]

If the soldiers were to be quartered in a town or village then the regimental quartermasters would chalk on the door of a house the regiment and company commander's name and the number of men that the property was to accommodate. If possible a regiment or company would be accommodated in the same village or town to make training easier, although sometimes as few as two or three men might quartered in a village so as to keep order.

The local population had no say in the matter, and having the 'best bed' and room was all very well, but many of the houses within a town might only have a couple of rooms and the occupants probably had just one bed which was reserved for the head of the household and his wife. This might be an inconvenience if a soldier stayed just a night or two, but could spell financial ruin if they stayed for months, or, if they were in a garrison town, years. True, the householders were to be paid for giving a soldier food and accommodation, but they may not be reimbursed until months later, if at all.

One civilian, Augustin Guntzer of Colmar in Alsace, left an account of soldiers billeted on him in 1633:

> I was onerously burdened with the quartering of soldiers. Therefore I had to argue with them often, because they wanted to have better food than I and my children have … In the night they took my housewares and took my wine from the cellar… often I found the tablecloth on the table, the mugs and glasses full of urine, the table cloth cut with a knife and other housewares defiled and destroyed. Then my two young daughters complained with crying eyes that the way that they were handled by the soldiers, they could not stay in the house. I went to the quartermaster for help, and I received as an answer that I had better get along well with the soldiers, so that the soldiers would not have reason to complain about me.

How long the soldiers remained with him Guntzer does not say, but rather putting the soldiers' activities down to ill discipline he saw it as a punishment from God 'for my sins.' Soldiers would return again to Colmar two years later and Guntzer would have to quarter two more soldiers who behaved just as

2 Wallhausen, *L'Art Militaire pour L'Infantrie*, p.151.

badly.[3] However, other civilians were not so naive as Guntzer, and fought back when the soldiers became unruly and took their revenge on any small isolated groups of soldiers they found.

Camping in the Fields

When there was no town or village nearby soldiers often had to quarter in open fields and would have to sleep under the stars or in tents. If there was time they might make themselves huts or cabins. According to Henry Hexham, they '[made] their huts of forks, lathes withes and straw or for if they were staying just one night, sticks and boughs or as such things as they can get.'4 Therefore a soldier's hut would depend on his foraging skills and what was available to hand, so some of these huts might be well built while others might just give the minimum of protection from the elements.

According to Edward Davies:

> A soldier in camp must make choice of two or three or more comrades, such as for experience, fidelity and conditions, do best agree with his nature, that be tried soldiers and trusty friends, to the intent that like loving brethren, they may support one another in all adverse fortune, and supply each others wants. As for example, having marched all day, and coming at night to the place where they must encamp, one of them chooseth out the driest and warmest plot of ground he can get in the quarter, which is appointed to his band [company] for [their] lodging place, doth keep all their cloaks, arms and baggage, whilst another makes provision to with one of their boys, in some adjoining village (if time and safety from the enemy doth permit) for long straw, both to cover their cabin, and make their bed of: during the time that another with a little hatchet (which with a leather bottle for drink, a little kettle to seeth [cook] meat in and a bag of salt, which areto be born of the boys amongst other baggage, and are most necessary things for encamping) doth cut down forked bows and long poles to frame and rear up the cabin withal, and provide timber, or firewood, if it be in winter, or when need requires, whilst another doth visit vniandiers and victualers (if any follow the camp) for bread, drink and other cates, if otherwise they be not provided by forage or picoree, and makes a hole in the earth, wherein having made a fire, stroken two forked stakes at either side, and hanged his kettle to seath upon a cudgel of wood upon the same, or that for roast meat he makes a spit, woodengauberds etc. And whilst thus everyone is occupied about their necessary occasions at one instant they may in due time make provision for all their wants and means of this league of amity amongst them, enjoy a sufficient time to rest their wearied bodies, which otherwise would be hard to be done.

Unfortunately, sources do not agree on how large a soldiers' hut should be; one description says that these huts should be able '[to] lodge two common soldiers and so you shall have 50 huts for each company, divided into ranks,

3 Quoted in Hans Medick and Benjamin Marschke, *Experiencing the Thirty Years' War: a brief history with documents* (New York: Bedford/St Martins, 2013), pp.76–77.

4 Henry Hexham, *The Art of War* (1638), p.21.

each rank consists of 25, every hut is to be six foot broad and seven foot long, each hut shall be distant one from another rank [by] two feet.'[5]

Whereas Sir Horace Vere, who served in the Dutch Army, said it was the quartermaster's duty:

> [to] go through every captain's quarters to see if the soldiers have built their cabins high and wide enough and have made their beds above the ground. Thecaptains ought every three weeks to get fresh straw to give their soldiers ... and to air their cabins and to keep their quarters swept every day very clean to avoid sickness.[6]

Robert Ward, however, writing some 25 years later, said this responsibility had passed to the sergeants of the company to make sure that:

> The soldiers build their huts even and keep exactly the measurements so the streets may be even and that if it be possible that the huts be built all of one height and after one and the same fashion ... All the doors of the huts must be open to the lane that is between the ranks of the huts.[7]

A company of 200 to 300 men would need between 100 to 150 huts per company since most sources agree that there should be two soldiers to a hut. In the Swedish Army there appears to have been three men to a hut or tent which was to be nine feet square. However, if a soldier was accompanied by his family then they appear to have occupied his hut, rather than another soldier.

Davies also suggests that:

> Whilst a soldier is in the camp, he ought never to lie out of his clothes, his piece [musket] ready charged must lie by his side, his furniture at his girdle [side], which is his flask, match and touch box, his rapier very ready, and his poinado [dagger] likewise at his girdle.[8]

Meanwhile the corporals and the regimental provost and his men were to make sure that the camp was kept clean, especially if they were quartered in the same place for some time.

Sometimes a commander might quarter his cavalry in a nearby town, while his infantry were quartered in the fields, but when a regiment was quartered in the field the horses, whether for the cavalry or artillery, needed stabling. John Cruso, who wrote *Militarie Instructions for the Cavalrie* in 1632, records that 'to lodge or encamp the cavalry, a special care must be had of the commodity of water, and where they may be under shelter: for one cold or rainy night might ruin the cavalry, nothing hurting a horse sooner then cold or wet.'

5 British Library Harl no. 6,344, *A Short military treatise concerning all things needful in an army*, ff.160–169.

6 TNA SP 9/202/1/18, Compendium of the Discipline of the Art of War under Sir Horace Vere, 1603–1625.

7 Ward, *Animadversions of Warre ...*, Book 2, pp. 32, 38.

8 Davies, *The Art of War and England's Training*, p.18.

51. (left, below and following page): Details of a military camp. Spanish siege of Breda 1624–1625. Jacques Callot, 1628 (Rijksmuseum)

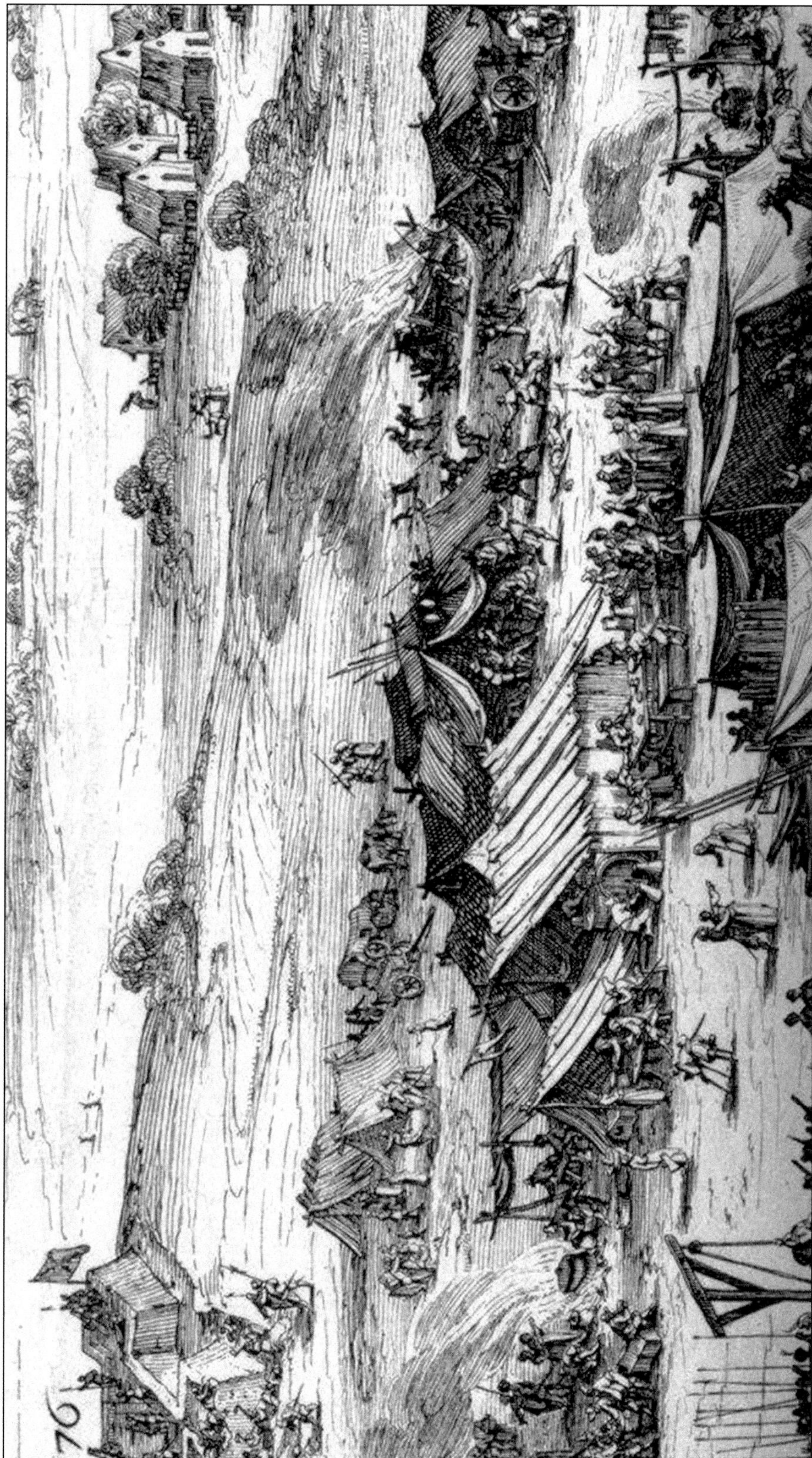
76

Cruso also suggests that each troop of cuirassiers were to be:

> 13 foot broad and the huts of the horsemen are 10 foot broad and 8 foot long for one horseman and his boy. And betwixt two huts there is two foot of space for the drain of rain water, dropping from the thatch or covers of the huts. These huts have their chief doors or passages towards their heads of their horse and a small opening into the street where they lay their hay and straw, every one behind his own hut ... a street of five foot broad [is] between the horseman's huts and the mangers [or stables] for their horses... Ten foot [is allowed] for the stables of their horses, which are placed with the heads towards their huts, and every horse hath four foot in breadth for his litter and eight foot for two horses; according to the length of their huts.[9]

It was essential for the 'boy' mentioned by Cruso to be quartered with the cuirassier so that he could help him into his armour. The harquebusier had no such problem and Cruso suggests that:

> [The] companies of harquebusiers have also 180 foot depth for the quartering of their ... huts ... but these have but 15 huts in every file for 30 horse, having also two streets (as the cuirassiers) ... being of 12 foot broad and eight foot deep for two harquebusiers and eight foot for the litter of their two horses and 10 foot for their stable. And five foot for a street between their huts and the mangers for their horses.[10]

The officers' and trumpeters' tents or huts were at the end of each street.

How many tents were issued to Wallenstein's Army is not known, but contemporary illustrations of encampments show tents were composed of two upright poles and one horizontal pole with a single sheet of canvas stretched over them and staked to the ground. The front and back appear to have been left open.

Officers had more elaborate tents. Johan von Wallhausen shows circular tents used by the officers, with cone tops and small flags on the top, secured to the ground by about 14 tent ropes. Although, a painting of Sir Horace Vere has a soldier guarding a rectangular shaped tent about seven feet tall and about 12 to 14 feet long with possibly six or seven small windows and a doorway with a crescent top. The roof tapers up. The tent cords are fastened to where the walls are attached to the roof and two cords are also tied to the poles holding up the roof. Presumably the walls are pegged down.

A colonel might not have just one tent, according to Thomas Raymond, who served in Colonel Packenham's Regiment in the Dutch service:

> My colonel had a kitchen tent, a servants' tent, a lodging tent for himself and another, the largest and fairest tent of all, wherein he eat, gave audience to his officers and

9 John Cruso, *Militarie Instructions for the Cavalrie being a facsimile of the edition* (Kineton: The Roundwood Press, 1972), ed. Brigadier Peter Young, pp.66–67.

10 Cruso, *Militarie Instructions for the Cavalrie*, pp.66–67.

52. Detail of a military camp. Spanish siege of Breda 1624–1625. Jacques Callot, 1628 (Rijksmuseum)

> entertained. Which also was our church having there every Sunday morning a sermon preached by the chaplain to the regiment.[11]

Johan von Wallhausen, who wrote a manual on cavalry and infantry at the beginning of the seventeenth century, suggests that these roads should be '16 paces wide' and each tent, or hut, should have a frontage of eight paces. Whereas lieutenants were allowed 16 paces, and ensigns and captains 24 paces. However another contemporary source suggests that the road should be '10 foot broad'.[12]

In addition space was set aside for huts and stalls of sutlers, which were to situated furthest away from those of the officers. Contemporary paintings of camp scenes by artists such as Philips Wouwerman or David Teniers the Younger, often show these sutler tents which are much taller than the soldiers' shelters and are distinguished by having laurel wreaths, a tankard, or a flag hanging from one of the tent poles outside. There are also several tables outside where the soldiers could sit to drink and eat.

With all the people in the camp there was a large amount of human and animal waste, and even the excrement soon built up even after a day. Several

---

11 Thomas Raymond (ed. G. Davis), *Autobiography of Thomas Raymond* (London: Royal Historical Society, 1917), p.37.

Wallhausen, *The Art Militaire pour L'Infantrie*, p.127; British Library Harl. 6344, *A Short military treatise concerning all things needful in an army*, ff.160–169.

manuals recommended that an army should set up an encampment by a river where the waste could be thrown to get rid of it, or even be buried. Unfortunately during the seventeenth century bacteria was unknown, so it was believed that bad smells were believed to spread diseases, therefore if an army stayed in an encampment too long then disease might break out such as typhus which is said to have destroyed many armies throughout history.

During the seventeenth century it was also known as 'camp fever' and 'gaol fever' since it thrives in filthy conditions, as well as being called the 'burning ague'. It was also known by enemy's name such as 'the Hungarian disease' or 'the Swedish disease'. It is caused by the *Rickettsia prowazekii* bacteria and is highly contagious, being spread from person to person by lice, which feed off an infected individual. The human body is the perfect environment for the louse, but when the body gets too hot due to fever or too cold due to death, the lice tries to find another human host to live upon. Meanwhile the bacteria in the lice's stomach multiplies and passes into its intestines where it is excreted and can stay active for many days in dried faeces. During this time the louse will have bitten its new host, who then scratches the itch, and if they break the skin the bacteria enters the bloodstream.

Typhoid was also a common disease in armies, similar to typhus and spread in the same way, although caused by different bacteria. During the first week the infected person's temperature rises, accompanied by headaches, malaise and a cough, before becoming delirious, and spots may appear on the body. Their diarrhoea has a green appearance and the liver and spleen become enlarged. After about four weeks death occurs in between 10 to 20 percent of suffers.

Dysentery, or the 'bloody flux', is also spread by unhygienic conditions, via organisms such as bacteria or parasitic worms which are found in food or water contaminated by human faeces. The sufferer's symptoms can include a high fever, fatigue, headaches, nausea or vomiting and abdominal pains which can lead to complications to the internal organs including kidney failure. However, all types of dysentery result in severe diarrhoea, which sometimes contains blood, hence the name 'bloody flux', which can lead to organ failure or death due to dehydration if left untreated.

The skeletal remains of the mass graves show that syphilis was common among the solders. Sores or legions would appear all over the body, especially around the genital area. One of the 'cures'often used was mercury, either taken orally, injected, or mixed with other ingredients to form a cream which was then rubbed into the sores.

These sores would usually disappear after a time without treatment, but the mercury could cause madness and damage to the nervous system.

Of course typhus, dysentery, and typhoid are all modern names for these diseases, but the most feared disease, which was blamed on the movement of soldiers, was plague, which is mentioned as the cause of death in many burial registers. Bubonic plague was spread by the fleas on black rats (*Rattus Rattus*). After they had gorged themselves on a rat infected by the *Pestis* bacteria the fleas then fed on humans and so passed the infection on. Once infected, the sufferer developed buboes, usually on the neck, armpits and groin. It the plague spread to the lungs then the sufferer would develop pneumonic plague which was spread from human to human by coughing or sneezing. Medicine books are full of cures for the plague, but on infection death would almost certainly follow.

Fortified Camps

In a hostile country a commander might fortify his camp. The military engineer Samuel Marolois recommends a ditch, six to eight feet broad and five to six feet deep 'and the parapet of the same breath and height', whereas Robert Ward suggests that redoubts should be dug to defend the passages to the camp. For passages where the approach of the enemy was least expected then Ward recommended a ravelin or triangular redoubt, which was to contain 30 or 40 men. However, for passages where the approach of the enemy was more likely, square redoubts were to be erected to protect between 80 to 100 men. Ward further adds that:

These redoubts are to be relieved every night before sunset with fresh companies from the main camp; where no soldier is to pull off his armour or set down his pike or musket until they be all entered the work and the sentinels set out in their due places.

The camp would be divided into areas for the cavalry, artillery and infantry divided by wide streets. These areas were further divided and allocated to a regiment and a company would be allocated an area of land within the camp on which to quarter. A space was also allocated for the regimental baggage.

Probably the most famous fortified camp was that created by Wallenstein near Nuremberg during the summer of 1632, and known as the Alte Veste. The Imperialists worked daily building their own fortified camp which was protected by palisades, ditches and other earthworks which protected Wallenstein's artillery. It had a radius of 2¼ miles and encompassed the villages of Stein, Zirndorf, Altenberg, Kreutles, and Lower Asbach and to the north was the Alte Veste. A plan drawn up two years later by Paul and Hans Trexel shows that the camp had about 30 half redoubts, 16 square redoubts, and a large star fort which were joined by earth parapets, all of which were protected by wooden stakes and a moat. There was also a large star fort outside this wall and six square redoubts guarded the nearby river. The infantry appear to have been in tents, while the cavalry were housed in wooden huts. As late as 1904 the remnants of three of the half redoubts could still be seen, and measured 26.3 feet wide and about five feet high. Part of the wall had also survived and measured 3.25 feet high and 18.3 feet wide, although the height of these fortifications was much greater in 1632 and had been worn away over the centuries. The ditch was almost five feet wide.

The area from Stein to Alterberg was allocated to Wallenstein's Army, and the remainder of the camp was for the troops belonging to the Catholic League. The artillery park was between Lower Asbach and Altenberg.

Gustavus Adolphus fortified the nearby city of Nuremberg, which was no less impressive than that of Wallenstein's camp, but now has been almost forgotten. Illustrations show that the Swedish fortifications surrounded almost the entire city and had about 40 bulwarks and square redoubts. There

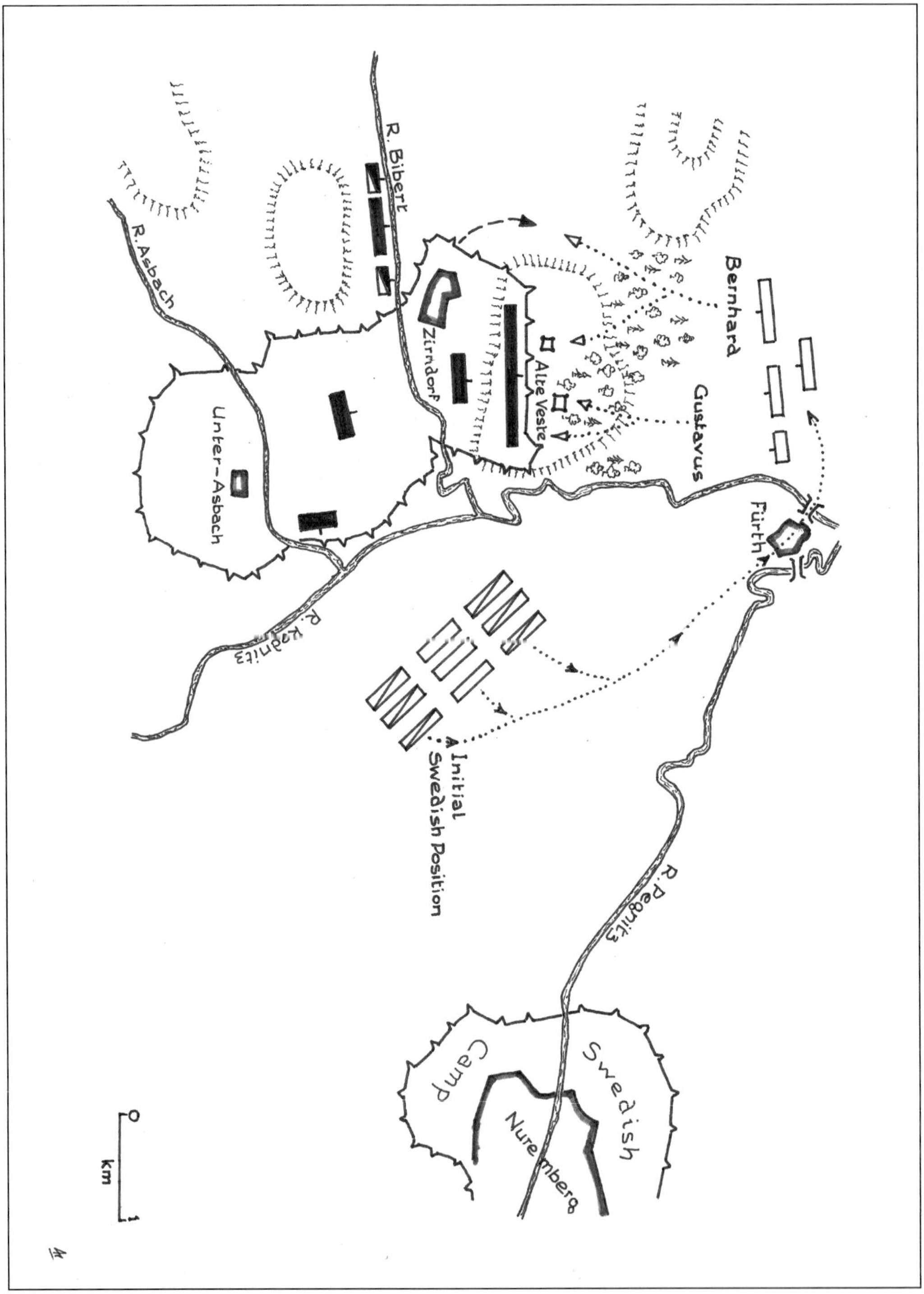

Map 1 Plan of the Alte Veste

were gaps in the line but these were protected by natural defences such as rivers. The infantry camped around these fortifications in tents, while the cavalry quartered in huts nearer to Nuremberg.

During the summer both sides clashed. Count Isolani's light cavalry patrolled the area against any Swedish raiding parties and they managed to push the Swedish outposts closer to Nuremberg. It soon became a battle of wits as to who would overcome starvation and the disease. Wallenstein's Army had the advantage because his camp's lines of communications were linked to the Palatine, Bavaria, and Vienna and so could easily be resupplied; unlike the Swedish camp, which could only depend on provisions from Nuremberg, which also had to feed its own population.

According to Sydnam Poyntz, Gustavus, 'puffed up with his great victories … [and] swallow[ed] up in conceit', thought Wallenstein would be easy prey, but:

> [He found] Wallenstein strongly entrenched and would not come out to fight. But there their lay one against the other for the space of three months and every day skirmishing. At last two so great armies lying so long there a great famine grew in the Swedish Army, though he had all the benefit [of] the city of Nuremberg could yield, for he lay in the town almost all that time; at the last the Swedish horse were driven to that need that they were constrained to ride ten or twelve miles for a bottle of hay: and then many times they were catched up by the Croats and come short home and many taken prisoners in every corner. For Wallenstein had stopped two passages, that they could go a pillaging but one way towards Saxony, and the king grew angry to see his army pent up and like to endure a long famine.[13]

Skirmishes between both sides occurred daily, but no major battle took place. Finally, according to Poyntz, 'one night the king having heated blood with drinking … vowed in that heat presently to set upon and beat this new proud General out of his trenches, and to use his words to 'pull the fox out of his den'.[14]

On 31 August Gustavus established four batteries to bombard the trenches of Wallenstein's camp, but although a reported 27 pieces fired all day on 1 September, nothing was achieved, therefore the following day he decided to reposition his artillery and on 3 September he began his attack on the Alte Veste.

A newssheet records:

> The king of Sweden (having all his forces joined together) took a resolution to give an assault upon the said castle [Alte Veste], as the strongest quarter of of Friedland [Wallenstein]. And on the 24 August [OS] being St Bartholomew's Day having placed his cavalry in battle array in a valley… his Majesty caused an onset to be made, which skirmish did last from 9 of the clock in the forenoon till

13 Sydnam Poyntz, *A True Relation of these German Warres from Mansfield's going out of England which was in the year 1624 until this last year 1636 whereof myself was an eyewitness of most I have here related as followeth* (Tonbridge: Pallas Armata, 1992), vol. 2, p.71.

14 Poyntz, *A True Relation*, p.71.

53. Swedish cavalry and infantry in 1632. *Theatrum Europaeum*. (Michał Paradowski's archive).

night, where were slain on both sides many officers and soldiers. On his majesty's side there died the general of artillery names Torzam, Colonel Ergung an earl of Eberstein General Major Boctius, a lieutenant-colonel and Captain Creilsheim and some other officers and 500 common soldiers. Besides these some officers were hurt and likewise 1000 soldiers, all which were brought into Nuremberg to be cured. General Banier was shot the day before through the left arm. The Duke Bernard of Saxe Wiemar from the beginning to the end (as also his Majesty) on foot in the middest of the fight, is said to have performed an incredible slaughter amongst the enemy. And behaved himself so valorously he hath not his like in the world.

On the enemy's side (as is advertised by prisoners) there were slain eight colonels, amongst them a Fugger, who hath commanded 1000 cuirassiers and being hurt was taken prisoner and brought to Nuremberg where he soon died. Item Don Cavarra Aldobrandino and Colonel Caesar, item 30 captains of horse and of foot and a great number of soldiers the certainty whereof is not yet known. Some prisoners do report that Friedland said oft times 'If the king gets this hillock from me then I will no more believe that there is a God in heaven.'[15]

Another newssheet records that after assaulting one side of the camp:

The same day his Majesty made a trial upon an old house … that being situated in a wood on a high place [which] did command over the camp of the enemy. Which if his Majesty had won thence he might have had advantage to dislodge the enemy, But it could not be, by reason that already the enemy had entrenched himself therein, having cut down the wood that stood about it.

Notwithstanding in this assault they did so engage one the other by their often cannonadoes, musket shot and fierce skirmishes, that this action (which lasted from 10 in the forenoon until night) did but little differ from a battle, for all the old soldiers do testify that they never saw, nor heard of the like skirmish.

On both sides are fallen many brave soldiers and it is thought there are of ours some 1500 soldiers slain and prisoners. Amongst others the White regiment and the company of his Majesty's Guard are much lessened. The losse of our officers high and low (which is also the greatest) is of about one hundred heads; the chief of the slain are general Major Boetius, Lieutenant-Colonel Septer, The Rittmeister Creilsheim, Lieutenant-Colonel Berthel. The chief of the grooms of his Majesty's horse named Nilsen, much sorrowed for and many others whose names I have not yet learned. The hurt are Colonel Reisten, Colonel Bert, 4 earls viz de Castel, d'Erbach, d'Eberstein and de la Tour. The prisoners are Colonel Dorstenson, General Commissary of the Ordinance and Colonel Eric Hands, Swedish.

The soul of one of the king's boots was taken away by a musket shot, without any harm: Duke Bernard of Wiemar had his horse slain under him, himself undamaged. The prisoners of the enemy do report that General Wallenstein's horse was slain under him and that 8 colonels were left dead in the field of whom they name one Aldobrandino and one Mario. The King of Sweden has taken three

15 TNA SP101/30, Advise from Norimberg [*sic*] the last of August and other parts the 3 and 4 of September stil vet.

54. Military camp at the siege of Jülich 1621–1622. Pieter Snayers. (Rijksmuseum)

> cornets. It's strange that on the 4th of this month when the King caused the retreat to be sounded the enemy did not leave his advantage to fall on our rearward.[16]

However, Wallenstein would not be drawn into battle, thereby forcing Gustavus to either storm his fortified camp or lose face by retreating. Therefore Gustavus had no choice but to order an attack. According to Robert Monro:

16 TNA SP101/30 Extract of a letter from Furt 6 September 1632, f.13.

> His Majesty commanded strong parties of commanded musketeers out of all brigades, led by a colonel, a lieutenant-colonel and a competent number of other inferior officers, to lead on the party towards the hill, to force a passage or entry unto the enemy's works; which being hardly resisted, the service went on cruel hot on both sides, so that the parties were no sooner entered on service, but it behooved the reliefs to be incontinent ready to second them, death being so frequent among the officers and soldiers, that those who were hurt rejoiced, having escaped with their lives, seeing the effect the service desperate on our side, losing still our men without gaining any advantage over our enemies, being always within their close works, while as we, both officers and soldiers, stood bare and naked before them, as marks to shoot at, without any shelter whatsoever, but the shadow of some great trees, being in a wood, so that we lost our best officers and soldiers, while as the basest sort durst not lift head in the storm.[17]

The colonel who led this attack was probably Colonel Wilhelm Burt of the White Regiment, who was carried from the field wounded. At the beginning of the attack the Swedish General Johan Baner was shot in the arm, but his wound was so severe that he would not see action again that year.

Meanwhile more Swedish regiments tried to storm the defences, Monro continues:

> The service continued in this manner the whole day, so that the hill was nothing else but fire and smoke, like to the thundering echo of a thunderclap, with noise of cannon and musket, so that the noise was enough to terrify novices, we losing still our best soldiers, grew so weak in the end, that the brigade of foot had scarce bodies of pikemen to guard their colours, the musketeers being almost vanished and spent by the continuance pf hot service, where the service was not alone among the foot in pursuing of the hill, but also about the hill without the wood, on the wings the horsemen furiously charged one another, being also well seconded by dragoons and musketeers, that do come on fresh with the reliefs.[18]

At one point Wallenstein's Croats seem to have charged the Blue Regiment which suffered heavy losses. According to Monro at 1:00 p.m. he was ordered to take command of 500 musketeers since their commander, Count von Thurn, had also been wounded. Leaving his own regiment in reserve, when he arrived he found:

divers officers and soldiers lying bloody on the ground … perceiving the enemy sometimes to fall out with small platoons of musketeers to give fire on us, and to spy our actions, returning again as their powder was spent to trap them the next time, I advanced a sergeant with twenty four musketeers to lie in ambush … which they perceiving came out no more, but one single man to spy.[19]

With his plan to ambush the enemy musketeers having failed, Monro returned to the main body of the musketeers, but a sniper, with a 'long piece'

---

17 Monro, *Monro, His Expedition*, p.148.

18 Monro, *Monro, His Expedition*, pp.148–149.

19 Monro, *Monro, His Expedition*), p.149.

who was hiding in a tree, shot him 'above the haunch bone on the left side'. Fortunately, the musket ball hit Monro's 'iron clicket of my hanger [sword]' which took the force out of the bullet, although he does admit, 'I lost much blood.' He remained at his post until he was relieved by 500 musketeers of his own regiment commanded by Lieutenant-Colonel John Sinclair.

Finally Bernard von Saxe-Weimar managed to capture a part of the outer defences, but the Swedes could not exploit his success since night had fallen, which put a stop to the fighting. The fighting was not renewed the following day. According to Wallenstein:

> The enemy stayed upon the hill until ten o'clock, but when hardly pressed he quitted the woods again with a loss of 2,000 men (or, as I am told, more, for the woods are full of dead whom he could not carry away, and prisoners say that dead and wounded were borne back throughout the day.)[20]

Gustavus withdrew his army to Nuremberg once more. According to Monro of the 500 musketeers he had taken command of at 1:00 p.m. about 200 had been killed and many others wounded. Sinclair returned to Monro's Regiment the following morning with just 30 officers and men, the rest having either been killed or wounded or who had deserted 'through plain fear'[21]

However, the Catholic forces did not come out of the encounter lightly. Colonels Fugger, Chiesa, Caraffa were among about 60 of Wallenstein's officers who were killed. Wallenstein later wrote to Ferdinand:

> The combat started right early and lasted most hotly all day. Many officers and men of Your Majesty's Army are dead and wounded … but I can by my honour assure your Majesty that all officers and men, on horse and on foot, behaved as bravely as I have rarely in my life experienced.[22]

Gustavus had had his first major defeat in the German War, and Protestant hopes, which had been so high after the battle of Breitenfeld the previous year, slumped. Soldiers who had flocked to his colours now began to desert. After leaving Nuremberg, Monro recalls that as a joke a soldier of the Swedish White Regiment jumped out from a bush and said he had seen the enemy. This made the whole brigade throw down their arms and run away towards another Swedish brigade in their rear who also panicked and fled. It was not until the fugitives came face to face with the pikes of Monro's Brigade that they finally rallied. The soldier who started the panic was severely punished, being 'cut and carved by the officers.'[23]

20 Mann, *Wallenstein, his life narrated*, p.634.
21 Monro, *Monro, His Expedition*, p.149.
22 Mann, *Wallenstein, his life narrated*, p.634.
23 Monro, *Monro, His Expedition*, p.152.

8

The Siege of Stralsund

Among the Emperor's enemies was Duke Bogislaw XIV of Pomerania, but in November 1627 his small army was forced to surrender and Bogislaw signed the Capitulation of Franzburg. In February 1628 he issued a proclamation to all the towns and cities of Pomerania to quarter Imperialist troops, however the city of Stralsund refused. Although technically in Pomerania, Stralsund, which is situated on the Baltic coast, was part of the Hanseatic League, and so did not bear allegiance to Duke Bogislaw. However, Wallenstein did not see it this way and wanted to secure the Baltic Coast for the Holy Roman Empire. Therefore he sent detachments to harass the city by examining all the wagons that left and entered it. The Imperialist general Hans George von Arnim demanded 150,000 thalers from Stralsund, but the council agreed to pay 80,000, including a down payment of 30,000 thalers. He also occupied the Island of Daholme which is situated opposite to Stralsund.

Stralsund stands on a triangular shaped island on the Baltic coast which was divided into four districts, St Mary, St Nicholas St Jacob, and St Jurgen, with a population of between 18,000 and 20,000 people. It is surrounded by water and like most large towns at this time was encompassed by a wall. Access to the city was by three dams or causeways which were guarded by three gates, to the north was the Knieper Gate, to the east was the Franken Gate and to the south was the Tribseer Gate. There were gaps in two other causeways which had led to the Hospital Gate and Kuter Gate, which no longer offered access to the city.

With growing Imperial harassment the inhabitants of Stralsund began to strengthen its fortifications. There are several contemporary plans of the siege of Stralsund, but none agree as to how the city was fortified before it began. One plan printed in *Theatrum Europaeum* shows that the Knieper Gate had three ravelins along the causeway and a network of three bastions protected the entrance to the causeway itself. These bastions, which were triangular in form with flanks so that an attacking force would be caught in a crossfire, were positioned side by side in a curved shape connected by a rampart. The ravelins, which were triangular shapes similar to the bastions, but without flanks, were positioned one behind another. Another ravelin was positioned on the city side of the Hospital causeway, which contained a gap. The Tribseer causeway had six bastions at its entrance, but unlike the Knieper

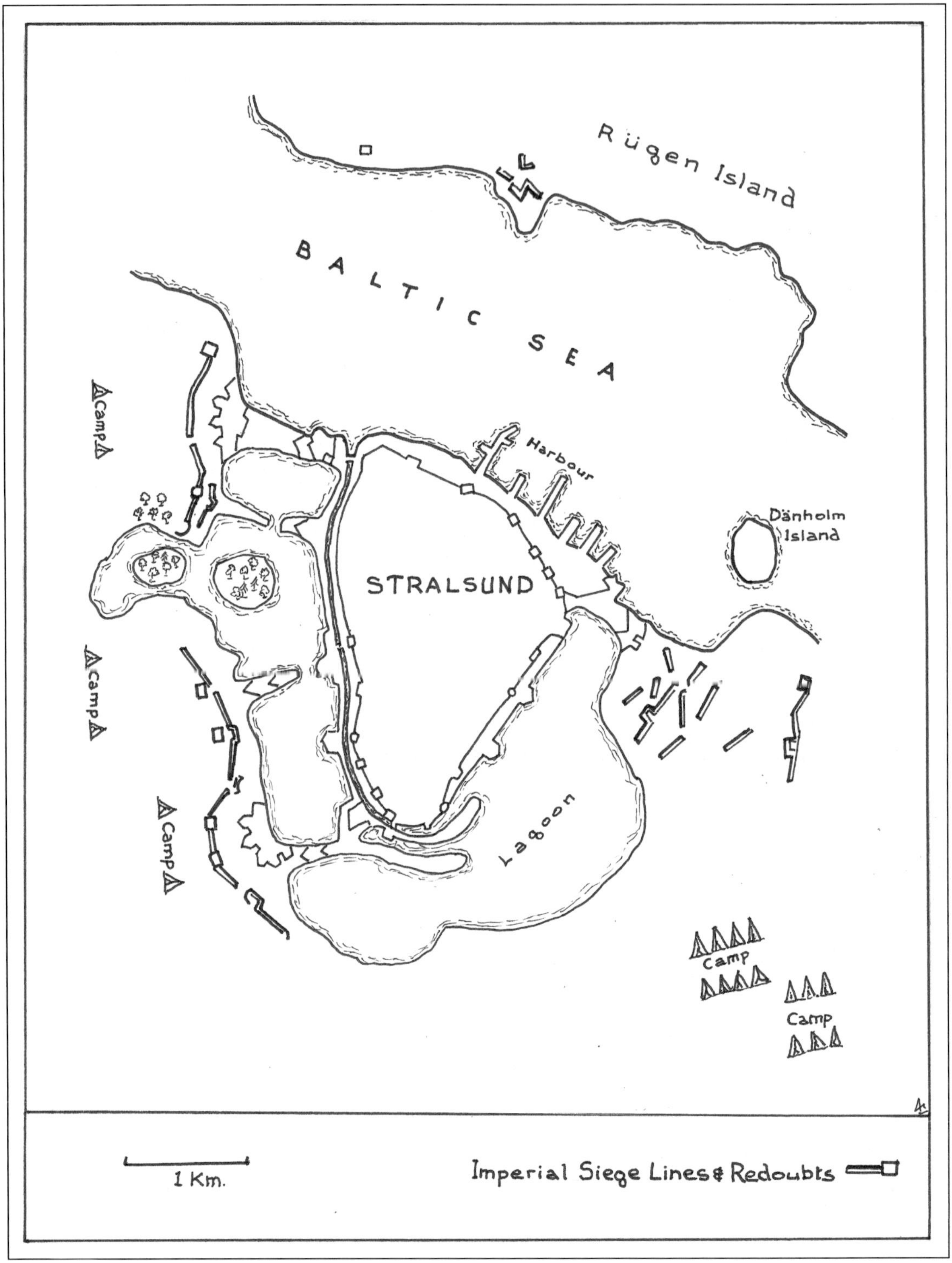

Map 2 The Siege of Stralsund, 1628

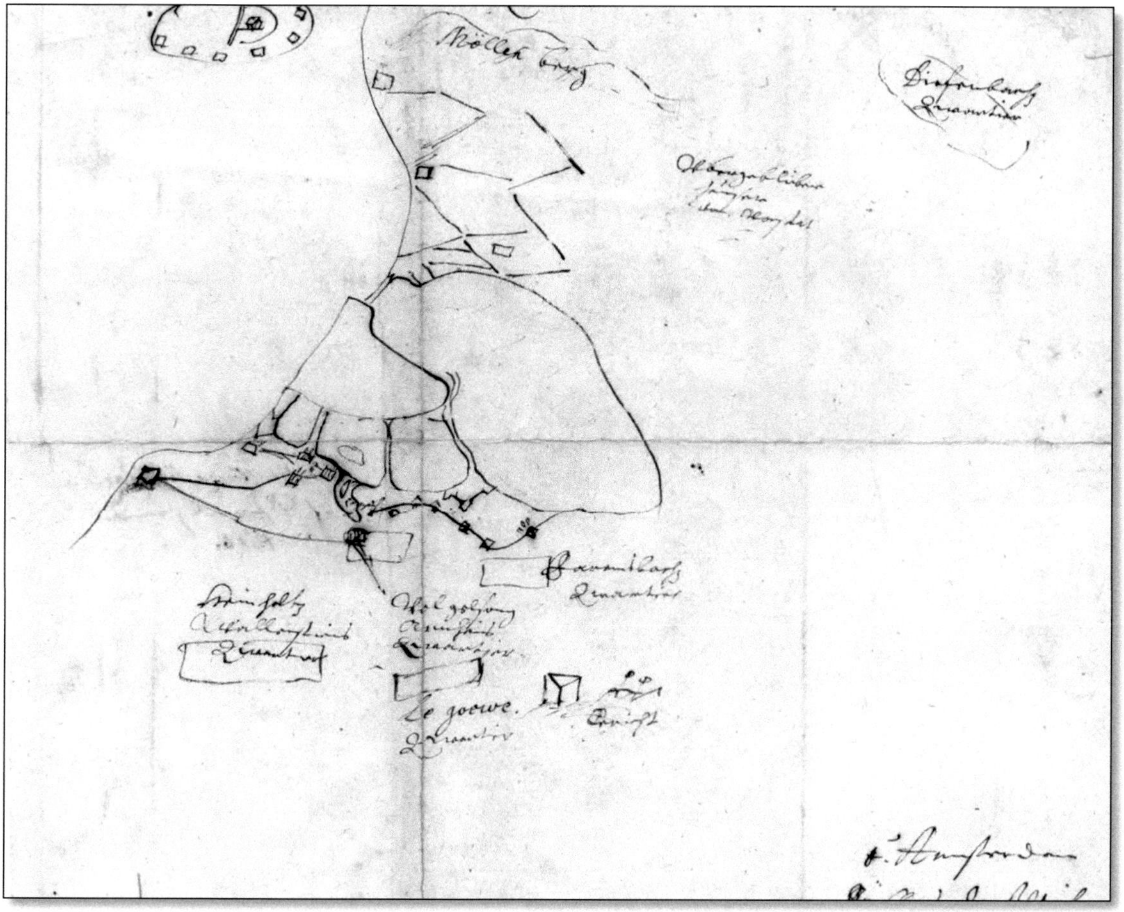

55. Map of the siege of Stralsund in summer 1628. (Riksarkivet, Stockholm)

causeway these were mainly positioned to the right of the causeway leaving a gap for traffic to pass. Although, like the Knieper causeway there were also three ravelins on the causeway itself, one behind the other. Despite not having access to the city, the Hospital and Kuter causeways also had several ravelins on them. The Franken causeway appears to have an earthwork with two bastions and behind it a large ravelin which blocked the causeway, with another bastion behind it which was part of the coastal defences.

The city's militia mustered about 1,400 strong, plus about 3,400 inhabitants who were willing also to defend the city, but the council realised that this force would not be enough. so on 8 May the city council appealed to Christian of Denmark for aid, who immediately ordered seven companies of Mackay's Regiment to reinforce the garrison of Stralsund, along with two Danish regiments of foot and a troop of horse under the command of Colonel Heinrich Holk, who would later join the Imperialist Cause.[1]

On 16 May Arnim laid siege to the city with about 14,000 men and the following day began to dig fortifications and batteries. On the evening of 17 May the Imperialist began to fire 21 to 24 pound balls into the city.

1 Monro, *Monro, His Expedition*, part I, pp.61–62.

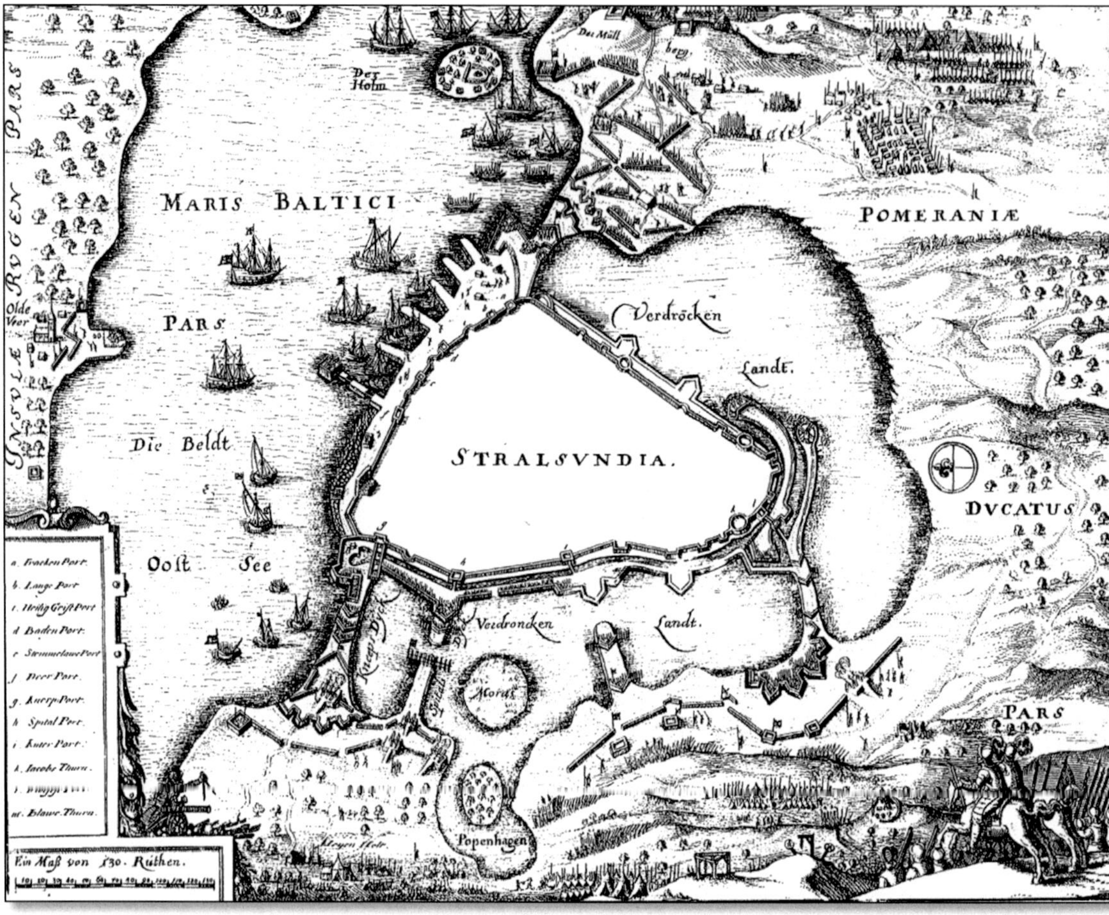

56. The Siege of Stralsund in 1628. *Theatrum Europaeum* (Michał Paradowski's archive).

Usually the commander of the besieging force had two options to capture a city, either he could decide to storm it, which might result in heavy casualties, or starve it into submission. Unfortunately for Arnim, and later Wallenstein, there was no Imperial navy to blockade it and Arnim soon found that ships could easily resupply it and Arnim could do little to prevent a detachment of Holk's force landing at the end of May. Therefore starving Stralsund into surrender was out of the question, so the only option for him was to take the city by storm. This would not be easy given that any storming party would have to attack over the three causeways since the city was surrounded by water. However this water prevented the garrison sending out sallying parties from these areas, which meant the Imperialists only needed to fortify the entrances to the causeways rather than encompassing the whole city with earthworks as was the usual practice.

On 25 May, the same day Holk arrived off the coast of Stralsund, the city's mayor, Krauthof, suggested to the council that the women, and children be evacuated for safety, which the council agreed to do.[2] This was a common

2 Ernst Heinrich Zober, *Geschichte der Belagerung Stralsund durch Wallenstein im Jahr 1628* (Stralsund: W. Trinius, 1828), p.140.

practice for a besieged town or city because it would make the provisions within the town last longer since there were fewer mouths to feed. On the other hand, a besieging general would try to prevent them leaving because the more people who stayed within a town or city, the quicker the provisions would be eaten. However, if the women remained in the town then they could help with its defence or treating the wounded. How many women and children did leave Stralsund is not known because there are accounts of women being in the city after this date.

Three days after Holk's arrival the rest of his force arrived, although this time the Imperialist artillery managed to de-mast one of the ships it still managed to enter Stralsund without loss. Mackay's Regiment was sent to the Franken Gate causeway, while 200 Danes were posted to the Tribseer causeway. Monro recalls, 'At our entry in this city, our travail and toil once begun, continued night and day for six weeks, till we grew hard with travail.'[3]

The Imperialists had not been idle in their preparations for the siege. According to the Theatrum Europaeum plan opposite the Tribseer causeway is shown a network of seven trenches with four square redoubts and two ravelins interspersed and a gun emplacement opposite the causeway, while opposite the Knieper causeway the Imperialists had constructed four trenches anchored to the north by a square redoubt and to the south by two gun emplacements opposite the Hospital causeway. A third gun emplacement with three trenches is shown in a forward position on the entrance of the causeway itself and curiously an Imperialist gun emplacement with supporting trenches is also shown within the city's defences which must have been erected at a later stage in the siege. The besiegers' works opposite the Franken causeway were a network of about 15 trenches plus an earthwork of three bastions, but no gun emplacements.

Robert Norton says of these gun emplacements:

> I would make choice of places to plant my ordnance, or make my batteries so against the weakest parts to make a breach in the most convenient place, bring them by trenches, as near as I can, within less that two hundred paces, and then having raised and plained the terraplenes and parapets made the platforms, cut and set out loops or placed the gabions[4] the whilst and planted pieces where they may most offend the enemy, endeavouring to ruin and embouch their defences, plying them so hard, that they may not have time to repair the old, not build new, nor retrench, as they else would do. And also make what slaughter I can, to weaken the adversary; and from each battery fit to shoot at the place [to make a] breach … and dismount [their artillery].[5]

These gun emplacements seem to have been ready by 30 May because between 9:00 a.m. and midnight and the following day the Imperialist from the Hospital causeway side fired a great many 'fire balls' into the city to try to

3 Monro, *Monro, His Expedition*, part I, p.63.

4 Gabions were large wicker baskets of various sizes filled with earth and stones to protect the artillery crews from enemy fire.

5 Robert Norton, *The Gunner's Dialogue with the Art of Great Artillery* (London: John Tap, 1628), p.26.

set it alight. These fireballs were usually fired from mortars and according to Robert Norton, were:

> Stone shot dipped in molten pitch, sulphur, rozen and turpentine mixed [in] equal parts; then being warm, roll in corn powder, with a cover of fustian dipped in molten Rochfire,[6] and dip it as at first, role it and cover it, until it be of fit hight for the piece; lastly dip it in Rochfire and fine corn powder and shoot it out of the piece without a wad.[7]

However, the guns of Stralsund were not silent and bombarded Wallenstein's defences, causing severe casualties to Niefenbach's Regiment, and Colonel Kehraus had his right arm smashed by a shot from the city.[8]

The besiegers' defences also made it difficult for anyone to enter the city from the land side, such as a woman who was captured in man's clothing trying to enter the city on 12 June with a letter. What the letter said is not recorded.[9]

Meanwhile, Gustavus Adolphus could not let Stralsund surrender to the Imperialist forces since it was the nearest port to Sweden. Therefore on the 31 May he sent 100 oxen, 100 tons of gunpowder and six half karthaunes to the city and then on 23 June/3 July he sent two Swedish commissioners on a fact-finding mission along with 600 soldiers under the command of Colonel Fritz Petrovitz Rosladin, Lieutenant-Colonel James MacDougal, and Major Semple, the majority being Scottish soldiers. These were sent to Knieper Gate to reinforce the militia who were stationed there.[10]

On 2 June it was said that 120 fireballs were fired into the city but did not cause any damage; the following day Wallenstein summoned the city to surrender. His demands included that the garrison be disbanded, the fortifications dismantled and that the remaining 50,000 thalers be paid.[11]

It was a common practice for a besieging force to offer terms, which would often be rejected, but if it was judged that the governor of the town surrendered too quickly then he would be judged a coward and ridiculed; if on the other hand he held out after it was considered impractical then he, and the town's population, would have to suffer the wrath of the besieging force, especially if the town was stormed. Holk rejected these terms, although the city's council appear to have sent a delegation to negotiate with Wallenstein.

Further Danish reinforcements arrived on 7 June with six half karthaunes, and that night the garrison made a new fortification in front of the Tribseer Gate, with the half karthaunes being installed the following day and beginning an artillery duel with the besiegers' guns. That evening a detachment sallied out of Stralsund from the Franken Gate to disrupt the besiegers' works and

6 Rochfire is a mixure of sulphur, gunpowder and mutton 'sewer', which was used to bind it so that it could cover grenades, pikes and arrows.

7 George Philipp Anton Neubur, *Geshichte der under des Herzogs von Friedland Oberbefehl von der Kayserlichen Armee uebernommene belagerung Der Stadt Stralsund* (Stralsund: Christian Lorenz, 1772), p.13; Norton, *The Gunner's Dialogue*, pp.28, 30–31.

8 Zober, *Geschichte der Belangerung Stralsund durch Wallenstein im Jahr 1628*, p.209.

9 Khevenhüller, *Annales Ferdinandi*, vol. 11, p.195.

10 Monro, *Monro, His Expedition*, part I, p.64.

11 Khevenhüller, *Annales Ferdinandi*, vol. 11, p.194

according to a chronicler of the siege, 'killed many' of them. The garrison sallied out again during the morning of the 10 June, this time from the Knieper Gate, but were forced to retire with the loss of three men.[12]

On 11 June, according to the chronicler, it was Arnim's turn to receive fresh troops and three days later the Imperialists erected a new earthwork opposite the Knieper causeway which was so close to that of the garrison's earthwork that they could literally throw stones at each other.[13] This is probably the three trenches and the gun emplacement shown on the Theatrum Europaeum plan at the mouth of the Hospital causeway.

On 20 June eight Swedish ships arrived off Stralsund bringing soldiers and ammunition for the city. However, the troops were not disembarked immediately, because although Gustavus Adolphus might have sent the city aid, it came at a price. This price was for Stralsund be become a Swedish base in Northern Germany for the next 20 years and that Sir Alexander Leslie should replace Holk as governor. It was not until the 3 July that the city council finally agreed and so the troops and ammunition were landed.

This has been seen as Gustavus Adolphus' intention to enter the war to protect the Protestant religion, but there is no mention of this aim in the Swedish State Papers, rather it was due to the wealth that Sweden and its nobility might accumulate from conquests in Germany that drove it to enter the war. Unfortunately, we will never know what Sweden's aims were, because Gustavus Adolphus was killed at the battle of Lützen in November 1632.

The day after the arrival of the Swedish ships the Imperialists bombarded the city once more, although they damaged some buildings, none of the population were hurt. That evening they attacked Knieper causeway and drove the defenders out of the trenches, but a counter-attack soon followed which recovered these trenches.[14]

Meanwhile Mackay's Regiment had not been idle since its arrival. One of the companies was placed on the an island which Monro called 'Hollomne', while three companies were posted to some 'scurvy outworks' outside the walls near the Franken causeway. Monro says that these were:

> Slightly fortified with a dry moat, the enemy lying strong before us … those that were relieved of the watch by five of the clock, were ordained again to meet by nine of the clock at night, and to watch again on the by watch till four of the clock in the morning, whereof the one half were appointed to lie in readiness at their arms without the port near the works, while as the others half were appointed also to lie in readiness at their arms on the Market place to attend all occasions of alarms, either within or without the Town; and thus watch nightly, relieving one another, for the space of six weeks.[15]

He adds, 'During our residence here, our orders were so strict that neither officer nor soldier was suffered to come off his watch, neither to dine or sup,

12 Khevenhüller, *Annales Ferdinandi*, vol. 11, p.195.
13 Khevenhüller, *Annales* Ferdinandi, vol. 11, p.195.
14 Khevenhüller, *Annales Ferdinandi*, vol. 11, p.196.
15 Monro, *Monro, His Expedition*, part I, p.64.

57. The Siege of Stralsund in 1628. Workshop of Frans Hogenberg, 1628–1630. (Rijksmuseum)

K
I
B
C
D
G
M
N
O
H
Felttmarsch
von Arnhei
auff
Possen
burg.etc
er bißher stehen auß
den Frieden vns bescher
Vngluck von vns Wehr.
Pourtraict de la ville Anseatique SRALSVND, auec le
Siege faict par le Generall de Wallenstein, duc de Fridland.
424

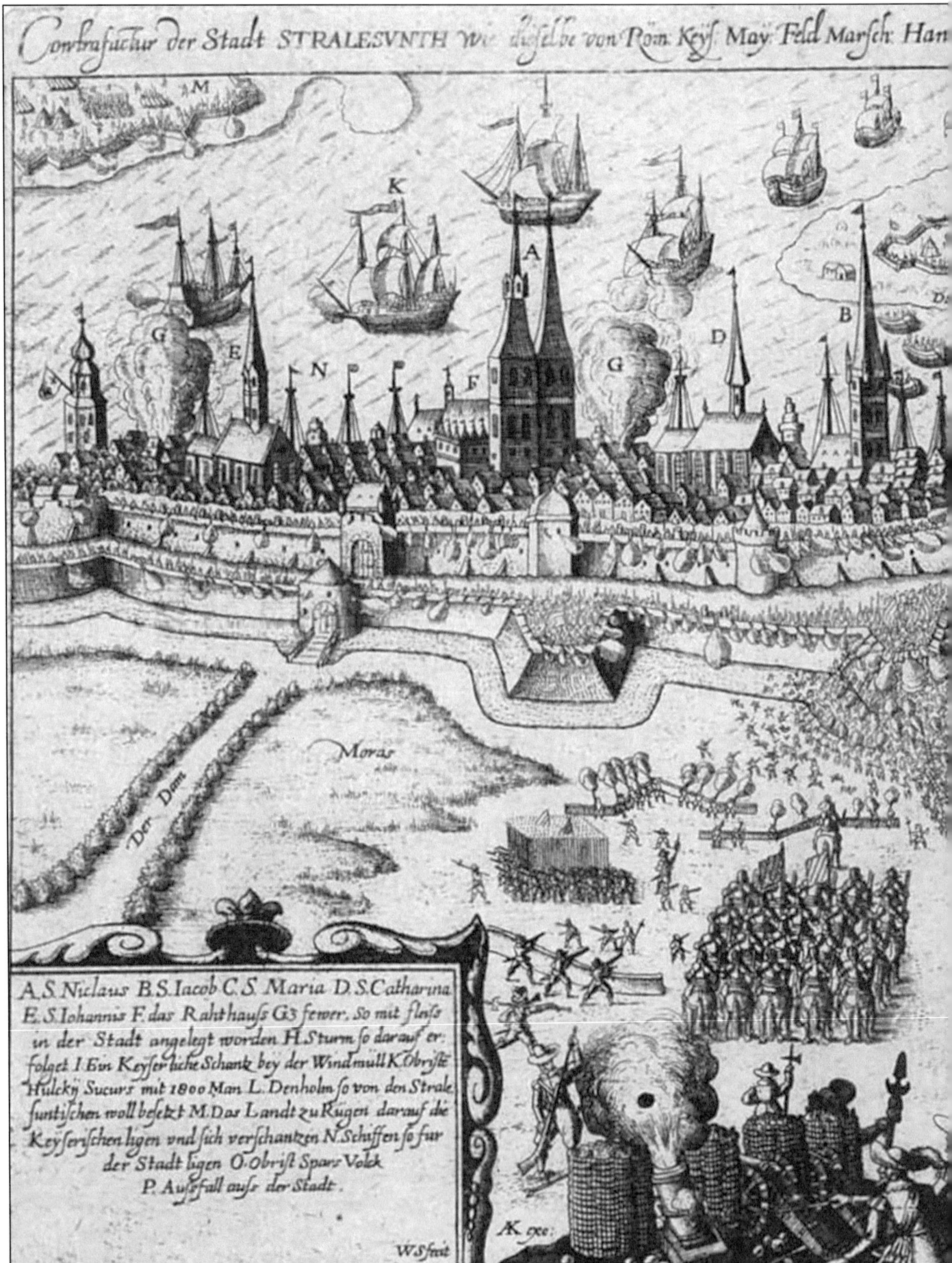
Contrafactur der Stadt STRALESVNTH wie dieselbe von Röm: Keys: May: Feld Marsch: Han
M
K
A
B
D
G
E
N
F
G
Moras
Der Dam
A.S.Niclaus B.S.Iacob C.S. Maria D.S.Catharina
E.S.Iohannis F.das Rahthauss G3 fewer. So mit fleiss
in der Stadt angelegt worden H.Sturm so darauf er:
folget I.Ein Keyserliche Schantz bey der Windmull K.Obrist
Hulcky Sucurs mit 1800 Man L.Denholm so von den Strale
suntischen woll besetzt M.Das Landt zu Rugen darauf die
Keyserischen ligen vnd sich verschantzen N.Schiffen so fur
der Stadt ligen O.Obrist Spars Volck
P.Aussfall auss der Stadt.
W.S.fecit
AK exc:

58. The Siege of Stralsund in 1628. Unknown author, from seventeenth-century pamphlet. (Staatsbibliothek zu Berlin)

but their meat was carried unto them.'[16] However, not all regiments had it so bad as Monro continues:

> The rest of the posts, above the walls, were also beset by the Dutch, but none had the half of our duties to discharge, by reason the whole approaches were made by the enemy to us, as being the weakest part. Notwithstanding, our great nightly watch and duty kept.[17]

Only Monro refers to a Dutch contingent, but it could have been commanded by Walter Leslie who is known to have joined the Dutch Army and was said to have been at the siege of Stralsund.

Despite appealing for help the city's council appears to have wanted the benefits of these soldiers, but not the problems that accompanied them, with the soldiers having to sleep in the streets rather being granted quarters among the population. Naturally after several weeks of this ingratitude the soldiers finally marched on the Burgomeister's house and demanded to be quartered with him. Monro records that on his first arrival 'the Burgers of the City did prove very ungrateful and unthankful to us, in not quartering our soldiers, as they ought to do.'[18] The Burgomeister complained to the governor, Colonel Holk, who assembled a council of war where the company, which by now had been reduced to 30 men and was divided into three corporalships, was to be court-martialled. It was decided that one soldier in each corporalship was to be hanged, by drawing lots from a hat and those who drew the piece of paper with a gallows on it were to be executed. Fortunately, the governor interceded on the two Scotsmen's behalf since it was his fault that they had not been allocated quarters, and they were allowed to return to their company, leaving only the third soldier – a Dane – to be hanged or as Monro put it, 'the Dane suffered justly for a Dane's fault.'[19]

However, another account states that the four companies of Mackay's Regiment lived in tents and huts outside the city since the citizens were complaining to the city's council that there were too many soldiers quartered upon them already, so the governor, Heinrich Holk, was asked to quarter these newcomers outside Stralsund. The source adds that it was only a few days rather than several weeks as Monro claims that these four companies mutinied and demanded to be quartered in the city.[20]

Meanwhile Mackay's Regiment continued to strengthen their earthwork, but as Monro states, 'the enemy [was] approaching fast', despite the regular sallies the companies made to prevent them.

> Till at last, the enemy did approach right under our work, where sometimes being so near we begun to jeer one another … We did also nightly take some prisoners of

16 Monro, *Monro, His Expedition*, part I, p.65.
17 Monro, *Monro, His Expedition*, part I p.64.
18 Monro, *Monro, His Expedition*, part I, p.64.
19 Monro, *Monro, His Expedition*, part I, pp.64–65.
20 Zober, *Geschichte der Belangerung Stralsund durch Wallenstein im Jahr 1628*, p.155.

> them, sometimes stealing off their sentries, which made many alarms in the night, and in the day time.'[21]

One of the chroniclers of the siege records on the 24 June, 'The Imperialists did ... [fire] 350 shots from great pieces, but damaged no more than a poor man, who remained at his work, dead.'[22]

On 26 June/7 July Wallenstein with about 11,000 men arrived and took personal command of the siege. After reconnoitring the city he decided that the weakest section was where Mackay's Regiment was stationed, which even Monro had to admit was 'inefficiency of the works, the wall not exceeding the height of a man'. It appears only now that Mackay's Regiment began to strengthen the fortifications further and prepare for an attack. A half moon earthwork was in an advanced position, but still unfinished. This was manned by 50 musketeers under Ensign Johnson of Mackay's Regiment.

According to Monro the Imperialists advanced shouting 'Sa, Sa, Sa' and drove Johnson's men back and the whole sector was, 'the hardest pressed'. He continues;

> For one hour and a half, the service being hot, sundry were killed of us, but three for one of the enemy, which finding himself resisted with valour, being relieved by a fresh supply of another thousand men, set on more furiously then before, where sundry of our officers were shot ... divers others were killed.[23]

Monro was one of those wounded, but as he was helped from the scene of fighting he could see reinforcements being sent to strengthen the line. These were the Scottish soldiers who had recently arrived with the Swedish contingent, but 'the enemy storming again with the third relief, which continued so long till a number of our officers more were killed and hurt.' Among those killed was Major Semple, and Lieutenant-Colonel MacDougal was captured. However, the garrison managed to beat off the attacks of the Imperialists, 'with great loss, with swords and pikes and butts of muskets'. It was rumoured that Wallenstein had some officers shot for retiring from the action because they were slightly wounded.[24]

The following day the Imperialist artillery '[fired at] the walls furiously the whole day, having shot at Frankendore [*sic*] near eight hundred shots', in preparation to storm the city again.[25] The attack came that night:

> The enemy furiously invade them, and they defended the works a long time, till in the end being pressed had, they retired to ... the ravelin, whereupon the enemy followed them with a stout and a cry, as if the town had been won, which did put the Burgers and the rest of the soldiers that were on other posts in great fear, thinking all was past recovery.

21 Monro, *Monro, His Expedition*, part I, p.65.
22 Khevenhüller, *Annales Ferdinandi*, vol. 11, p.196.
23 Monro, *Monro, His Expedition*, part I, pp.67, 68.
24 Monro, *Monro, His Expedition*, pp.69–70.
25 Monro, *Monro, His Expedition*, p.73.

> Notwithstanding this sudden fear, our soldiers valiantly and bravely defended the Ravelin with pikes and fireworks, the enemy having advanced bravely to the cutting of the palisades, pressing also to undermine the ravelin by working under it which our folks did hinder by countermining.[26]

Monro's mention of the attacking force resorting to mining is unusual because it took weeks, if not months, to dig a tunnel to undermine the enemy's fortifications rather than just a few hours. It would also take a long time for the besieged to countermine the enemy's tunnel. Therefore Monro, who was not present on this occasion, must be referring to something else. It may be that if the illustration in *Theatrum Europaeum* is correct then the ravelins blocked the whole of the causeway, so the Imperialists might have tried digging their way through the fortifications since they could not outflank it. Mackay's Regiment may have tried to prevent this.

After the attack the Imperialists tried to consolidate their position by building a new fortification, which appears on the plan of the siege published in *Theatrum Europaeum* and is mentioned by Monro:

> The enemy also have another foretell or advantage by reason of a new work, which was incomplete, betwixt the Ravelin and the outworks, where he did lodge himself, having the new works as a breastwork to defend him from our shot.
>
> The night thus passed furiously on both sides, not without great loss being well fought, both of the pursuer and defender, in the morning our soldiers ... being led with resolute officers they fall out pell-mell amongst the enemies and chase them quite out of the of the works again and returning with credit maintained still the triangle or ravelin.[27]

In 2010 two mass graves were discovered near this causeway, one containing 13 skeletons and the other 10. Artefacts found near the grave, such as pipes and ceramics suggest they were buried during the early part of the seventeenth century. The cause of death of the majority of these skeletons is unknown, although it has been suggested that they died from plague which broke out in Stralsund in 1629, rather than the siege. True, they were not buried according to the Christian fashion, facing east, but rather in a haphazard way, suggesting they were buried in a hurry. However, both graves contained only male skeletons and an examination of the skeletons reveals that the majority were between 21 to 25 years old when they died. They were on average 166 cm (5 feet 5 inches) tall and all showed signs that they were in poor health while alive. Only two had unhealed wounds, including one injury to the head which was possibly caused by a sword. One reason why they are considered to have been plague victims, rather than siege casualties, is that none of their teeth show signs of them being pipe smokers. However, not all soldiers smoked and smoking was also a civilian pastime, although we

26 Monro, *Monro, His Expedition*, part I, p.74.
27 Monro, *Monro, His Expedition*, part I, p.74.

59. Infantry engaged in hand-to-hand combat. Johann Jacob von Wallhausen, ***Ritterkunst***, 1616. (Michał Paradowski's archive)

will never know for sure since a soldier might receive a gaping wound but if the weapon missed his bones then there would be no signs on his skeleton.[28]

However, a third grave was also found near to Franken Gate causeway, and there can be no doubt that this person died during the siege since they were buried where they fell. Among the artefacts scattered nearby were six pikes, three swords and two muskets, one of which was still loaded. Both the skulls of the skeletons were touching each other and their left arms were underneath each other's body. The first skeleton was about 1.66 m (5 feet 3 inches) tall and was 45 to 50 years old. His left arm was broken and the right one shows marks of having been hit with a blade, but his mortal wound appears to have been a pistol shot to the chest. The second skeleton was 1.82 m (5 feet 11 and a half inches) tall and between 18 to 22 years old. A hole in his fourth thoracic vertebra, which is located in the centre of the back, suggests that he was stabbed in the back by a pike or similar weapon. Other artefacts included a Pomeranian shilling dated 1622 and a clay whistle. Whether they were friends or enemies is not known.[29]

Meanwhile, the situation looked desperate for the city and so Holk decided to plead for reinforcements from Christian IV in person, and so left Lieutenant-Colonel Alexander Seaton of Mackay's Regiment in charge. According to a chronicle of the siege from 2:00 a.m. on 3 July the Imperialist artillery bombarded the earthworks on the Franken and the Knieper Causeways, which lasted all that day and into the night, during which time 1564 shots had been fired, 'but there was little harm done to the buildings'. A ravelin in front of the Knieper port was damaged, but being made of earth it was quickly repaired.[30]

After these attacks Wallenstein sent a trumpeter to the city and managed to negotiate a truce with Seaton, who agreed, despite having orders not to do so. Between 6 and 9 July the official City Chronicler, Jacob Hasert, recalls that a delegation from Stralsund met with Wallenstein, who 'received the municipal deputies very graciously; he had chairs offered to them, and when the salutation met, Syndicus Hasert vividly described the former misery of the city.' During these talks the deputies tried to defend themselves against accusations that they were rebels against the Emperor's authority.[31] How far these negotiations would have gone is not known because once Holk returned on 9 July and broke the truce and hostilities commenced once more. Whether Wallenstein was serious about these negotiations is uncertain because on 17 June he had written to Arnim,

> My Lord can always treat with the Stralsunders, but agree to nothing, much less cease the works, for they are rascals and must be punished; that I proceed with them

28 Usually smoking a clay pipe wears away part of the tooth where the smoker usually places his pipe.

29 Konze, et al., 'Der Stralsund Laufgraben von 1628…', pp.208–209.

30 Khevenhüller, *Annales Ferdinandi*, vol. 11, p.199.

31 Konze, et al., 'Der Stralsund Laufgraben von 1628 …', p.217.

> somewhat gently is just to put them off their guard, for the evil that has been done I certainly will not let them off lightly.[32]

During this 'calm time' as Monro calls it, 'the soldiers that in six weeks before, were wounding and killing one another, are now coming and discoursing together as friends.'[33]

Holk had managed to secured the services of Colonel Lord Spynie's Regiment, which disembarked during the 9 and 10 July, and some Danish artillery arrived on 12 July, but Christian of Denmark had only sent enough supplies for the city to hold out, because while Wallenstein was distracted by the siege he was building up his army once more on the Island of Usedom. Lord Spynie's Regiment was said to have been reduced to four companies shortly after its arrival, since it was chosen to conduct a sortie on the Imperialists' siegeworks. The regiment was supported by Colonel Mackay's Regiment. 'They went on with boldness and confident resolution,' recalls Monro,

> and falling into the enemy's works, they forced the enemy to retire and to give ground, even to the body of their army. And delighting in the shedding of their enemy's blood… they pursued them hard following them unto their main reserve or battle, where they seized their cannon, but the enemy being too strong, and his forces still augmenting, they were made to retire with the loss of some brave cavaliers.[34]

On 3 August Christian IV decided to withdraw Mackay's and Spynie's Regiments from Stralsund so that they could join him at Wolgast, where his army had just landed. By this time Mackay's Regiment mustered only 400 men out of the 900 which had landed at Stralsund. Of these 'I do not think one hundred were free from wounds received honourably.'[35]

The Imperialist garrison of Wolgast had quickly been overcome by the Danish and it appeared that the local population were about to rise up in support of the Danish king. This gave Wallenstein an excuse to abandon the siege and on 12 August he met Christian's smaller army about half a mile from Wolgast. The Danish Army was defeated with the loss of about 1,000 men and 600 captured, plus a further 500 were forced to surrender when Wolgast surrendered to Wallenstein. In the Danish Army's retreat Mackay's Regiment formed the rearguard.

However, the siege had cost Wallenstein dearly: on 25 August 1628 James Spens from Stockholm wrote to Sir Thomas Coke, the Secretary of State, that the garrison, 'manfully helped the town and sustain in a few days more than 10 assaults with loss to the enemy of about 10,000 [men] as is alleged.'[36] No

32 Quoted in Don McNair, *The Struggle for Stralsund, 1628–1630* (Farnham: The Pike and Shot Society, 2012), p.30.

33 Monro, *Monro, His Expedition*, part I, p.76.

34 Monro, *Monro, His Expedition*, part I, p.78.

35 Monro, *Monro, His Expedition*, part I, p.80.

36 TNA SP 95/3/19 Spens to Coke 25 August 1628.

doubt this figure of 10,000 men is an exaggeration, but whatever the true figure the garrison suffered just as badly, as Monro recalls:

> Many rose here is the morning, went not to bed at night, and many supped here at night, sought no breakfast in the morning. Many a Burger in this city coming forth in his holy days clothes, to take the air, were never home again till he was carried quick or dead, where some had their heads separated from their bodies, by the cannon; as happened to one lieutenant and thirteen soldiers, that had their fourteen heads shot from them by one cannon bullet at once: who doubts of this, may go and see the relics of their brains to this day, sticking on the walls, under the Port of Frankendore in Stralsund.[37]

Stralsund was not the only siege that Wallenstein's Army was involved in: after his dismissal eight regiments of foot and six of horse took part in the siege of Magdeburg under General Johan von Tilly. In an age when atrocities were regularly reported, the sack of Magdeburg in May 1631 would send shock waves across Europe for its brutality.

37 Monro, *Monro, His Expedition*, part I, pp.65–66.

9

The Battle of Lützen, A Case Study in Tactics

The most famous battle that Wallenstein fought was at Lützen on 16 November 1632. After failing to draw Gustavus Adolphus into battle at Weissenfels on 12 November, Wallenstein decided to dispersed his army into winter quarters, which was the usual practice for armies at that time of year. Although it is surprising he did this knowing that the Swedish Army was so close. Lützen was to be his headquarters, while other detachments were sent to the surrounding towns, and General Gottfried von Pappenheim was sent with a large force to Halle, about 30 miles from Lützen.

However, hearing that Wallenstein had dispersed his army Gustavus Adolphus planned to surprise him at Lützen, before the general could gather his army once more. Fortunately for Wallenstein a detachment of Croats and dragoons were guarding a bridge over the Rippach as well as a village of the same name. On 15 November this outpost clashed with the Swedish Army and Colloredo was able to draw in several Imperialists regiments which were supported by Isolani's Croats. When the main body of the Swedish Army arrived, who were able to outflank the Imperialists at a ford about a mile downstream, they decided to withdraw. However, they had bought Wallenstein several hours to recall the surrounding detachments of his army and by now it was too dark for the Swedes to attack that day. Among the orders Wallenstein sent was the one to Pappenheim which read, 'The enemy is marching towards us. Your honour should drop everything and route himself hereto with all troops and guns to be with us in the early morning.' He added: '[The enemy] is already at the pass where yesterday the road was bad.' No doubt the other commanders received similar orders, but this one gained iconic status since it was found on Pappenheim's body with his blood on it.

Gustavus hoped to have launched his attack early in the morning of the 16 November, but now he was further delayed since his army would have to cross the Flossgraben canal, which was used to transport wood to the Saxon salt mines. He appears to have built some rafts which helped his army to cross the canal, but by now Imperialist troops from the surrounding towns and villages had begun arriving.

According to an anonymous account:

60. The Battle of Lützen. Pamphlet frcm the seventeenth-century. (Riksarkivet)

> As every [Imperialist] regiment came in, so were they put into order, which continued all night long … At 10 at night did Wallenstein begin to think of the places most advantageous for the planting of his ordnance; some of which having mounted upon the windmill he began to cast up a trench of earth about them.[1]

Unfortunately, no details of the strength of Wallenstein's Army has survived, but Diodati records, 'The whole army did not exceed the figure of 12,000 men.' A letter believed to have been written by Hans von Munchhausen, who was the major of Colonel Theodor Comargo's Regiment, also estimated that Wallenstein had '6,000 foot and 6,000 horse'. On the other hand Heinrich Holk estimated there were about 8,200 infantry, but he does not comment on the strength of the cavalry. These figures do not include Pappenheim's force. As to the artillery, estimates vary from between 21 and 26 guns.[2]

Wallenstein is said to have learnt from Gustavus' tactics and formed his infantry up in a new style, having discarded the outdated 'Spanish tertio' formation. This is incorrect: even the name 'tertio' is misleading since German accounts never refer to formations by this name. They are always referred to as 'battles' 'squadrons' or 'battalions'. Even in his book *A Discourse of Military Discipline* published in 1634 and dedicated to King Philip IV of Spain, Gerat Barry mentions four types: a large 'battle square' which could be composed of between 1,000 and 10,000 men, a smaller 'squadron square', which appears to be formed of fewer than 1,000 men and a 'cross battle' which was formed by about 1,500 men divided into four and was formed in the shape of a cross. Even though Barry refers to them as squares, some were more rectangular in shape having between 61–72 files by 26–31 ranks depending on how many infantry a general had and how many formations he required. The fourth formation Barry suggests is the 'triangle battle' whereby one man was in the first rank, three in the second, five in the third and so on. Unfortunately, he does not say why this formation should be used and probably never was on the battlefield. Barry Gerat also shows a 'squadron square' with a hollow centre, presumably where the musketeers could retire if the formation was attacked by cavalry.[3]

Printed sources showing the formation of Wallenstein's Army vary considerably. The illustrations in *Theatrum Europaeum* show four large bodies of infantry drawn up in a diamond shape, with bodies of musketeers on the four corners of each formation. The cavalry are drawn up on each wing in the traditional style and the right wing, which included a fifth body of infantry is behind Lützen. Whereas the *Swedish Intelligencer* shows the Imperialist centre as formed from eight bodies of infantry in a single line with no musketeers attached to the four corners. A regiment of cavalry is in the centre, although both illustrations correctly show musketeers deployed in a sunken road in front of the Imperialist position.

1 Anon., 'The Battel of Lützen, 1632 …', (repr. Rushworth, 1721, pp.291–305).

2 G. Wittrock, 'Fyra Relationer om Slaget vid Lützen', *Historisk tidskrift*, vol. 52 p.304; Henrich Holk's account printed in Lorenz, *Quellen zur Geschichte Wallensteins*, p.500.

3 Gerat Barry, *A Discourse of Military Discipline* (Brussels, 1634), p.125. He sometimes refers to these rectangular squares as 'squadrons of broad front'.

However, a hand-drawn plan discovered in the Austrian Archives shows that Wallenstein had planned to deploy his army with six regiments of foot in the centre and four or five in the second line and two regiments of foot in the third with six regiments of horse on the either flank, with two behind the infantry. Which seems conclusive until one considers that it shows several regiments which were with Pappenheim and would not join the battle until that evening. Since its discovery it was believed that the plan shows Wallenstein's deployment at Lützen, but in fact it shows Mansfeld's and Suy's Regiments of Foot, which were not present at the battle, but they were at Weissenfels a few days before.

However, while researching for her biography of Pappenheim, Barbara Stadler discovered another plan which superseded the Weissenfels battle plan, and is now believed to show the Imperialists' deployment. This new plan, by Colonel Lobl, shows

that Wallenstein does not seems to have left any gaps in his lines in anticipation of Pappenheim's arrival. Instead he formed his army up according to the regiments he then had at his disposal. The infantry are shown as being drawn up from left to right: Colonel Theodor Comargo's Regiment of Foot, J. Ph. Breuner's Regiment, Colonel Francesco Grana's and Friedrich von Breuner's Regiments which formed a single battalion, Rudolf von Colleredo's and Colonel Andreas Matthais Kehraus' Regiments also forming a single battalion and finally Berthold von Waldstein's and Henrich Julius von Saxe-Lauenburg's Regiment taking the place of honour on the right. The second line was formed of Colonel Wilhelm, the Margraf von Baden-Baden's Regiment on the left and Hans Gottfried von Breuner's Regiment on the right. Finally there was a commanded body of men.[4]

The five battalion front is confirmed by Heinrich Holk, who records that:

> [Wallenstein's] battle was a threefold: 5000 foot in five brigades amidst two brigades of 1000 and six companies of horse, two and two mixed; lastly five companies of 500 infantrymen and two squadrons of 12 companies of commanded cavalrymen. Towards Lützen in the castle and in the town were 400 men.[5]

According to the anonymous account Wallenstein is said to have drawn up his army:

> into one mighty front; which he divided into three bodies. His right wing of horse (whose end was near the town of Lützen) was committed to the Count Rudolf Colloredo, that day sergeant-major general of the army. This wing had also commanded musketeers besides some others that were lodged in the gardens of the town aforesaid. This wing having the advantage of of the wind mills, and their hills, by the town side, made us of those natural batteries for the planting of nine pieces of ordnance; the mills and millers house serving them also for a good shelter ... The left wing opposite to the right wing, was led by Colonel Hendrick Holk, newly

4 Barbara Stadler, *Pappenheim und die Zeit des Dreissigjährigen Krieges* (Winterthur: Gemsberg-Verlag, 1991), p.729.

5 Henrich Holk's account printed in Lorenz, *Quellen zur Geschichte Wallensteins*, p.500.

> made Lieutenant Field Marshal unto Pappenheim, who but commanded until Field Marshal Pappenheim should be come into the field.[6]

The 500 infantrymen mentioned by Holk are the commanded men shown on the plan, although the 400 musketeers appear to have been redeployed to the gardens of the town during the battle. Diodati also refers to '5 divisions of infantry, of 2 others Divisions and a reserve supported [them]'. The anonymous account records that the Imperialist Army gave the appearance of being 'in one mighty front'.[7]

In his *Sulle Battalia,* Raimondo Montecuccoli, who was present at Lützen, suggests;

> The first line of battle is constituted more solidly than the second. This is because it has to sustain the momentum of freshly arrayed enemy forces which may be advancing as a single, unified front. Such a line must abound with men.[8]

He also states that the infantry formations:

> [Have] customarily been formed in five different ways. 1. A square of men; 2. A terrain rectangle; 3. a double square; 4. an oblong rectangle; and 5. a rectangle the horizontal and vertical dimensions of which are determined according to a given ratio, the space which each soldier takes up marching in battle three feet in breath and seven in depth.

He continues:

> A battalion can never fight effectively if it has more than six or seven ranks. This is because the pikes are eighteen feet long. The hands occupy three feet of the shaft and thus the remaining part extends fifteen feet beyond the first rank. The second rank in addition to the space.[9]

How did Wallenstein draw up his infantry at Lützen? According to one anoymous account, 'Wallenstein's discipline is to march 10 files deep in a file.'[10] However, this account is unrealiable in places, so it could be wrong in this case. Montecuccoli on the other hand states that, 'in the Imperial army it is customary to make the battalions seven men deep placing the remainder in front. If the total is between 300 and 400 pikes Friedland [Wallenstein] made the number of ranks in even, so that the ensigns would be stationed exactly in the middle of the unit, i.e. the fourth row.'[11] Whether Wallenstein actually adopted the seven man deep formation is not known since many of his earlier battles have not been described by his contemporaries, but it

6 Anon., 'The Battel of Lützen, 1632 …' (repr. Rushworth, 1721, pp.291–305).
7 Anon., 'The Battel of Lützen, 1632 …' (repr. Rushworth, 1721, pp.291–305).
8 Barker, *The Military Intellectual and Battle*, p.104.
9 Barker, *The Military Intellectual and Battle*, p.90.
10 Anon., 'The Battel of Lützen, 1632 …' (repr. Rushworth, 1721, pp.291–305).
11 Barker, *The Military Intellectual and Battle*, p.90.

could have been as a result of the Swedish victory over Tilly at the battle of Breitenfeld.

According to Sydnam Poyntz, 'Wallenstein to make his army seem bigger, had together all the women, struggers and boys of the camp of the camp with horses and wagon jades to stand together to make as it were a great troop with sheets for their flags.' Poyntz is the only one to mention this, but whether true or not this ploy did not do Wallenstein much good: as Poyntz adds, 'when they saw the cannon shoot so fast upon them, [they] run all away; though soldiers were sent to keep them together.'[12]

Montecuccoli also suggests that, 'It is essential to make sure that the wings of the battle order are equipped identically and are the same strength, the presumption being that there is no set of circumstances, no foe and no location which affords more advantage on one side than on another.'[13]

According to Holk this is precisely what Wallenstein did, 'on the right wing 36 cornets and on the left 36.'[14] However, he did not draw up his cavalry in the traditional style, i.e. positioned in two straight lines on each flank. According to the Weissenfels and Lützen plans Wallenstein drew up his cavalry so that they covered the flanks of his entire army. According to Diodati, Imperialist cavalry 'was deployed equally on the right and left wing in stairs order, well covering the one and the other flank of the army, advancing when necessary to attack enemy, joined by the infantry.' This 'stair order' is described in a military manuscript as being 'More ready for a fight in the rear then in the front. And if the enemy should follow so close as you must needs come to it that is but either turning to the right or to the left as you shall think fit and you are ready for a fight.'[15]

Therefore it would appear that Wallenstein was preparing to fight a defensive action, and feared that the Swedish cavalry would try and outflank him.

He deployed Holk's Regiment of Cuirassiers, Terzka's and Desfour's Regiments of Cuirassiers (who formed one body), Hagan's Regiment of Harquebusiers, Drost's Regiment of Harquebusiers were on the right wing, while Götz's and Piccolomini's Regiment,[16] Leundersshaim's Regiment of Harquebusiers and Loyers' and Lohe's Regiments of Harquebusiers (which formed a single squadron) were on the left.

However, according to the anonymous account, 'the battle of middle ward was commanded by the Duke of Friedland [Wallenstein] himself, whose place was said to be in the head of that great regiment of Piccolomini's Horse, which was in the very middle of the foot regiments.'[17] This is the regiment

12 Poyntz, *A True Relation*, p.126.

13 Barker, *The Military Intellectual and Battle*, p.108.

14 Henrich Holk's account printed in Lorenz, *Quellen zur Geschichte Wallensteins*, p.500.

15 British Library Harley Mss 6844, An anonymous military manuscript, f.166.

16 Early in 1632 Piccolomini's Regiment were described as harquebusiers, but in the 1633 list there were cuirassiers. Exactly when they were converted into cuirassiers is not known, but they appear to have been heavily armoured at Lützen if not full cuirassiers. Also if they were cuirassiers this would balance both cavalry wings, two squadrons being cuirassiers and two harquebusiers.

17 Anon., 'The Battel of Lützen, 1632 …' (repr. Rushworth, 1721, pp.291–305). Henrich Holk's account printed in Lorenz, *Quellen zur Geschichte Wallensteins*, p.500.

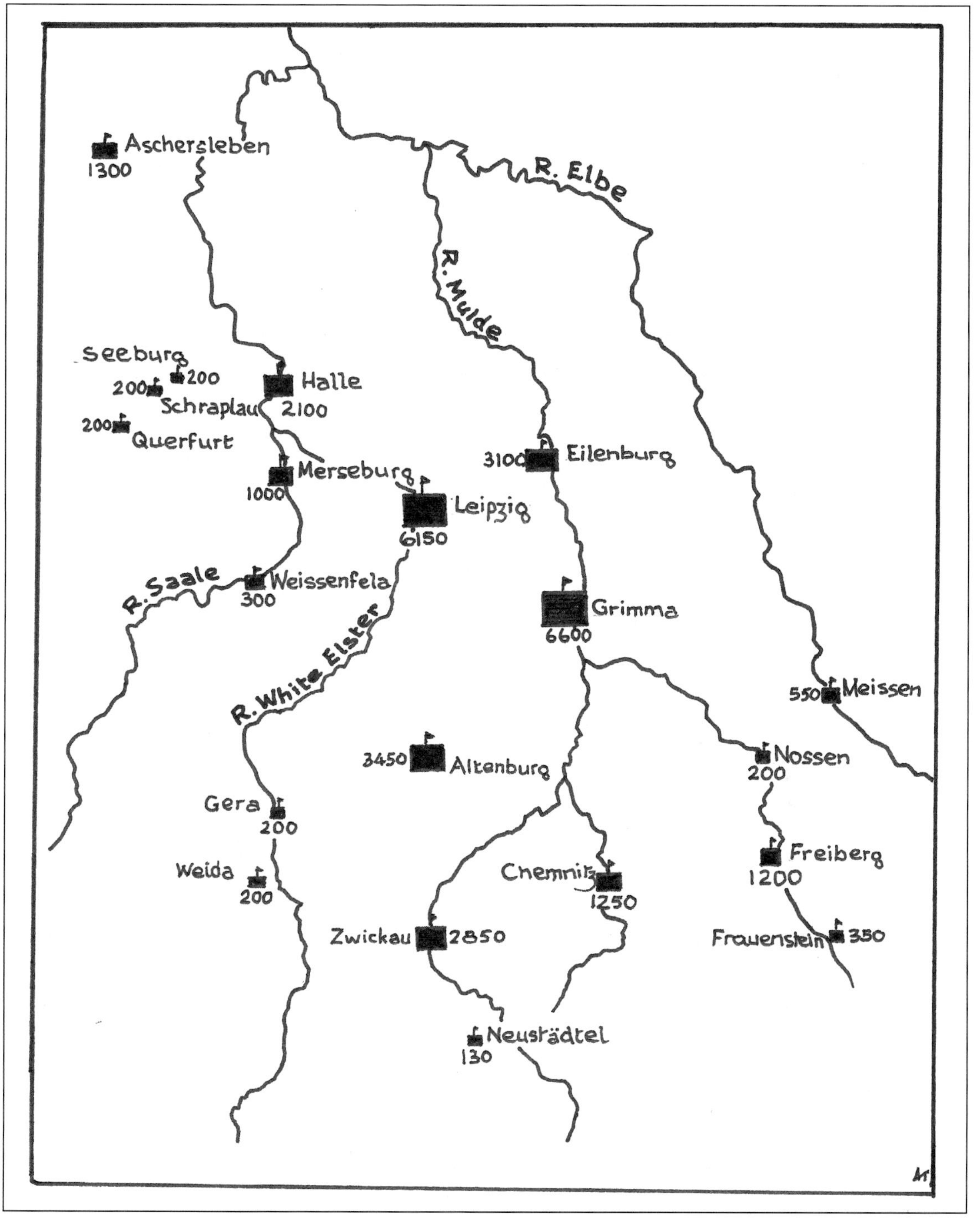

Map 3 Wallenstein's deployment prior to the Battle of Lützen

61. Plan of the Battle of Lützen, drawn by unknown Swedish officer, taking part in the fight. (Riksarkivet)

of horse shown in the illustration shown in the *Swedish Intelligencer* as being drawn up in the centre of the front line infantry battalions. Although this account seems to be in error, because Piccolomini himself claims that Colonel Götz's Regiment of Cuirassiers 'was ahead of me on my right hand', which would suggest that he was on the left wing. Holk also records that on 'each wing had 150 musketeers in front of the cavalry.'[18]

Montecuccoli suggests that:

> One must also mention the reserve squadrons which are posted behind the infantry. The rationale is that the footman cannot be overturned like cavalry, the disorder of which often results in the collision with a relief force of the very same arm. It may be added that, if the enemy is thrown into confusion by the infantry these reserve squadrons can pursue him, thus allowing the unmounted soldiers to remain in good order. Avoiding the possibility of their dispersion and preventing any inconvenience. Such bodies of horse are made up of 200 full cuirassiers, the most suitable instruments of combat for creating stability, providing support and absorbing shock. The ranks are composed of 50 horse and files of four.[19]

In the Weissenfels plan both Loyers' and Breda's Regiment were drawn up in four small formations, possibly deployed in 200 strong squadrons as described by Montecuccoli behind the first line of infantry. By the time of Lützen, Westphalia's, Lindelo's and Breda's Regiments of Harquebusiers were positioned behind the first line of infantry, probably to compensate for a weaker front line of infantry. The harquebusier regiments of Westromb and Gouschier, formed a reserve behind the infantry reserve. There was also Isolani's Croats which were positioned on each wing.[20]

Gustavus Adolphus is usually credited with introducing regimental artillery, but the Catholic League's Army certainly had them before the Swedish intervention in the Thirty Years' War and at least some of the Imperialist regiments of foot had them, usually two to a regiment.

In 1628 Robert Norton wrote a treatise on artillery in which he records the best way to deploy the artillery:

> There are divers opinions therein; some say it is best to plant them in the front, to disorder the enemy, and cause them to break their ranks at first; which others disliking, say, that will hinder their own party from many advantages, and difficult to retire them: some would plant them them in the flanks: and some would have some of them in the front and some in the flank: And lastly, some would have them behind the Army, that upon a sign given, their own squadrons may open away for the gunner to play upon the enemy's troops or squadrons. But wheresoever they are planted, care must be had, that the musketeers appointed for guards, not any other firearms, approach within 100 paces of the ordnance, lest untimely firing them work mischief to the party. But having viewed beforehand the place appointed for battle,

18 Henrich Holk's account printed in Lorenz, *Quellen zur Geschichte Wallensteins*, p.500.

19 Barker, *The Military Intellectual and Battle*, p.108.

20 The positions of the regiment are as those given in Schurger, *The Archaeology of the Battle of Lützen, an examination of 17th century military culture*, pp.238, 242

> if any eminent rising place be there near, to lodge the ordnance thereon, they may thence most safely play upon the enemy in front, flank and traverse, with wonderful advantage and hope of victory.[21]

Wallenstein is believed to have had 24 pieces of artillery, nine 24-pounders, two 16-pounders, two 14-pounders, four 12-pounders, a 10-pounder and six 7-pounders, although the accounts disagree on how these were deployed. One states that seven guns were on the left wing, 14 on the right and three were in the centre. Whereas another account states there was a battery of nine artillery pieces established near the windmills, but George Fleetwood says that Wallenstein established an artillery battery near to the windmills, of 'thirteen half cartours', which is also the number mentioned in the anonymously authored *The Great and Famous Battle of Lützen.*[22] Wallenstein also established a smaller battery on his left wing, which according to Dalbier consisted of 'four demi cannon and two quarter cannon.'[23]

The Swedish Order of Battle

During the night of 15/16 November, while Wallenstein was gathering his army at Lützen, the Swedish Army appears to have been afraid that the Imperialists would attack them during the night, since the anonymous account records that:

> [They laid] all night in Battalia, every regiment lying down in the same order that they had marched, with their arms by them. The pikemen they stuck up their pikes… and every rott [file] (that is every six men) of musketeers bringing their muskets to their rottmaster [file leader], he set them right up with their mouths [barrels] upward, and bound them together with a piece of match, where they stood ready at hand for all occasions.[24]

Gustavus' army was larger than Wallenstein's: according to Swedish figures it numbered 13,882 infantry and 6,810 cavalry or a total of 20,692, with an additional 616 infantry being sick and so were not present with their regiments. A document in the Dresden Archive put the figure at 15,000 infantry and 6,350 cavalry or 21,350 in all. However, the document in the Dresden archives appears to have rounded the strength of the regiments up or down.[25]

The infantry drew up with four brigades in the front line and four in the second. The four brigade's in the first line consisted of the Green, Blue, Yellow, and Swedish Brigades, which mustered 2,036, 1,110, 1,221 and 1,594

21 Norton, *The Gunners Dialogue with the Art of Great Artillery*, pp.22–23.

22 Surrey History Centre LM/2040, Letter from George Fleetwood to his father, one of three letters known to exist; *The Great and Famous Battle of Lützen*, 1633, p. 15.

23 TNA SP81/39/250–253, Colonel Dalbier's account quoted in Wilson, *The Thirty Years War: A Sourcebook*, p.176.

24 Anon., 'The Battel of Lützen, 1632 …' (repr. Rushworth, 1721, pp.291–305).

25 G. Droysen, *Die Schlacht bei Lützen* (Göttingen, 1865), pp.96–98.

officers and men respectively, although the Swedish Brigade only had 267 pikemen to protect its 1,068 musketeers. The Green Brigade was not the same brigade that Sir John Hepburn had commanded at Breitenfeld the previous year, but was made up of Bernard of Saxe-Weimar's Green Life Regiment, Wilderstein's Black Regiment, and Leslie's Scottish Regiment. Despite having 16 companies Leslie's Regiment mustered just 360 musketeers, 24 pike and 192 officers. Only the Yellow and Blue Regiments were strong enough to have formed one brigade, the other brigades were made up of three regiments of foot. Behind the first line were 180 musketeers and 48 officers of John Henderson's Regiment of Foot.

The second line of infantry was formed from Duke Wilhelm von Saxe-Weimar's Brigade, composed of his own and three regiments of the Elector of Saxony's Army, Knyphausen's Brigade composed of his White Regiment; Thurn's Brigade formed from his own Black Regiment and three additional regiments and Mitzlaff's Brigade was formed from three regiments. Ohm's Regiment of Horse formed the reserve for the Swedish second line.

Both wings of cavalry were formed from six cavalry squadrons in the first line and six in the second. Only Bernard von Saxe-Weimar's Life Regiment was strong enough to form two squadrons, the Småland Regiment was place on the right wing next to the Swedish Brigade. The front line cavalry squadrons were interspersed with 198 musketeers of Brandenstein's Regiment and the 600 musketeers of Lowenstern's Regiment of Foot, which gives an average of 80 musketeers between squadrons.

According to tradition Gustavus Adolphus introduced a new formation of infantry to the fighting in Germany, which were more mobile than the lumbering formations the Catholic Armies had used up to then. However, the 'Swedish brigade' formation had been developed by the Dutch at the beginning of the seventeenth century and adopted by the Danish, before Gustavus Adolphus 'introduced' it to the battlefields of Germany. Although the Swedish infantry drew up six deep, the Dutch were in formations eight or 10 deep. However, the Dutch had abandoned this formation during the 1620s since it was too complicated.

Terrain

According to the *Swedish Intelligencer*, 'The country was a goodly vast level and *campania* as corn lands could be; even as far also as the eye could see.' The battlefield has changed very little since these words were written, although the town of Lützen has increased in size since 1632. Across the battlefield runs the Leipzig–Lützen Road, which appears to have been a sunken road and bordered on both sides by a ditch for drainage. According to the anonymous eyewitness, 'All night and [the] next morning his [Wallenstein's] dragoons and pioneers wrought with their spades about the highway, and to make the ditches or drain by it, serve them for a breastwork to lodge their musketeers.'[26]

26 Anon., 'The Battel of Lützen, 1632 ...' (repr. Rushworth, 1721, pp.291–305).

Map 4 Dispositions of both sides at the Battle of Lützen

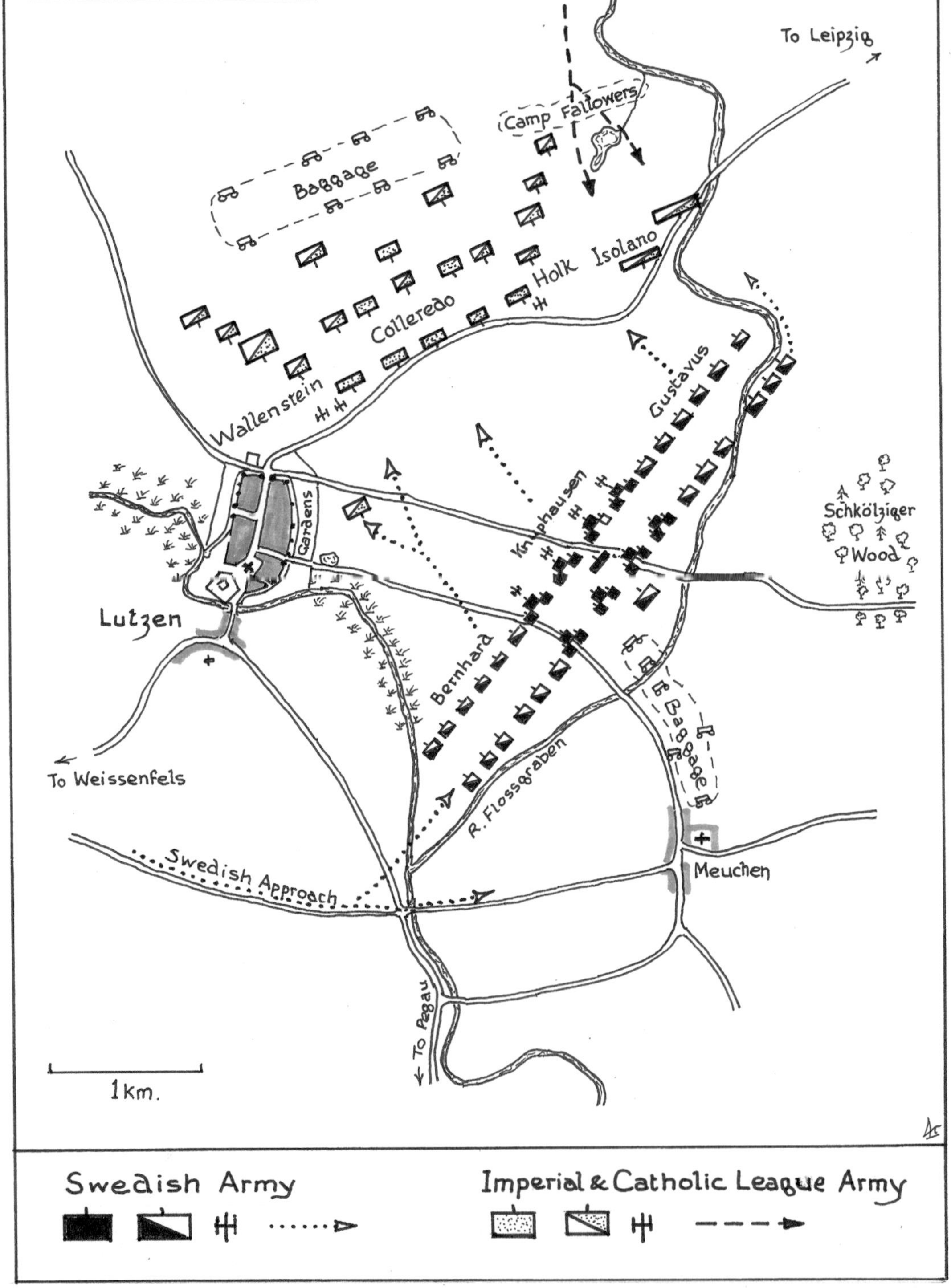

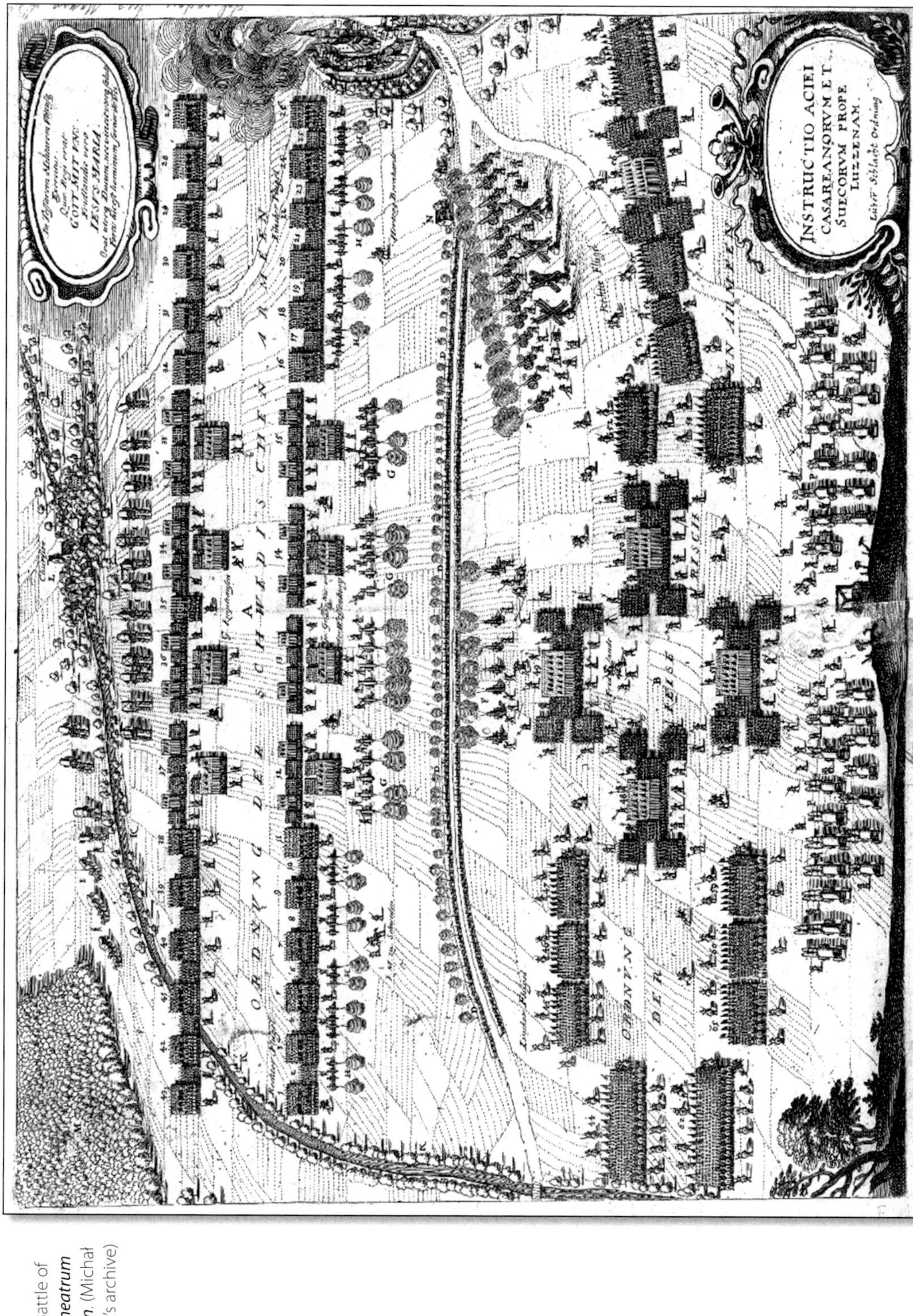

62. The Battle of Lützen. ***Theatrum Europaeum***. (Michał Paradowski's archive)

According to this account Wallenstein:

> [Placed] some commanded musketeers down into it, it served them as well as a trench or breastwork. This was so troublesome for the King's horsemen, that many of them were overturned and left behind in the getting over to charge Wallenstein; for indeed there were divers gaps through it, which the horse jostling for, overturned one another. The ground also behind the ditch, had two little risings, and those did Wallenstein make choice of, for planting some pieces [or ordnance].[27]

This information was said to have come from 'two English gentlemen' who were prisoners of the Imperialist Army. Sydnam Poyntz also records that 'in the front of his [Wallenstein's] camp lay a long dry ditch which he filled full of musketeers.'[28] In his *Sulle Battalia* Montecuccoli refers to this ditch, which 'brought the greatest possible advantage to the Imperials in the battle of Lützen.'[29]

Holk also refers to a wood on left hand on the Imperial battle lines. Unfortunately the site of this wood has been lost. Holk also mentions another wood on the Imperialist left wing, but this was '[to Gustavus'] advantage and a small hill, [within] a musket shot from [our] battle.' This may be the wood *Theatrum Europaeum* refers to as being where the Swedish planted their artillery. Close to Lützen were three or four windmills. George Fleetwood, who wrote to his father on 22 November, recalled that 'close to the town stood four windmills, which is fortified by nature very strong; there they planted nine pieces of ordinance, and [in] two or three other places of advantage they had 12 pieces more.'[30]

On the morning of the 16 November Gustavus Adolphus is said to have ridden to each of his brigades to raise morale by giving them words of encouragement. According to the anonymous eyewitness the army made 'a horrid clashing of their armour and with cheerful vows and acclamations.' Gustavus offered a prayer: 'Jesu, Jesu, Jesu, Vouchsafe thou this day, to be my strong helper; and give me courage this day to fight for thy glory, and Honour of thy great name's sake.'[31] The Swedish field word for the day was 'Gott mit uns' [God with us] while the Imperialists' was 'Jesus Maria'.

The Opening of the Battle

Precisely when the battle began is not certain. Some reports state that it began at about 9:00 a.m., although George Fleetwood estimated it was at 8:00 a.m. that Gustavus fired '[his] first shot … and so advanced towards the enemy'. Although he does later add that 'the battle joined about 10 of the clock.' Certainly other sources put the battle beginning at 10:00 a.m.,

27 Anon., 'The Battel of Lützen, 1632 …' (repr. Rushworth, 1721, pp.291–305).
28 Poyntz, *A True Relation*, p.72.
29 Barker, *Military Intellectual and Battle*, p.126.
30 Surrey History Centre, LM/2040, George Fleetwood to his father, 22 November 1622.
31 Anon., 'The Battel of Lützen, 1632 …' (repr. Rushworth, 1721, pp.291–305).

although later sources hedge their bets by saying between 9:00 and 10:00 a.m.

The battle opened when the Swedish artillery commenced firing, which:

> [Fired[Several salvos with three half cannons, which the enemy answered with a battery, which he had cast up at the windmills near the town and which he continued with other batteries, he had at the side of Scheiditz [Skolzig] ... and there was heavy firing with pieces but one hour on both sides.

An anonymous account records:

> The armies being come within cannon shot, the great ordinance began to play one upon another terribly. The air roared and the earth trembled, and those many hearts that seared not dying, were yet very loath to have no more play for their lives ... Wallenstein surely [had] a great advantage over the king's Army for his ordnance being ready planted upon steady and fixed batteries, the cannoniers raversed their pieces and delivered their bullets with more aim than the king's men could.[32]

However, Colonel Dalbier contradicts both these sources as to the extent of the bombardment of the Imperialists' lines:

> At about 9am we caught sight of the enemy in order of battle and waiting for us. They had hidden their troops well, behind a large ditch and had planted their cannons. The king wasted no time. As he could not make use of his cannons, he started marching on his enemy, at the head of his Swedish cavalry.[33]

Lord Praissac recommended in his Art of Warre that, in battle:

> The artillery ought to be so placed that it hinder not the passage of the battalions, and that it may easily discover those of the enemy. For the most part the infantry is within the body of the army, in several Battalions, disposed chequer wise: the cavalry on their wings and rear in several squadrons, and the artillery according to the convenience of the place, so the Front of the Army or on the flanks of the Battalions.[34]

Praissac continues: 'The artillery must play so soon as they begin to discover the battalions of the enemy; making the battery fully and speedily to disorder and scatter them before they come to give battle.'[35] Whereas Robert Norton suggests:

> According to the distance I would choose a piece that in a straight line can shoot home ... be it with *Demi Culverin, Saker* or *Falcon,* and plant my piece as near parallel to the champion plain as I can, that the shot may range and shoot at girdle

32 Anon., 'The Battel of Lützen, 1632 ...' (repr. Rushworth, 1721, pp.291–305).

33 TNA SP81/39/250–253, Colonel Dalbier's account quoted in Wilson, *The Thirty Years War: A Sourcebook*, p.175.

34 Lord Du Preissac (transl. John Cruso), *The Arte of Warre, Or, Militarie Discourses* (1639), p.27.

35 Du Preissac, *Arte of Warre*, p.27

> height, unless the ground be stony, for then would I place my shot short of them, that grazing amongst the stones, the stones may do them more spoil then the shot of itself can do, by far; but in no case would I shoot wide or over them, for that were both loss and shame also.[36]

The larger guns, such as the culverin, had a maximum range of 2,100 paces, so that they could probably hit the enemy forces even before they advanced and would be able to fire several shots until the enemy came within point-blank range of 400 paces. By now the smaller artillery pieces would have begun firing; the sakeret or minion had a range of between 280 to 1,400 paces and a falcon from 260 to 1,200 paces, so the battalions would be under constant fire.

According to Fleetwood, 'at our first falling on they likewise set the town of Lützen on fire, which did us much inconvenience, the wind blowing the smoke just upon us.' Another account states that due to this smoke the Swedish Army could not see 'four paces' in front of them.[37]

With this distraction Wallenstein ordered his Croats on the right wing to circle behind the Swedish Army and attack it from behind. Fleetwood continues:

> The enemy had ordered the Crabates [Croats] to fall round about upon our rear, which the king perceiving gave command to the Finns under the command of Stalhandske to march upon them, which he did diligently. And having eight companies, he charged them with four companies, putting them to flight;but upon his retreating (according to expectation) they charged him so that they put him to the worst, till being received by his four companies (set for the purpose) he charged them so sore that he so routed them that the whole day we were no more troubled by them.[38]

Unfortunately, since Fleetwood's Regiment was not present at Lützen we do not know where he witnessed these events, but he may have been on the Swedish right wing. However, Wallenstein appears to have sent the Croats on both wings forward because Lieutenant-Colonel Relinguen is said to have received orders for his regiment, which mustered about 300 men, to charge four regiments of Croats commanded by Isolani who was on the right wing of Wallenstein's Army. One pamphlet relating to the battle recalls that Relinguen:

> performed [this] with so much bravery and courage, that he twice pierced through them and brought back three standards, leaving behind one of his own. All his officers were wounded, and he himself in the second onset had his arm shot through with a pistol bullet, which forced him to retire. Isolani, general of the Croats, lost

36 Norton, *The Gunners Dialogue*, p.22.

37 Surrey History Centre, LM/2040, George Fleetwood's letter to his father, 22 November 1632. Field Chancellery Diary quoted in Richard Brzezinski, *Lützen 1632:, Climax of the Thirty Years War* (Oxford: Osprey Publishing, 2001), p.52.

38 Surrey History Centre, LM/2040, George Fleetwood's letter to his father, 22 November 1632.

> his life, with a great number of his men, Eighteen of his companies charged some German regiments that guarded the baggage, but they were stoutly opposed, the combat [was] fierce, the assaults reiterated, the earth dyed crimson, and burdened with carcasses. The Croats were driven back, though not without some disorder of the German horse, recoiled amongst the carts.[39]

This pamphlet is incorrect: Isolani was not killed at Lützen, but died in 1640. Moreover archaeological evidence suggests that the Croats put up a severe fight and reformed two or three times, before finally being driven off the field, but not before some had plundered the Imperialist baggage train.

The Foot Come to Grips

According to the anonymous *The Great and Famous Battle of Lützen*, published in 1633,

> All this while were the four Foot Brigades of the Swedish Battle, pell-mell at it: And they (even by [the] *Spaniards* confession) got ground apace of those Imperialists whom they had attacked. And now also did *Stolhausche* (who certainly had an *item* given him of the king's death, or great danger) charged so fiercely towards that very place, that he beat off the Imperialists, and recorded the body; which he brought off naked, after it had been a full quarter of an hour in the enemy's possession. And now was Piccolomini's soundly peppered …

As the Swedes advanced, the Imperial battery commanders probably followed the advice given by Raimondo Montecuccoli:

> As soon as the foe begins to come into view, the battery of heavy artillery is made ready and goes into action, forthwith routing and disordering him. Gradually as the two armies approach, the other smaller pieces discharge, and then the muskets and all other weapons join in, and this the adversary is continuously subject to injury.[40]

On the other hand Montecuccoli's counter to artillery fire, in that the attacking force should march at the open order, i.e. three feet apart:

> thus rendering the incoming fire useless. For it is a general rule when there is something that cannot be resisted, it is necessary to give way. Another instance would be if the foe had posted all of his guns in the same place. In order to deny the crews the opportunity of delivering additional blows, one would have to charge the position very quickly and defer coming to grips with the enemy in other sectors.[41]

However, there are accounts of regiments not having opened their ranks during an artillery bombardment, including Robert Monro who was then

---

39 Anon., *The Great and Famous Battle of Lützen…* 1633, p.13.
40 Barker, *The Military Intellectual and Battle*, p.140.
41 Barker, *The Military Intellectual and Battle*, p.140.

serving in Colonel Donald Mackay's Regiment in the Danish Army, who recalls that a lieutenant and 13 soldiers had their heads shot off from one cannon bullet.

Montecuccoli continues: The moment the troops become subject to bombardment, they rush toward the enemy, presupposing ... that there is no advantage of putting off the actual clash of arms. Thereby the damage which an adversary's guns can wreak is avoided and the soldiers do not become discouraged.[42]

When these formations advanced upon the enemy's infantry, according to Gerat Barry:

> Coming within reach of the musket then the first ranks of the wings of musketeers are to march in this manner; the first ranks stepping some two or three paces forward having cocked their matches, then with readiness and expedition all those of the first ranks (their muskets being upon their rests or forks) to discharge at once, permitting other ranks to proceed, then presently those of the second rank to step up before the first rank, as the battle or battalion do march, and so to discharge as their former fellows had done before, and then the third rank before the second and the four, before the third, and so all the other ranks consequently with this kind of double march and at the train of the last rank those of the first to follow up again, and so consequently the rest. But if chance that the squadron of pikes be distressed or constrained to retire, they are to discharge at the enemy, retiring back upon a counter march, and with speed fall back into their rank, to give place to the next ranks, and no time be idly employed.[13]

It is generally believed that Gustavus Adolphus introduced the practice of firing by three ranks in a 'Swedish volley'. However, the English writer Gervase Markham, in his 1625 drill book, also mentions this type of firing, describing it as an 'ancient and vulgar manner of discipline', because:

> In teaching to give volleys ... (which is that the whole volley shall be given of all the shot in one instant as well of them behind as before [in front]) is utterly to be condemned for either the hindmost must venture to shoot their fellows before through the heads or else will over shoot and so spend their shot improfitably. Besides the volley being once given, the enemy comes on without impeachment or annoyance.[44]

Meanwhile as the Swedish advanced, according to the newssheet *The Battel of Lützen*:

> On the Swedes side the chief of the spoil light upon the two middle most Brigades of foot belonging unto Grave Neeles and Colonel Winckle's. The imperialists charged with so much fury and with battalions of two or three thousand in a regiment, they by force drove the Swedish to retreat in the plain field, and (as the most say),

42 Barker, *The Military Intellectual and Battle*, p.141.

43 Barry, Gerat, *A Discourse of Military Discipline* (Brussels, 1634), p.134.

44 Gervase Markham, *The Souldiers Exercise* (London, 1643), p.9.

> even then recovered their seven pieces of ordnance, Grave Neeles, Colonel of the Lifeguards, (which is the Yellow Regiment) was there shot a little above the knee, of which, being carried off spoiled, he after died. Out of this Brigade, did the imperialists carry away seven colours, and to tell the truth, the King's own company, which served here among the Guards, lost their own ensign or Standard Royal too. He that had carried the colours was after seen with his sword in his hand but his clout missing.[45]

The Green and Swedish Brigades were less mauled in the battle since their flanks were protected by their cavalry and the Blue and Yellow Regiments respectively. Why were these two regiments so badly cut up? As the Swedish cavalry regiments on the right wing manoeuvred to come to grips with those on Wallenstein's left the four infantry regiments under Gustavus Adolphus' command also shifted to the right, which opened a gap in the Swedish centre. Nils Brahe, the commander of the Swedish front line of infantry, must have been horrified to see a large lap opening up in his centre and quickly sent word to Gustavus for their return. The King sent word that the Yellow and Swedish Brigades would be returned presently, but events would overtake the front line of the Swedish infantry. Seeing their opportunity, some Imperialist cavalry swooped on the gap between the Yellow and the Blue Regiment and both these regiments were cut to pieces.

When it came to hand-to-hand fighting Johan von Wallhausen suggested that musketeers not only use their muskets as a club, but also their bandoliers, musket rests, helmets and fists. Certainly there are many references during the English Civil War to musketeers 'falling on' with 'clubbed muskets'.[46]

Major Munchhausen of Comargo's Regiment records that the regiment 'attacked three regiments' supported by Piccolomini's and Götz Regiments of Horse. No doubt General Hans Philip von Breuner's Regiment of Foot, which was on the right of Comargo's Regiment, also played a part in the destruction of the Yellow Brigade, but the regiment is not mentioned by Diodati, who recalls that:

> the enemy was recoiled by Colonel Piccolomini with his regiment and Götz's, which from this side flanked our infantry so well, that although the enemy tried several times to penetrate into it, he still did not succeed, also a large number of yellow coats, advanced in determined readiness, their muskets covering the pikes, and were attacked by our infantry and completely overthrown on the place, and this whole division almost at a moment transformed into a mountain of the dead, gave a wonderful sight. No better fortune met the Blue coats, who were attacked by Colonel Piccolomini.

Even the Imperialist history of the war had to admit that it was 'odd to see how in half an hour the yellow coated Swedish regiment was cut down, so that they afterwards lay dead with their arms in [the] order [they had

45 Anon., 'The Battel of Lützen, 1632 …' (repr. Rushworth, 1721, pp.291–305).
46 Wallhausen, Johan Jacob von, *Kriegkunst zu Fuss* (Oppenheim, 1615).

fought] having seen them alive a little before [fighting]with great bravado and bravery.' Of the 1,017 men the regiment had begun the battle with, it mustered only 324 shortly after the battle with an additional 273 wounded.[47]

Piccolomini takes up the narrative:

> The Blue Regiment, the most esteemed by the king … advanced to Götz's Regiment, which was in front of me on the right … I immediately charged it, which lowered the pikes, but making half a caracol, I took them from the flank, where I cut it to pieces and took their colours … After I had defeated that infantry, I attacked again a cavalry regiment and dispersed it and at that time many of my soldiers came to tell me the king is dead.[48]

Piccolomini added that he 'had defeated two of the best regiments' of the Swedish Army.[49]

The 'caracol' is often mentioned in later sources when describing an attack by Imperialist cavalry, who made slow plodding attacks, whereas the Swedish cavalry used the more progressive cavalry charge.

However, a treatise translated from French into English in 1678 includes the paragraph:

> Horse must fire by ranks and by files, and are to detach by caracol gaining the [upper] hand if possibly they can; that is to say, using their endeavour to have the enemy on the right. They should be detach[ed] at a trot, then put on the gallop, and having discharged [their firearm] return to their bringer up.[50]

The 'bringer up' was the last man in a file. At the 'trot' and 'gallop' is hardly the 'caracol' mentioned referred to modern sources on tactics. It is obvious that this treatise was originally written in the late 1630s or 1640s, but these movements are also mentioned in Wallhausen's *Art Militaire a Cheval* which was published in 1616, although he does not refer to this manoeuvre by the name 'caracol'.[50]

True, Wallhausen does show cuirassiers shooting at each other with their pistols, but during the English Civil War, Captain Richard Atkins records that he attacked Sir Arthur Hesselrige, who was in cuirassier armour, and fired at him at point-blank range with his carbine. When this failed Atkins 'struck him a good while [with his sword] and tried him from head to saddle and could not penetrate him nor do him any hurt.' Despite Atkins' claim, Hesselrige did have a number of wounds insomuch that prayers were said for his recovery, but Atkins had tp practically hold his pistol to Hesselrige's breastplate before he could inflict any damage.

An anonymous military manual which appears to have been written during the late 1620s or 1630s, suggests that 'as for the cuirassiers they must never use

47 Khevenhüller, *Annales Ferdinandi*, vol. 12, pp.193–194; Brzezinski, *Lützen 1632*, p.87.

48 Angang, 'Piccolominis bref om Slaget vid Lützen', in *Historisk Tidskrift* vol. 14 1894, p.89.

49 Angang, 'Piccolominis bref om Slaget vid Lützen', in *Historisk Tidskrift* vol. 14 1894 p.89.

50 Archibald Lovell, *The Military Duties of the Officers of Cavalry Containing the Way of Exercising the Horse according to the Practice of this Present time* (London: Robert Harford, 1678), pp.14–15.

the caracol, but make directly upon the enemy and so break upon him for if they wheel about they are already half beaten, nay the harquebusiers themselves ought not to do it when you are with all your forces near to one another.'[51]

Andre Schurger suggests that the 'Blue Regiment' which was attacked by Götz and Piccolomini was not Winckle's Blue Regiment which formed the Blue Brigade on the centre left, but that commanded by Eric Hand, which belonged to the Swedish Brigade. In 1636 Hand's regiment would become the 'New Blue Regiment', but as will be discussed below it was almost certainly the 'Old' Blue Regiment that Piccolomini and other sources are referring to. According to an account of the battle, 'The Swedes Brigade fared something better because near unto the Horse: And yet there came not above four hundred off alive or unwounded.'

After having dealt with the Yellow Brigade Piccolomini's Regiment reformed close to the Swedish infantry. It was probably at this time according to Captain Silvio Piccolomini, who commanded a troop in Piccolomini's Regiment:

> It is certain that we can thank God and the Holy Madonna for not all being dead, because basically we were standing a quarter of an hour at a distance of twenty paces from an infantry squadron … escaping miraculously … because of the cuirasses of proof, saving the lives of [many of those present].[52]

Silvio Piccolomini was probably exaggerating here because cuirasses or breastplates were usually only pistol proof.

Once it had reformed Piccolomini's, along with Götz's Regiment, charged the Swedish Brigade. However since this brigade had its flank protected by Swedish cavalry on its right and the remnants of the Yellow Brigade on its left, it was less mauled by the Imperialist units. The official figures state that of the 1,335 soldiers which made up the Swedish Brigade, 87 killed or missing and 374 wounded during the battle.[53]

How these infantry regiments met the Imperialist cavalry is not recorded, but Gervase Markham suggests that when repelling cavalry the infantry should fire single volleys when surrounded by the pikes:

> So that the volley is given entirely and without impeachment or trouble to one … another. Whereas to shoot over one another's shoulder or by making the first man kneel, the second stoop, the third bend his body, the fourth lean forward and the fifth to stand upright and so deliver their volley both rude and disorderly, bringing great danger to the soldier and placing them in such a lame and uncomely posture.[54]

51 British Library Harley ms 8644, *A short practice concerning three military points, marching, lodging and fighting*, f.175.

52 Quoted in Schurger, *The Archaeology of the Battle of Lützen*, p.271.

53 Anon., 'The Battel of Lützen, 1632 …' (repr. Rushworth, 1721, pp.291–305); Brzezinski, *Lützen 1632*, p.87.

54 Gervase Markham, *The Second Part of the Soldiers Grammar* (London: A. Matthews, 1627), p.23.

While in 1635, *A Regulation Made by the Late King Lewis XIII...* states that when the infantry are confronted by cavalrymen:

> Then the foot make a Battalion with four strong platoons or parties for skirmish and double rank of pike to resist the horse, whilst three ranks of musketeers shall prepare to give their volley at the first pistol shot, which is ten to twelve paces from the foot; then if the pikes with swords in hand pursue them vigorously, without doubt the squadron will be put into great disorder and all by the means of good musketeers who have had the right art of pitching on their men and have made as many fall as they have fired shot, being thereto taught by their good discipline.[55]

The Death of the King

Seeing the slaughter of the Yellow and the Blue Brigades and with the Swedish Brigade in danger of also being overrun, Gustavus Adolphus took the Småland and Ostgota Regiments of Horse, along with the Finnish Horse and rode over to the centre to stabilise the situation. However, they ran into musketry from an Imperialist infantry and Colonel Frederick Stenbock of the Småland Regiment was wounded along with Lennart Nilsson Bååt, the lieutenant-colonel of the Ostgota Regiment, which must have also disordered these two regiments. Nevertheless Gustavus Adolphus pressed on. Having been separated from his cavalry and with only a few retainers and reformadoes, and due to a fog or mist they blundered into some Imperialist cavalry.

According to Sydnam Poyntz, Piccolomini's Regiment:

> At the first coming made a wonderful breach through the King's Finlanders, who are light horsemen, but lighting upon a Brigade of the King's infantry, thinking to break threw through them also, the foot received them with such a volley of shot they were constrained to retire. And the Finlanders with their light horse wheeling about upon their rear, that in that retreat there was such a confusion that both horsemen came pell-mell over the dry ditch, that those musketeers which were laid to gall the enemy could not hurt the enemy, but must shoot their own. But Wallenstein supplying that fault with new forces the enemy retired, but the ditch was quickly filled up and levelled in that encounter with horse and men that lay dead therein.[56]

According to Dalbier, 'The king leading the advance guard of the Swedes and Finns against the right wing of his enemy and was shot by a musket in his left arm, in such a manner that the bone entirely smashed.'[57] This was presumably from a musketeer which was positioned between the Imperialist cavalry squadrons or from a soldier in Comargo's Regiment of Foot. Whereas a French pamphlet records it was a pistol shot, which:

55 Printed in Lovell, *The Military Duties of the Officers of Cavalry ...*, p.28.

56 Poyntz, *A True Relation*, p.73; Barker, *The Military Intellectual and Battle*, p.108.

57 TNA SP 101/30 unfolio letter Lieutenant-Colonel Dalbier, An extract of a letter from Frankfurt 15 December 1632

> pierced the king's arm and broke the bone. When those next [to] the king saw him bleed, they were amazed and cried out *The king is wounded.* Which words the king heard with much distant and repining, fearing it would abate the valour of his men: wherefore dissembling his grief with a joyful and undaunted look. He sought to qualify the fear of his soldiers with these masculine words; '*The hurt is slight comrades, take courage, let us make use of our odds, and return to the charge*'. The commanders that were about him, with hands lifted up, earnestly besought him to retire: but the apprehension of frightening his men, and his ambition to overcome prevailed.[58]

With these words of encouragement the Småland Regiment is said to have charged once more, but could not rescue their king. The pamphlet continues:

> The loss of blood and the grief which he felt in the agitation of his body, enfeebled much his spirits and voice, which caused him to whisper in the ear of the Duke of Saxon Lauenburg; *convey me hence, for I am dangerously wounded,* He had scarcely ended his speech and turned head to retire, when a cuirassier marking his retreat advanced upon the gallop from the battalion of the enemy and discharged his carbine full in the shoulder of the king, with this insulting speech; *And art thou there then? Long it is that I have sought thee.*[59]

Dalbier records that Gustavus Adolphus:

> charged on the enemy himself. By his side were volunteer cavaliers, amongst them the Duke Franz Albrecht of Saxe-Lauenburg and two gentlemen. According to the reports later made by the Duke of Launeburg of the events, the king sustained a wound on his arm, was covered in blood and shouted to the Duke of Lauenburg. 'Please my cousin give me assistance, I am badly wounded and I need to retire from here'. As he got hold of the royal horse's bridle to turn him around, an enemy came up behind the king and fired his pistol through the king's back. The king fell off his horse. A gentleman bane Luchart who was following the Duke of Lauenburg killed the man who shot the king. Meanwhile our side was retreating and the king stayed where he fell."[60]

According to a later pamphlet, which quoted a letter written at Delft on 20 November 1632, Gustavus Adolphus had 'been shot twice through the body and once through the arm, and at evening [he] received the news that the victory was on his side. He joyfully thanked God and having cheerfully recommended his soul he died 36 hours after he was shot, thus much I remember.'[61]

Unfortunately, the eyewitness at Delft was mistaken. The newsheet continues:

58 Anon, *The Great and Famous Battle of Lützen…*, p.10.
59 Anon, *The Great and Famous Battle of Lützen…*, p.11.
60 Colonel Dalbier's account in TNA SP81/39/250–253, quoted in Wilson, *The Thirty Years War: A Sourcebook*, pp.175–176.
61 TNA SP101/30/223, *Extract from a letter from Delft,* 20 November 1632.

> When the king had received this mortal wound, which pierced him through and through he fell from his horse, and gave up the ghost, with nothing but *My God* in his mouth. He that made this accused shot was beaten down with a storm of Harqubusados, and sacrificed to the indignation of the Swedes. But while the Groom of the kings chamber, and diverse others lighted to raise the body, the charge began again more seriously then ever, the enemy having taken notice of this blow, and concluding that all was now finished.[62]

This charged forced Gustavus' attendants to remount their horses, but seeing that there was no choice they were forced to withdraw from the scene leaving the king's body where he had fallen. Only Gustavus' groom of the chamber remained behind and was cut down by the Imperialists.

According to the *Swedish Intelligencer* an unnamed cuirassier officer mortally wounded Gustavus Adolphus and as the Swedes tried to rescue him, 'the cuirassiers charged so fiercely in upon the Swedish; that they were not able to bring off the dying king.' True, the Piccolomini's Regiment was forced to retreat, but these two accounts hardly suggest a slow plodding attack usually associated with cuirassiers.[63]

Gustavus Adolphus' death sent shockwaves throughout Europe, with many not willing to believe it and that he had only been 'dangerously hurt'. Fortunately for the Swedish Army the fog or mist which had made Gustavus blunder into the Imperialist cavalry, shielded his death from the rest of his army. Although for the Swedish Army the day looked bleak, and Jacobus Fabrucius, the king's chaplain records, saw the Småland Cavalry Regiment return without the king:

> No one wanted to answer my question, where the king was, until a passing field preacher shouted 'the king is wounded'. I was shocked about that and turned to the place where I had seen his Royal Majesty moving. But instead I met Colonel Ernst von Anhalt-Bernburg, Lieutenant-Colonel Winkler and Lieutenant-Colonel Rehlinger along with other high-ranking officers, who asked if I have seen their men … Two members of the Royal Office rode by and shouted, 'It is a rout' but I responded 'Make a stand, our flight provoke all others to flee'. In search for my king I met a lot of fleeing musketeers and cavalrymen and a Livonian nobleman named Lieutenant-Colonel Tiesenhausen, whom I ordered to stand. But the more we were shouting the faster they were running, because they thought they were pursued by the enemy, not seeing far because of the fog.[64]

After this attack Comargo's Regiment appears to have fallen back and reformed with the Baden's Regiment of Foot which had been in the second line of infantry.

62 Anon, *The Great and Famous Battle of Lützen … faithfully translated out of the French copy* (1633), pp.11–12.

63 William Watts, *The Swedish Intelligencer, the third part* (London: Nathaniel Butter and Nicholas Bourne, (1633), p.173.

64 Quoted in Schurger, *The Archaeology of the Battle of Lützen*, p.330.

With the death of Gustavus Adolphus and the retreat of the Swedish Army to its original position, the crisis had come for the Swedes. The battle might have ended with a Swedish withdrawal, but Duke Bernard von Weimar consulted with Dodo von Knyphausen on the army's next move. Unfortunately, there are few accounts of what happened during the second half of the battle, but they decided that the army should continue to fight and Bernard charged the Imperialists at the head of Prince Anhalt's and Count Lowenstein's Regiments.

> The fight became obstinate on both sides, the charges redoubled, and carcases piled up, the pikes broken and the difference come to be decided by dint of the sword. The eye of man, nor that greater of the world ever beheld a joust more furious. The Imperialists strove to hold their advantage recovered, and the Swedes to dispossess them of it.

The Duke did wonders that day. Thrice like lightening shot he through the forces of the enemy … before he had constrained the enemy to abandon the cannon and his post.

> The winning of this opened him the way to the conquest of another; for this valiant Prince pressed the Imperialists so hard that he again disranked [i.e. disordered] them, and compelled them to quit another post, guarded with 13 cannon. His dexterity in the drilling of his men, in the opening and shutting of his ranks was such, that they received little or no hurt from the enemy cannon. The Duke undaunted, pierced through the clouds of smoke, displaced the enemy, and made himself master likewise of this place, and of the cannon and drove the enemy to a confused retreat. The slaughter was great and the Swedes well blooded, made good use of their advantage., and the disorder of their foes, passing over their bellies, killing all that came in their way and stopping their ears against all motives for quarter.[65]

Sydnam Poyntz records that by the afternoon there was little enthusiasm for taking prisoners. 'At the beginning great store of prisoners were taken on both sides', but as the day wore on 'no more prisoners [were] taken... [as] everyone strove to save himself'. Poyntz claims that such was the fierce nature of the battle he was captured three times, but was rescued twice and managed to escape the third time.[66]

Dalbier continues:

> We carried on fiercely and around 2pm. Our side was able to seize the enemy batteries [on the Imperialists' left] which we hastily spiked. Upon seeing that no enemy soldiers were attempting to retrieve them, Monsieur de Knyphausen ordered the nails taken off and fired large calibre balls and ordered continuous fire on the enemy.

65 Anon, *The Great and Famous Battle of Lützen*, pp.14–15.
66 Poyntz, *A True Relation*, pp.126–127.

63. (above, below, facing page): Swedish troops in 1631/1632. ***Theatrum Europaeum.*** (Michał Paradowski's archive).

> Around 3pm nobody remained on the enemy left wing and the right wing was fought by Duke Bernard of who came with very few men as he thought we had lost the battle. Monsieur de Knyphausen was still holding two infantry brigades, Duke Wilhelm [von Saxe-Weimar and his own] and the cavalry regiment of Colonel Ohm, under the banner of which all on our side, who had come back in disorder, regrouped. So that the Duke Bernard arrived he found it all in good order. As we were reassembling, a little time passed without any musketry being fired. Also the heavens cleared so that we could see what was left of the enemy, namely two blocks of infantry and a few standards of cavalry that were standing behind a ditch near three windmills. The enemy realised then that our army was still firm and ready to fire; so they fired too when Duke Bernard arrived. This lasted until nightfall at about 7pm, when the moon disappeared and we ceased fire.[67]

As the fighting continued Colonel Adam Trcka's Regiment of Horse came under severe pressure and Hagen's Regiment, which was station behind Trcka's was ordered forward. However, Hagen's Regiment refused to advance and withdrew. Hagen would claim that fleeing Croats had ridden through his regiment, which effected the morale of the regiment. The Swedish cavalry appears to have pursued Hagen's Regiment and managed to capture a least one colour, but fortunately for Wallenstein the other Imperialist cavalry regiments on this wing managed to plug the gap.

67 Colonel Dalbier's account in TNA SP81/39/250–253, quoted in Wilson, *The Thirty Years War, A Sourcebook*, p.176.

The Imperialist Right Wing

According to George Fleetwood:

> At our first falling on they likewise set the town of Lützen on fire, which did us much inconvenience, the wind blowing the smoke just upon us. Duke Bernard's [the Green Brigade] and Winckles [Blue] Regiments were commanded upon the cannons at the mill; the other cannon were soon taken and nailed, but those at the mills three times we had in our possession and were again beaten from them.[68]

It is usually said that during early seventeenth century battles the artillery remained where it had been planted that morning, but according to one pamphlet:

> The artillery advanced, and began to thunder, and to enter divers battalions, and to make legs and arms fly from one place to another. The smaller shot was also so violent, that the squadrons encountered in the palpable darkness caused by the smoke without knowledge of their parties. This furious shock continued two hours, with equal loss to both, victory opening her arms to embrace now one side, then another.[69]

According to Holk, 'The Duke [Wallenstein] fought for two hours against the [Swedish] infantry with four horse regiments, namely Holk, Trcka, Piccolomini and Desfour and he was encircled completely until Holk sent the cavalry to second him.'

> Colonel Winckle's Blue Regiment likewise found as hard a treatment. Himself (brave man) was shot in the arm a little above the elbow, and in the hand and carried out of battle. His lieutenant, Caspar Wolff was slain upon the place, and most of his colours taken. These two Brigades [the Yellow and Blue] were of the flower of the Army; old soldiers of seven or eight years service, (the most of them) and whom the king had there placed, for that he most relied on them. These old blades stood to their arms stoutly … [and] their dead bodies now covered the same ground, which they had defended.[70]

Despite not being present at the battle, Count Galleazzo Priorato recalls in his history of the war:

> The Swedes encouraged each other, with loud shouts of 'Victory, Victory' and the Regiments of Winckle and Sticknitz[71] coming unto them [the Imperialists] the following files making good the place of those that were slain in the former they got at last through the trench [sunken road] and passed on into the midst of Wallenstein's

68 Surrey History Centre, LM 2040 George Fleetwood's letter to his father, 22 November 1632.
69 Anon., *The Great and Famous Battle of Lützen*, p.16.
70 Anon., 'The Battel of Lützen, 1632 …' (repr. Rushworth, 1721, pp.291–305).
71 Although there was a Colonel George Matthais von Stechnitz, who commanded a weak regiment of horse which was position in the second line of the Swedish Left wing, Priorato seems to be referring to a different officer.

> forces. Here the Imperialist Horse hastening in, in close ranks and giving upon the Swedes Foot, with their swords in hand, who were not seconded by their horse by reason of the difficulty they found in descending the ditch, yet with their musket shot and pikes withstanding the violence of the enemy and charging upon the Imperialist Horse, coming on all sides close up unto them and breaking their first ranks the Imperialists broke in upon them with such violence, as that the wounded and half dead being by the horse trod underfoot and the strong an able cut in pieces by the sword, both these Battalions were little less then consumed with so much honour though as that witnessing their loyalty and writing it in Characters of blood it is worthy observation, that many soldiers as they lay gasping and giving up the ghost did notwithstanding with their swords prick the horses in the bellies that trampled upon them.[72]

Priorato's account of the war should be used with caution, but in 2011 a mass grave of 47 soldiers was discovered in the area where the Blue Regiment is believed to have fought. They show signs of having been attacked by cavalry as described by Priorato. Isotope tests on the teeth show that apart from one who came from Sweden, all were Germans, which the muster roll of the Blue Regiment confirms. Only five skeletons show signs of sharp force trauma which was the cause of death (perimortem),73 probably caused by a sword cut. One skeleton is estimated to have been between 15 and 19, had several sword cuts to the back of the head. Several other skeletons showed signs of injuries caused by swords or knives to the head, although these do not appear to have been the cause of death. Thirteen to 20 skeletons showed signs of blunt force trauma, including one with cranial trauma, whereby the cause of death was caused by 'the body colliding with a hard, flat or blunted surface.' A further 22 to 24 skeletons show signs of having been killed by a gunshot wound to the face and neurocranium, and for 11 of them, the ball that had killed them was still in the skull. A further two skeletons were probably killed by gunshot wounds to the face. Eight skeletons had lead balls in their hip joint, iliac bone, lumber vertebrae and abdominal area, and some fractures on other skeletons' thighs and lower legs could also have been caused by 'projectile trauma'. It is said that soldiers of the Blue Regiment were veterans and 12 skeletons show signs that had been wounded in the head before, which had healed (antemortem trauma). These wounds were around the cranial vault or the nasal bone, one had been wounded in the head four times before he was killed at Lützen. In fact 21 or 44.7 percent of these skeletons showed signs that they had previously received about 30 wounds to their thighs, forearms and lower legs which had healed, so they may have received them while fighting the Poles or even at the battle of Breitenfeld the

72 Priorato, *An History of the Late Warres and other State Affairs*, p.132.

73 Antemortem means before death; whereas perimortem would mean that it was caused at the time of death, and postmortem after death. Therefore an Antemortem wound would have showed signs of healing, if not being completely healed, whereas a perimortem wound was often the cause of death.

year before. At Lützen the Blue Brigade lost 206 men killed or missing and 381 wounded during the battle.74

Priorato also mentions the actions of the Green Brigade:

> The battle grew hotter then before, one battalion fighting with another not only with muskes but with pikes and swords. Whilst on this side blows were thus dealth about the Duke of Weimar appeared no less hardy on the other side, nor the Imperialists less courageous... For the Swedish Foot giving on in close ranks upon the Miller's houses and the Ditch manfully made good by the *Romanists* [Imperialists] and the *Casarian* [Imperialist] Cannon from the windmills and the Swedish cannon which were planted just against them playing reciprocally one upon another, though the Imperialists shot playing upon the Swedes on the flank, did them small hurt, yet were they so withstood by musket shot, and by the valour of the *Austrian* Commanders, as *Weimar* seeing he was not able to effect his intended design.[75]

Such was the fierceness of the battle at one point it was said that the Green Brigade had to seek shelter behind a miller's house. The exact position of this house has now been lost, and it would certainly so have been large enough to shelter a whole brigade from Imperialist gun fire, nevertheless according to the muster rolls the Brigade lost 379 killed or missing and 223 wounded during the battle.

At one point Priorato recalls that the Swedish cavalry which formed the front of the left wing:

> seconded by Wildestein's Regiment of Foot [which formed part of the Green Brigade] facing about to that part which lies between Lützen and the Windmills,fell upon the Imperialist on the flank and so renewed the fight that grew so hot on boths sides that nothing but clouds of smole and lightenings of fire were to be discerned.[76]

The *Swedish Intelligencer* records that:

> In this sore bickering, the spoil on the Imperial side, fell mostly upon old Breuner and Young Wallenstein's Regiments, both of which were here killed, with [a] full half, if not two thirds of the soldiers. These regiments performed their duties so valiantly, and Wallenstein himself took such special notice of them, that he [for] a long time after (if not still) maintained them in his own house at Prague.'[77]

Unfortunately, no returns of casualties for the Imperialist Army have survived for the battle of Lützen, but given the nature of the fighting the *Swedish Intelligencer* cannot have exaggerated greatly.

---

74 Nicile Nichlisch, et al., 'The Face of War: Trauma analysis of a mass grave from the battle of Lützen', PlOS 2017 12 (5) <www.ncbi.nlm.nih.gov/pmc.articles/PMC5439951> (accessed 28 March 2018); Brzezinski, Richard, Lützen 1632, Climax of the Thirty Years' War (Oxford: Osprey Publishing Ltd, 2001), p.87.

75 Priorato, *An History of the Late Warres and other State Affairs*, pp.132–133.

76 Priorato, *An History of the Late Warres and other State Affairs*, p.133.

77 Watts, *The Swedish Intelligencer*, p.145.

Pappenheim Arrives

Since receiving the despatch from Wallenstein, Pappenheim had been force-marching his men to arrive at Lützen in time. Now with Imperialists being force back the field marshal and his cavalry finally arrived.

> The Duke possessed of this place and master of the field between two and three in the afternoon, thinking there was but one post to force, seated by the windmill, and guarded by three Imperial Regiments, endeavoured to remove them, sending in the meantime sundry squadrons to chase the fugitives. But then the fight grew more cruel then ever; for Pappenheim was returned from Halle.[78]

Precisely when Pappenheim arrived on the battlefield is not known, some accounts state it was before Gustavus Adolphus' death, while Sydnam Poyntz goes as far as to claim that it was Pappenheim who killed the King in an epic hand-to-hand fight. Poyntz was not alone in believing this, according to one pamphlet:

> Some imagined that it was *Pappenheim* that gave the blow, by reason he had often vaunted, that an ancient prediction was found amongst the records of his family, That a stranger king should die by the hand of a Pappenheim, with diverse scares in his body and mounted on a white horse.[79]

However, it appears that he arrived shortly after Gustavus' death, possibly shortly after midday. He immediately set about deploying his cavalry on the Imperialist's left, although it would still be sometime before his infantry would arrive.

According to Fleetwood, Pappenheim's arrival gave encouragement to the Imperialists:

> I believe had not so long continued, had it not been clear weather, for the mist was so great that when we had beaten them we could not see to follow the victory.
>
> At last when the [the Imperialists] were quite beaten and we had turned the cannons at the mills upon them, about 3 of the clock, there came on eight thousand soldiers, Pappenheim's Army, which charged again at the mills and gave so brave a salvo that the whole day we had not the like, which the remainder of Duke Bernard's Regiment (which are the most was but 50 strong, answered) with which the commander of the fresh army fell.[80]

However, his arrival only gave a brief respite to the Imperialist cause:

> After a little pause, the Count von Pappenheim, with his horse and dragoons arrived … By his coming was the charge thereabouts renewed. He put himself into the Imperial left wing (which was most distressed, and which had been reserved for him)

78 Anon, *The Great and Famous Battle of Lützen…*, pp.14–15.
79 Anon, *The Great and Famous Battle of Lützen…*, pp.11.
80 Surrey History Centre, LM/2040 George Fleetwood's letter to his father, 22 November 1632.

> to be opposite to the Swedish Right Wing; where he supposed the king in Person had commanded. Just as he was ordering his horse, he was struck with a bullet of a falconet, or small sling piece, about the shoulder of which he died presently; even so soon as he was taken down from his horse, to have been carried into Leipzig.[81]

Pappenheim had often been wounded, but this time it sent shockwaves through the Imperialist Army, since all those who saw him knew he had been mortally wounded. According to Fleetwood:

> The loss of this commander so astonished them all that the officers ran about him and the soldiers flung down their arms and ran away and the officers could by no means make them longer stand; for upon that Duke Bernard charged himself the mills, beating them from their cannon, and their lodged himself all that night.[82]

Among the cavalry with Pappenheim were the regiments of Sparr, Bonninghausen, and Lamboy, which performed very poorly during the battle. In its flight elements of Bonninghausen's Regiment met with the infantry regiments of Pappenheim's force struggling to get to the battlefield in time and told them the day was lost. However, the infantry regiments decided to continue their march to Lützen. Colonel Bonninghausen would gain the reputation of a coward, while the lieutenant-colonel of Sparr's Regiment, Albrecht von Hofkirchen, would be executed. Lohe's Regiment also left the field, but not before its colonel had been killed, even so its lieutenant-colonel was also put on trial, but acquitted.

After the battle Wallenstein wrote to General Johann Aldringen that the harquebusiers:

> [Had] failed to injure the foe, even a little, but on the contrary these troops had either thrown the other [friendly] cavalry into disarray as a result of being thrust back upon it or else had hindered the latter when it began to charge. Thus he unconditionally commanded all the commanders of horse to abolish the carbines and to supply such regiments with cuirasses.[83]

By now Piccolomini's and Götz's Regiments had reformed and once more charged, this time against the Småland and Ostagota Regiments who were forced to give ground. Croats and some of Pappenheim's cavalry even began to threaten the Swedish right flank again.

After ordering forward three cavalry regiments from the Swedish second line along with Mitzlaff and Thurn's Brigade of Foot, Bernard von Saxe-Weimar launched another attack on the village of Lützen. These three fresh regiments of horse under Anhalt, Brandenstein and Lowenstein now outnumbered the Imperialist horse on the right wing, since only three out

81 Anon., 'The Battel of Lützen, 1632 ...' (repr. Rushworth, 1721, pp.291–305); Brzezinski, *Lützen 1632*, p.87.

82 Surrey History Centre, LM/2040 George Fleetwood's letter to his father, 22 November 1632.

83 Barker, *he Military Intellectual and Battle*, pp.108, 110.s

64. Croat or Polish light horseman. Pieter Snayers. (Nationalmuseum, Stockholm)

65. Imperial harquebusiers in 1634. Pieter Snayers. (Nationalmuseum, Stockholm)

of the four regiments on that wing remained, Hagen's Regiment having withdrawn to safety and refused to advance.

Now the Swedish Army was given fresh impetus and was able to push forward again: 'A little after 3pm,' recalls Dalbier, 'our side regained the lost ground and reached the place where the king had fallen, He was found among the dead bodies, all his clothes had been stolen except his shirt on his back. As there was no coach available, he was taken away on an ammunition cart.'[84]

According to tradition that evening his body was taken to Lützen church, which is now dedicated to Gustavus Adolphus, and laid out on an old table, where his body was cleaned and sent back to Sweden.

With the right wing under severe pressure Wallenstein ordered Piccolomini with his regiment to go to the right wing, while Holk managed to rally elements of Pappenheim's cavalry and lead them forward once more, and so they managed to stabilise that wing and force back the Swedes.

However, due to a thick mist, 'you could not see anything beyond ten paces, especially when the muskets fired their salvoes.'[85] Many sources, but

84 Colonel Dalbier's account in TNA SP81/39/250–253 quoted in Wilson, *The Thirty Years War, A Sourcebook*, p.176.

85 Colonel Dalbier's account in TNA SP81/39/250–253 quoted in Wilson, *The Thirty Years War, A Sourcebook*, p.176.

66. Catholic cavalry fighting against Swedes in 1634. Pieter Snayers. (Nationalmuseum, Stockholm)

not all, refer to this mist during the battle, although at different times of the day. It has been suggested by modern sources that it was caused by the smoke from the burning town of Lützen and the fire of musketry, but these were veteran soldiers reporting the mist and they must have surely been able to tell the difference between smoke from a town and that caused by firearms, both of which have a very different smell. Some of the archaeologists excavating the battlefield did observe this fog, which does appear in November and is caused by high humidity.[86]

By now both sides were extremely tired, with the Swedish having two infantry brigades and a regiment of horse still uncommitted. What reserve Wallenstein still had is unknown, but news began to spread in the Swedish ranks that Pappenheim's infantry:

> [had arrived], and were beginning a fresh charge about the windmills ... Now was all the service (after half an hour's silence on both sides) turned unto the windmills. The Imperialists' courages, like the throws of a dying body, struggled hard at the last cast, for life: and made, for the time, as fierce a charge of it, as any had the day before passed.[87]

To counter this threat Knyphausen is said to have committed his last two brigades of infantry; his own, White Brigade and that of Duke Wilhelm von Saxe-Weimar's, to counter this newly arrived infantry.

Montecuccoli, under the heading 'Of causing dismay' records:

> In the battle of Lützen chance miraculously provided the aid which is otherwise obtained only by artifice. This is to say Reinach arrived from Halle with a fresh corps of infantry at the point when both armies were already abandoning the field. Both sides were tired and frightened and one was afraid that the aforesaid footmen might appear on the scene. It was commonly believed and has since become quite obvious that of Wallenstein had allowed these newly arrived formations to fight he would have won a complete victory.[88]

However Thomas Barker, the translator and editor of Montecuccoli's work, rightly points out,that Pappenheim's infantry were almost certainly exhausted by their long march and that Wallenstein and Holk were unaware of the Swedish Army's condition.

Among Reinach's Infantry was Augustin von Fritsch, who had joined the Catholic League's Army as a musketeer and would rise to the rank of colonel; he does not mention any fighting between Pappenheim's infantry and their Swedish counterparts. Instead, in the darkness he was sent to observe the enemy's movements near the windmills. He could see lights which he thought were the lighted match of the Swedish musketeers on guard, but:

86 Schurger, *The Archaeology of the Battle of Lützen*, p.249.

87 Watts, *The Swedish Intelligencer*, p.149.

88 Barker, *The Military Intellectual and Battle*, pp.155, 237.

> I saw, however, that they were only candles which the soldiers were holding as they looted the battlefield or visited the dead. From there I went over to see our big cannon, but there was not a single soldier of ours or the enemy's at that place.[89]

67. Officer in cuirassier armour. Jan Morszten the Younger, 1620–1600. (Rijksmuseum)

The night, and the exhaustion of both sides put a stop to the fighting. According to Sydnam Poyntz;

> we were scarcely laid down on the ground to rest and in dead sleep but come a command from the General [Wallenstein] to all colonels and sergeant majors to give in a note of how strong every regiment was found to be, but it seems finding every regiment very weak by the officers' relations, we had scarcely had one sleep for ourselves and our horses and as little victuals for both.[90]

With reports of his weakened army coming in, Wallenstein decided to abandon the field. Piccolomini had five horse killed under him that day and six musket bullets are said to have bounced off his armour. Duke Bernard von Saxe-Weimar and Kniphausen were also thinking about withdrawing from the battlefield when they heard the news that the Imperialists were drawing off.

Among the wounded was Berthold von Waldstein, who was 28 in 1632. He was taken to Frauenstein in Bohemia, it was said 'very ill hurt in the right shoulder … he died there within two days. And that his body with six other dead colonels had been set into the Church of the Cloister called Graben, the place where the first Popish Reformation was made.' A rumour spread that it was Wallenstein himself who had died, but it was soon dispelled.[91]

89 Quoted in Schurger, *The Archaeology of the Battle of Lützen*, p.330.

90 Poyntz, *A True Relation*, p.73.

91 TNA SP 101/30 f305 *Extract from a Letter from Nuremburg*, 7 December 1632.

Conclusion

In 1633 the Imperialists should have had the initiative in the war, since the Swedes and their allies were still reeling from the death of Gustavus Adolphus. However, Wallenstein also needed time to repair his army which had suffered terribly at Lützen. Recruits had to be found to bring the regiments up to strength again, 10,000 florins was sent on the artillery to replace the guns that had been lost and this money also went to supplying two guns per regiment. Examples also had to be made of those officers and regiments who had performed badly during the battle and those who had performed well.

Unfortunately, Wallenstein did not have the time. Despite being 49 he had been ill for some time with gout and other illnesses. Moreover, according to Dr Geoff Mortimer Lützen may have had a psychological effect on him just as Waterloo had on Wellington, when he wrote, 'I hope to God that I have fought my last battle. It is a bad thing to be always fighting … Both mind and feelings are exhausted … and I always say next to a battle lost, the greatest misery is a battle gained.'[1] Of course we will never know if Wallenstein was in the same state of mind, certainly who won the battle of Lützen is still debated today, although it must be remember that he had been fighting since 1618, or 15 long years which must have had an effect on him.

As early as June 1633 he had opened negotiations with the Electors of Saxony and Brandenburg. His proposals included:[2]

That people be free to exercise their religion

All Jesuits in the Empire be rooted out

Restoring all the exiled Bohemian lands

Giving satisfaction to the heirs of Elector Frederick of Palatinate

That Saxony and Brandenburg possess Silesia

1 Geoff Mortimer, *Wallenstein, the Enigma of the Thirty Years' War* (Basingstoke: Palgrave Macmilian, 2010), p.178; quoted in R. Holmes, *Wellington, the Iron Duke* (London: Harper Collins, 2003), p.254.

2 TNA SP 80/9/6 Points propounded by General Wallenstein, Leipzig, 25 June 1633.

The Swedish Army occupy Bavaria

If these proposals are true then there is no way that they would be acceptable to Ferdinand or to Maximilian of Bavaria: the former was a fanatical Catholic whose religious views were one of the causes of the war, and the latter would never agree to the Swedish Army living off his Electorate.[3]

Whatever his feelings, Wallenstein took the field once more in the summer of 1633 and defeated a Swedish Army at Steinau on 20 October, but the die had been cast and it was only a matter of time before he would be dismissed. This would come in his assassination at Eger in February 1634.

However, Wallenstein's death did not mean the end to the Imperial Army. Ferdinand II would not make the same mistake again in promoting one of his commanders to such a prominent position. Instead he appointed his son, Ferdinand King of Hungary, as the commander-in-chief. He along with the Cardinal Infante would win an outstanding victory at the battle of Nördlingen on 5–6 September 1634 which defeated the combined Swedish Army under Duke Bernard von Saxe-Weimar and Gustavus Horn. This battle forced Catholic France to declare war on Catholic Spain and the Holy Roman Empire.

However, Wallenstein's negotiations with John George of Saxony had shown that there was a willingness to negotiate, and talks began on 15 June 1634. On 30 May 1635 the Peace of Prague was signed whereby the majority of German rulers agreed to drive out the foreign invaders Many people saw this Peace as the end of the war, since many had believed the comet which had been observed over Europe just before the beginning of the war had been seen for 17 days, or to a superstitious people one day for each year the war was to last. Unfortunately, it is not known for how many days the comet was visible, but the war would be ended only by the moderate Emperor Ferdinand III, who had succeeded his father in 1637 and ordered negotiations be started to end the fighting. This would have been unthinkable under his hardline father, but even so it would not be until October 1648 that the war finally ended with the Peace of Westphalia. Yet this Peace would only take the German dimension out of the equation, because the war in Europe would continue between France and Spain, and would go on until the Peace of the Pyrenees in 1658.

Thanks to Wallenstein the Emperor would have a stronger army for the remainder of the war, and although the majority of the regiments were disbanded after the war, many continued to serve the Emperor long into the seventeenth century. Colonel Julius von Hardegg's Regiment would become the 11th (Johan George Prince von Saxony's) Infantry Regiment which served in both World Wars. Colonel Heinrich Duval Count Dampiere's Regiment of Harquebusiers, which was raised in 1619, became the 4th Cavalry Regiment in 1769 and in 1798 the 8th Count Montecuccoli's Bohemian Regiment of Dragoons. It fought in the First World War, and in 1938, although it was officially disbanded due to the Austrian Anschluss, it immediately reformed as the 11th Cavalry Regiment in the German Army, taking part in the Second World War.

3 Maximilian had secretly been raised from Duke to Elector by Ferdinand after he confiscated the title from Elector Frederick.

Appendix I

Senior Officers of Wallenstein's Army

Name	Major General	Field Marshal Lieut.	General of artillery	General of cavalry	Field marshal	Lieutenant General
Tieffenbach	10 Mar 1619	-	-	-	-	-
Marradas	18 Jun 1619	-	-	24 Oct 1622	24 May 1626	24 May 1627
Wratislaw	Dec 1625	-	-	-	-	-
Lobl	22 Jan 1626	-	-	-	-	-
Maestro	15 May	-	-	-	-	-
Aldringen	1627	-	15 Dec 1631	-	13 Oct 1632	-
Gallas	11 Apr 1629	-	22 Dec 1631	-	13 Oct 1632	16 Sep 1633
Courtenbach	11 Apr 1629	-	-	-	-	-
Virmond	6 Nov 1629	-	-	-	-	-
Montecuccoli	29 Jun 1630	-	24 Mar 1633	-	-	-
E. von	20 Aug 1630					
Furstenberg	27 Dec 1631	-	-	-	-	-
Cratz	28 Dec 1631	-	-	-	-	-
Merode	28 Dec 1631	-	10 Dec 1932	-	-	-
Traum	29 Dec 1631	-	-	-	-	-
Ilow	31 Dec 1631	8 Apr 1632	-	-	19 Oct 1633	-
Desfours	19 Jan 1632	-	-	-	-	-
Colloredo	27 Jan 1632	-	23 Dec 1632	-	-	-
Holk	21 Feb 1632	-	25 Aug 1632	-	31 Dec 1632	-
Haracourt	20 Mar 1632	-	-	-	-	-
H.P. von	1 Apr 1632	-	13 Oct 1632	-	-	-
Breuner		-	-	-	-	-
Schaffgotsch	8 Apr 1632	-	-	19 Oct 1633	-	-
Goltz	May 1632	-	-	-	-	-
Sparr	11 Jul 1632	-	-	-	-	-
Strozzi	24 Nov 1632	-	-	-	-	-
Piccolomini	31 Nov 1632	-	-	19 Oct 1633		

Name	Major General	Field Marshal Lieut.	General of artillery	General of cavalry	Field marshal	Lieutenant General
Gotz	5 Apr 1633	-	-	-	-	-
Baden	29 Jul 1633	-	-	-	-	-
Mortain	9 Oct 1633	-	-	-	-	-
Suys	11 Dec 1634	-	-	-	-	-
Rittberg	21 Feb 1634	-	-	-	-	-
Trczka	-	Oct 1633	-	-	-	-
Schlick	-	-	15 Jan 1626	-	2 Jun 1627	-
Torquanto						
Conti	-	-	2 June 1627	-	20 Jul 1629	-
Schauenberg	-	-	20 Jul 1629	-	-	-
Mansfeldt	?	-	24 Jan 1632	-	-	-
Toscana	-	-	15 Feb 1632	-	-	-
Hatzfeld	?	15 Aug 1633	1 Feb 1634	-	-	-
Grana	?	-	6 Feb 1634	-	-	-
Scherffenberg	?	15 Aug 1633	-	-	20 Sep 1625	31 May 1628
Collalto	-	-	-	-	30 Apr 1628	-
Arnim	-	-	-	-	1628	-
Nasseu	-	-	-	-	1 Jul 1629	-
Pappenheim	*	*	-	-	Nov 1630	-
Anholt	*	*	-	-	1628	-

Appendix II

Regiments Raised During Wallenstein's Time

Raised	Type	First Inhaber	Remarks
1616	Cuirassiers	Don Balthasar Maradas	Incorporated 1642
1616	Harquebusiers	Heinrich Dampierre	Disbanded 1623
1618	Harquebusiers	Puchheimb	Incorporated 1619
1619	Harquebusiers	Lobl	Disbanded 1628
1619	Harquebusiers	Meggau	Disbanded 1620
1619	Cuirassiers	Max von Liechtenstein	Disbanded 1620
1619	Cuirassiers	Albrecht von Wallenstein	Disbanded 1638
1619	Cuirassiers and Harquebusiers	Heinrich Dampierre (aka Florentine Regiment)	1628 converted to cuirassiers in 1867 became 8 Dragoon Regiment
1619	Harquebusiers	Solms	Disbanded 1619
1619	Harquebusiers	Hiesterle	Disbanded 1622
1619	Harquebusiers	Wallenstein's 2nd regiment	Disbanded 1624
1619	Cuirassiers	La Croix	Disbanded 1624
1619	Harquebusiers	Paul Palffy	Disbanded 1621
1620	Harquebusiers	Herberstein	Disbanded 1622
1620	Harquebusiers	Ernst Montecuccoli	Disbanded 1622
1620	Harquebusiers	Max Rudolph von Saxe Lauenbug	Disbanded 1622
1620	Harquebusiers	Aldobrandi	1622 entered Papal service
1620	Harquebusiers	Des Fours	Disbanded 1622
1620	Harquebusiers	Karl Dampierre	Disbanded 1622
1620	Harquebusiers	Auersperg	Disbanded 1622
1620	Harquebusiers	Julius Heinrich von Saxe Lauenburg	1621 converted to cuirassiers; disbanded, 1625
1620	Harquebusiers	Spott	Disbanded 1622
1621	Harquebusiers	Stadl	Disbanded 1621

Regiments of Horse

Raised	Type	First Inhaber	Remarks
1621	Harquebusiers	Miniati	1622 entered Papal service
1621	Harquebusiers	Avandagno	Disbanded 1628
1621	Harquebusiers	Goltz	Disbanded 1621
1621	Harquebusiers	Khunen	Disbanded 1622
1621	Harquebusiers	Nachod	Disbanded 1622
1621	Harquebusiers	Karl Liechtenstein	Disbanded 1623
1621	Cuirassiers	Holstein	Disbanded 1625
1621	Cuirassiers	Khain	Disbanded 1622
1621	Harquebusiers	Julius Heinrich von Saxe Lauenburg	Disbanded 1622
1623	Cuirassiers	Paul Palffy	Disbanded 1624
1623	Cuirassiers	Neuhaus	Disbanded 1624
1623	Dragoons	Pechman	Disbanded 1624
1624	Harquebusiers	Strozzi	-
1624	Harquebusiers	Cratz	Incorporated 1632
1624	Harquebusiers	Auersperg	Disbanded 1625
1625	Harquebusiers	Pechman	1630 converted to cuirassiers; in 1631 incorporated
1625	Harquebusiers	Franz Albert von Saxe Lauenburg	Disbanded 1649
1625	Cuirassiers	Merode	Disbanded 1632
1625	Harquebusiers	Des Fours	Disbanded 1628
1625	Harquebusiers	Scherffenberg	Disbanded 1631
1625	Harquebusiers	La Motte	1633 converted to cuirassiers; in 1660 disbanded
1625	Harquebusiers	Hebron	1628 converted to cuirassiers; in 1642 disbanded
1625	Dragoons	Hebron	1628 converted to harquebusiers then to an infantry regiment
1625	Cuirassiers	Max Rudolph von Saxe Lauenburg	Disbanded 1628
1625	Harquebusiers	Julius Henrich von Saxe Lauenburg	1626 converted to cuirassiers; in 1650 disbanded
1625	Dragoons	Des Fours	Incorporated 1626
1625	Croats	Isolano	Incorporated 1641
1625	Cuirassiers	Luigi Gonzaga	Disbanded 1627
1625	Harquebusiers	Schaffgotsche	Disbanded 1626
1626	Harquebusiers	Dohna	Disbanded 1628
1626	Cuirassiers	Brunswick	Disbanded 1630
1626	Harquebusiers	Schellhardt	Disbanded 1628
1626	Harquebusiers	Johann von Gotz	1631 converted to cuirassiers; in 1639 or 1640 disbanded

Raised	Type	First Inhaber	Remarks
1626	Dragoons	Ernst von Montecuccoli	1628 converted to cuirassiers; in 1634 incorporated
1626	Cuirassiers	Dietrich von Cratz	Disbanded 1628
1626	Dragoons	Pechmann	Disbanded 1627
1626	Croats	Gall	Disbanded 1627
1626	Croats	Zrinyi	Disbanded 1628
1627	Cuirassiers	Verdugo	Disbanded 1628
1627	Harquebusiers	Ilow	Disbanded 1628
1627	Harquebusiers	Gropell de Medici	Disbanded 1628
1627	Dragoons	Barwitz	Disbanded 1628
1627	Cuirassiers	Hussmann	Disbanded 1632
1627	Harquebusiers	Stessel	Disbanded 1630
1627	Harquebusiers	Julius Heinrich von Saxe Lauenburg	Disbanded 1628
1627	Harquebusiers	Lobl or Lobel	Disbanded 1628
1627	Harquebusiers	Sparr	Disbanded 1629
1627	Cuirassiers	Pernstein	Incorporated 1634
1628	Croats	Stephen Draghi	Incorporated 1628
1628	Harquebusiers	Jacob Dampierre	Disbanded 1631
1628	Harquebusiers	Hydou	1632 converted to cuirassiers; in 1642 incorporated
1628	Harquebusiers	Lopez de Gradin	Disbanded 1628
1628	Harquebusiers	Brandenburg	Disbanded 1628
1628	Harquebusiers	Hieronymus Colloredo	1635 converted to cuirassiers; in 1649 disbanded.
1628	Croats	Hrastovacky	Disbanded 1628
1629	Cuirassiers	Ottavio Piccolomini (Old)	1635 entered Spanish service
1629	Harquebusiers	Hareancourt	1630 converted to cuirassiers,disbanded 1640
1629	Harquebusiers	Haugwitz	Disbanded 1643
1629	Cuirassiers	Schaffgotsche	Disbanded 1631
1629	Harquebusiers	Hatzfield	Disbanded 1632
1629	Cuirassiers	Sparr	Disbanded 1631
1630	Cuirassiers	Capua	Disbanded 1631
1630	Dragoons	Dohna	Incorporated 1634
1630	Cuirassiers	Holk	
1630	Harquebusiers	Bonnighausen	1635 converted to cuirassiers; disbanded 1650.
1630	Harquebusiers	Schaffgotsche	Disbanded 1631
1630	Croats	Losy	Disbanded 1639
1630	Hussars	Forgach	Disbanded 1632
1630	Croats	Corpes	Disbanded 1630

Raised	Type	First Inhaber	Remarks
1630	Croats	Morzin	Disbanded 1631
1631	Dragoons	Bohm	Disbanded 1635
1631	Cuirassiers	Bucquoi	Disbanded 1638
1631	Harquebusiers	Eckstadt (Vitzthim)	1634 converted to cuirassiers; disbanded 1636
1631	Cuirassiers	Rangono	Incorporated 1632
1631	Cuirassiers	Bredow	Disbanded 1640
1631	Harquebusiers	Morzin	1631 converted to cuirassiers; reduced 1636.
1631	Cuirassiers	Johan Winz	Disbanded 1642
1631	Cuirassiers	Mothaillon	Disbanded 1632
1631	Cuirassiers	Bentivoglio	Disbanded 1633
1631	Dragoons	Gotz	Incorporated 1636
1631	Cuirassiers	Cirey	Disbanded 1632
1631	Harquebusiers	Montrichier	Incorporated 1634
1631	Cuirassiers	Trcka	Disbanded 1649-50
1631	Dragoons	Ilow	Renamed 10th Dragoon Regiment in 1873
1631	Harquebusiers	Saviyeux	Disbanded 1636
1631	Harquebusiers	Leyen	Disbanded 1632
1631	Dragoons	Butler	Incorporated 1641
1631	Harquebusiers	Vehlen	1635 converted to cuirassiers, disbanded 1650
1631	Croats	Hrastovacky	Incorporated 1642
1631	Croats	Corpes	Disbanded 1649
1631	Croats	Orossu	Disbanded 1633
1631	Dragoons	Gallas	Incorporated 1636
1632	Harquebusiers	Konig	Incorporated 1634
1632	Harquebusiers	Lobkowitz	1635 converted to cuirassiers, incorporated 1638
1632	Harquebusiers	Westphalen	1635 converted to cuirassiers, disbanded 1652
1632	Cuirassiers	Baden	Incorporated 1633
1632	Dragoons	Gallas	Incorporated 1636
1632	Dragoons	Holk	Incorporated 1636
1632	Cuirassiers	Vitzthum	1636 entered Spanish service
1632	Harquebusiers	Czernin	Disbanded 1632
1632	Cuirassiers	Asseburg	Disbanded 1649–50
1632	Harquebusiers	Loyers	1635 entered Spanish service
1632	Harquebusiers	Goschutz	Disbanded 1638
1632	Harquebusiers	Hagen	Disbanded 1632
1632	Harquebusiers	Leutersheim	Disbanded 1638
1632	Harquebusiers	Lamboy	Incorporated 1639
1632	Harquebusiers	Herman Baden	Disbanded 1634
1632	Harquebusiers	Gronsfeld	Incorporated 1634
1632	Cuirassiers	Bonninghausen (1st Regiment)	Incorporated 1642

Raised	Type	First Inhaber	Remarks
1632	Cuirassiers	Bonninghausen (2nd Regiment)	Disbanded 1644
1632	Cuirassiers	Lohe	Incorporated 1638
1632	Cuirassiers	Westphalen	Disbanded 1637
1632	Cuirassiers	Ottavio Piccolomini (New)	Disbanded 1734
1632	Dragoons	Sparr (1st Regiment)	Disbanded 1634
1632	Dragoons	Sparr (2nd Regiment)	Incorporated 1635
1632	Dragoons	Merode	Disbanded 1633
1632	Dragoons	Bonninghausen	Disbanded 1637
1632	Harquebusiers	Fontinelli	1634 entered Spanish service
1632	Harquebusiers	Drost	Disbanded 1635
1632	Dragoons	Trcka	Incorporated 1636
1632	Croats	Blaskovits	Disbanded 1636
1632	Croats	Dornberg	Incorporated 1649
1632	Croats	Batthyanyi	Disbanded 1635
1632	Croats	Beygott	Disbanded 1634
1632	Croats	Keglevich	Incorporated 1640
1633	Dragoons	Gall	Incorporated 1647
1633	Cuirassiers	Peter Gotz	Incorporated 1634
1633	Harquebusiers	Zaradetzky	Incorporated 1642
1633	Cuirassiers	Mannsfeld	Disbanded 1636
1633	Dragoons	Aldringen	Disbanded 1642
1633	Harquebusiers	Vehlen	1635 converted to cuirassiers, disbanded 1646
1633	Dragoons	Henderson	Disbanded 1637
1633	Dragoons	Piccolomini	Disbanded 1643
1633	Croats	Revay	Incorporated 1635
1633	Croats	Kossetzky	Disbanded 1635
1633	Hussars	Peter Forgach	Disbanded 1640
1634	Cuirassiers	Mercy	Disbanded 1679
1634	Cuirassiers	Versa	Incorporated 1637
1634	Cuirassiers	Schlik	1636 entered Spanish service
1634	Cuirassiers	Traun	Incorporated 1638
1634	Cuirassiers	Lissau	1636 entered Spanish service
1634	Cuirassiers	Sylvio Piccolomini	Disbanded 1649
1634	Cuirassiers	Schonickel	Disbanded 1642
1634	Cuirassiers	Scherffenberg	Disbanded 1679
1634	Cuirassiers	Vernier	Incorporated 1638
1634	Cuirassiers	Trappola	Disbanded 1650
1634	Dragoons	Bracht	Disbanded 1637
1634	Cuirassiers	Aescher	Disbanded 1636
1634	Dragoons	Matthias Gallas	Incorporated 1649–50
1634	Cuirassiers	Furstenburg	Incorporated 1636
1634	Dragoons	Furstenburg	Incorporated 1636
1634	Croats	Ludwig	Disbanded 1642
1634	Hussars	Lengyel	Disbanded 1636
1634	Hussars	Kovacs	Disbanded 1639
1634	Croats	Tischler	Incorporated 1639

Regiments of Foot

Raised	First Inhaber	Remarks
1613	Stander	Disbanded 1660
1618	Saxe Lauenburg	Disbanded 1651
1618	Colalto	Disbanded 1651
1618	Furstenburg	Disbanded 1623
1618	Fugger	Disbanded 1621
1618	Creange	Disbanded 1618
1619	Tieffenbach or Teuffenbach	Disbanded 1649
1619	Nassau	1635 entered Spanish service
1619	Fuchs	Disbanded 1623
1619	Schaumburg	Incorporated in 1642
1619	Schwendi	Disbanded 1622
1619	Rudolph Colloredo	Disbanded 1622
1620	Kollonits	Disbanded 1622
1620	Traun	Disbanded 1622
1621	Wallenstein's	1634 Incorporated
1621	Max Liechtenstein	1636 Incorporated
1621	Schlik	Disbanded 1631
1621	Paradiss	Disbanded 1623
1621	Aldobrandini	Disbanded 1622
1621	Karl Liechtenstein	Disbanded 1628
1622	Dohna	Disbanded 1623
1623	Rudolph Colloredo	Disbanded 1623 or 1624
1623	Baldiron	Disbanded 1624
1623	Pechmann	Disbanded 1624
1623	Lodron	Disbanded 1624
1625	Desfours	Disbanded 1625
1625	Rudolph Colloredo	Disbanded 1649
1625	Wratislaw	Disbanded 1636
1625	Cerbon	Disbanded 1631
1625	Aldringen	Incorporated 1642
1626	Dohna	Disbanded 1635
1626	Merode	Disbanded 1633
1626	Holstein	Disbanded 1636
1626	Brunswick	Incorporated 1630
1626	Franz Albrecht Saxe Lauenburg	Disbanded 1631
1626	Pallant	Disbanded 1650
1626	Rudolph Saxe Lauenburg	Disbanded 1628
1626	Nogarol	Incorporated in 1642
1627	Verdugo	Disbanded 1628
1627	Wolfgang von Mansfeldt	Disbanded 1628
1627	Fahrenspach	Disbanded 1628
1627	Sulz	Disbanded 1648
1627	Conti	Incorporated 1634
1627	Hebron	Incorporated 1643
1628	Wangler (the elder)	Disbanded 1645
1628	Morando	Incorporated 1640
1628	New Colalto	Disbanded 1632
1628	Brandenburg	Incorporated 1630

Raised	First Inhaber	Remarks
1628	Savelli	Disbanded 1632
1629	Berthold von Waldstein	Incorporated 1642
1629	Hardegg	Became no 11 Regiment
1629	Perusis	Incorporated 1632
1629	Anolt-Bronckhorst	Incorporated 1630
1629	Maximilian von Waldstein	Disbanded 1809
1629	New Schaumburg	Later became 50th Infantry Regt
1629	Witzelben	Incorporated 1633
1629	New Aldringen	Incorporated 1632
1630	Holk	1634
1630	Geramb or Cramb	Disbanded 1649
1630	Scherffenberg	Incorporated 1632
1630	Lobel	Incorporated 1637
1630	Baden-Baden	Disbanded 1631
1630	Butler	Disbanded 1632
1630	Baldiron	Disbanded 1631
1630	Liechtenstein	Disbanded 1637
1630	Jechtersheim (Ascanio)	Disbanded 1633
1630	Posen	Incorporated 1636
1631	Ilow	Incorporated 1631
1631	Traun	Incorporated 1650
1631	Pappenheim	Incorporated 1640
1631	Bohm	Disbanded 1637
1631	Trcka	Incorporated 1634
1631	Schrenkh	Incorporated 1637
1631	Rittberg-Ostfriesland	Disbanded 1631
1631	Rasfeld	Disbanded 1634
1631	Wolfgang von Mansfeldt	Incorporated 1631
1631	Fahrenspach	Disbanded 1632
1631	Suys	Incorporated 1632
1631	Gotz	Incorporated 1619
1632	Paradiss	Incorporated 1637
1632	Ernest von Montecuccoli	Disbanded 1636
1632	Zinzendorff	Disbanded 1636
1632	Morzin or Marasin	Disbanded 1634
1632	Philip von Breuner	Disbanded 1636
1632	Arco	Incorporated 1638
1632	Hatzfeld	1635 entered Spanish service
1632	Pallant	Disbanded 1650
1632	Moriamez	Disbanded 1632
1632	Gil de Haes	1635 entered Spanish service
1632	New Trcka	Incorporated 1642
1632	Webel or Waevel	Incorporated 1642
1632	Schaffgotsche	Disbanded 1635
1632	Rostock	Disbanded 1637
1632	Rivarra	Disbanded 1636
1632	Rudolph von Liechtenstein	Disbanded 1636
1632	Funk	Disbanded 1650
1632	Schlik	Disbanded 1650
1633	Mercy	Disbanded 1650

Raised	First Inhaber	Remarks
1633	Stranz	Disbanded 1633
1633	Camilo Gonzaga	Disbanded 1637
1633	Burian von Waldstein	Disbanded 1637
1633	Diodati	1636 entered Spanish service.
1633	Puchheimb	Incorporated 1634
1633	Baden-Baden	Incorporated 1638
1633	New Schaffgotsche	Disbanded 1636
1633	Don Felix	Incorporated 1640
1634	Brisigell	Disbanded 1638
1634	Zweyer	Disbanded 1650
1634	Annenberg	Disbanded 1638
1634	Wolkenstein	Incorporated 1637
1634	Wolfsegg	Incorporated 1637
1634	Solis	Incorporated 1638
1634	Herrera	Disbanded 1636
1634	Eynon	Disbanded 1637
1634	Furstenberg	Disbanded 1637

Appendix III

Coat Colours

Nils Brahe's Uppland Regiment (Swedish, undated)	Grey coats
Duchy von Brunswick-Wolfenbüttel (2 regiments, *c*.1620)	Blue coats
Conrad von Burgsdorf's regiment, (Brandenburg Army 1646)	Blue coats faced silver lining
Collalto's Regiment (Imperialists, 1630)	Blue coats
King of Denmark's Regiment (1620)	Light blue coats faced white
Danish 'Red' Regiment	Red coats, with red, blue and yellow breeches
Ehrenreiter's 'Red Regiment' (Swedish, late 1620s)	Red coats
Frei Company (Saxony, 1631)	Blue coats faced yellow
Count Mathias Gallas' Regiment (Imperialists, 1645)	Grey Coats
Goldstein (Saxony, 1620)	Yellow coats
Haimhausen's Regiment (Catholic League, 1621)	Blue coats and red coats[2]
Erik Hand's Östergötland Regiment, (Swedish)	Blue coats
Karl Hard's Västergötland Regiment (Swedish, 1630)	Grey coats
Julius von Hardegg's Regiment (Imperialists, 1632)	Blue coats faced red
Julius von Hardegg's Regiment (Imperialists, 1635)	Red coats faced blue
Adam von Herbersdorff's Regiment (Catholic League, 1621)	Blue coats faced white

The following coat colours can be identified:[1]

Hohendorf's 'Red Regiment' (Swedish, late 1620s)	Red coats
Hustavus Horn's Regiment (Swedish, 1630)	Grey coats
Klitzing (Saxony, 1631)	Blue coats faced red
Colonel von Kracht (Brandenburg, 1620)	Grey coats faced blue
Johan Lilliehook's Västergötland Regiment (Swedish, 1630)	Grey coats
Loser (Saxony, 1631)	Red coats faced white
Donald Mackay's Scottish Regiment (Swedish, 1630)	Grey coats
Hans Nohten's 'Blue Regiment' (Swedish, late 1620s)	Blue coats
Okant Regiment (Swedish, undated)	Blue coats
Ake Oxernstierna's Regiment (Swedish, 1628)	Black coats
Odoardo Duke of Parma's Regiment of Foot (1635)	Green cassocks
Hans George von Ribbeck's (formerly Rochow) Regiment (Brandenburg Army 1646)	Blue with green lining
Elector of Saxony's Life Regiment	Blue coats (1633 and 1643)
Schaffenburg's Regiment (Imperialists, 1630)	Yellow coats
Scherschadel (Saxony, 1631)	Black coats faced yellow
Schleinitz's Regiment (ex Loser's, Saxony, 1635)	Red coats faced white
Schlieben (Saxony, 1620)	Red coats
Schmidt's Regiment (Catholic League, 1621)	Silver grey coats with red facings and grey breeches
Schwalbach (Saxony, 1631)	Red coats faced yellow
Sperling's Södermanland Regiment (Swedish, 1632)	Red and blue coats
Maximilian von Teuffel's 'Blue Regiment' (Swedish, late 1620s)	Blue coats
Count von Thurn Regiment's Regiment (Swedish, late 1620s)	Blue coats
George Friedrich von Trott (Brandenburg Army 1646)	Blue with yellow lining
'Unidentified militia regiment from Ortenau'	Red coats

Unknown Regiment of Foot in Parma's Army (1635)	Yellow Cassocks
Unknown Regiment of horse in Parma's Army (1635)	Yellow Cassocks
Unknown 'German' Regiment (Swedish, late 1620s)	Yellow coats
Colonel Winckle's Blue Regiment (Swedish, 1631–32)	Blue coats
Hans Wrangel's Regiment (Swedish, undated)	Blue coats

Ehrenreiter's Regiment, which later became Hohendorf's, and Nohten's Regiments, were known as the Red Regiment and the Blue Regiment respectively, while Teuffel commanded the Blue Regiment, before being appointed the commander of the Yellow Regiment; it is his former regiment that Hoppe is referring to. There have been various theories put forward as to why a regiment was known by a colour rather than its colonel, some say its refers to the colour of the ensigns, whereas others believe it was the colours of the regiment's coats, and some say both. However there are other regiments which meet these conditions which are known by the name of their colonel. It may be that these regiments enjoyed a special status within the army.

1 Ernstberger, *Hans de Witte, Finanzmann Wallensteins*, p.207, Parker, *The Thirty Years War*, p.192; Israel Hoppe, *Israel Hoppe's Burggrafen zu Elbing Geschichte des ersten schwedischpolnischen Krieges in Preussen nebst Anhang* (Leipzig: Duncker and Humblot, 1887), ed. Dr M. Toeppen pp.112, 138, 141, 230, 247, 270, 417, 469; Hans de Witte, p287; Hanauer, *Trente Guerre Ans a Haguenau*, pp.138, 138, 175; Parker, *The Thirty Years War*, p.192; Curt Jany, *Geschichte der Königlich Pressischen Armee bis zum 1807* (Prussia: K Siegismund, 1928) p.100; Gregory Hanlon, *The Hero of Italy, Odoardo Farnese, Duke of Parma, his soldiers, and his subjects in the Thirty Years War* (Oxford: Oxford University Press, 2014), p.83, quoting a document in the Biblioteca Comunale Passerini-Landi di Piacensa Ms Pallastrelli 126, Chronicle Boselli, 109; Karl von Reitzenstein, *Der Feldzug des Jahres 1621* (München: Zippner, 1891), p.147; Dr Hans Wertheim, *Der Tolle Halberstädter Herzog Christian von Braunschweig im Pfalzischen Kriege, 1621–1622* (Berlin: International Bibliothek GMBH, 1929) vol. 1, p.112, 394.

2 In 1621 the colonel's company of Colonel Haimhausen's Regiment is believed to have had blue coats, whereas his lieutenant colonel's company had red coats. However, whether this was two different issues of clothing with one colour replacing the other or each company having its own coat colour is not known.

Appendix IV

Swedish Army Colours Seen at Wittenberg, 3 September 1631[1]

276 horse in 4 blue and white cornets [of his Majesty the King of Sweden
130 horse [with] 1 black and gold cornet
66 horse [with] 1 black and gold cornet
48 horse of the King's Horse
218 horse [with] 2 blue and red cornets
84 horse [with] 1 white cornet
85 horse [with] 1 orange colour cornet
79 horse [with] 1 yellow cornet
67 horse [with] 1 red cornet
110 horse [with] 1 blue cornet
63 horse [with] 1 blue and red cornet
126 horse [with] 2 parakeet green cornets
178 horse [with] 2 blue cornets
92 horse [with] 8 green cornets
448 horse with 8 blue cornets
213 horse [with] 2 red cornets
1,284 foot in 13 old white ensigns
327 foot in 4 ensigns [colour not given]
778 foot with 12 blue/ and white ensigns with moon and stars, 4 entirely from the poles
534 horse [with] 7 white cornets, Colonel Halles
383 foot in 8 ensigns, 7 blue, 1 white
730 foot in 16 ensigns, among them 4 red and white, 7 red and 1 white
808 foot in 12 ensigns, 4 blue, the others entirely old and worn
744 horse in 11 blue cornets
435 horse in 6 green cornets
461 horse in 6 blue cornets
340 horse in 10 blue cornets

1. H.K.H. Prins Gustaf, Duke of Upland, *Arkiv till upplysning om Svenska Kriegens och Krigsinrättningarnes Historia* (Stockholm: Norstedt, 1861), tredje Bandet no. 910, pp.80–81.

570 horse without cornets
149 horse without cornets
406 horse without cornets
80 horse without cornets
737 foot with 6 ensigns, I white, 1 yellow, 4 orange with white crosses

Colour Plate Commentaries

An Introduction to the Colour Plates

by Mark Allen

Anyone researching the armies of the seventeenth century will soon realise that there is often little primary documentation and what there is needs to have every last drop of useful information dragged from it. Wallenstein's Army is no different. We are enormously lucky that in at least one aspect we have an asset that few other areas of comparable research can boast of. With the possible exception of the Swiss, no other nation has preserved, catalogued and collated their own and captured colours, flags, standards and guidons, together with other trophies of war, like the Swedes. The 'trophe' section of the Armémuseum in Stockholm's digital galleries carries over 8,000 items of captured items, a further 3,000 plus images are available from the watercolour books of the artist Hoffman who recorded these captures in the later 17th century. Unlike most nations, Sweden looked to preserve these items, and rather than leaving them to rot in churches, catalogued them and left us an amazing legacy. Many of these flags, which is where I need to concentrate, were captured as cities were taken and arsenals ransacked. Indeed the most memorable revision of attribution came about when the Swedish curator Eva Turek debunked a long-held belief that a set of colours were those of the Generalissimo Wallenstein's regiment, taken on some far-flung battlefield, and replaced that notion with the more prosaic theory that they belonged to the Regiment of the Prince of Liechtenstein and were taken whilst the Swedes were besieging Prague in 1648, and occupied the Prince's house, the regiment itself having been disbanded in 1624 (Eva Turek, 'Under False Colours', Stockholm 1996). Which explains the dilemma, whilst these flags are beautifully preserved, attempts to determine to which regiment they belonged are difficult in the extreme. The original research on the 'Wallenstein' colours was undertaken by Alfred Mell of the Austrian Army Museum, in Vienna, but much has been left to amateurs, including many by Zinnfiguren enthusiasts and historians anxious to find references for their work. Much is this is insightful, but there are a number of dubious attributions for which there is little documentary evidence.

Away from flags and banners, there is also little evidence for regimental coat colours, the author has listed a few, where they are known, but generally we are in the dark. By the 1670s the Imperial Army was beginning to regulate their German regiments into grey/white coats, and it may well be that this process started sooner. In Rome there is a series of paintings celebrating the victory of Catholic arms, at the Battle of the White Mountain, painted, according to record, by Pieter Snayers, but in a somewhat naive style. In these pictures the Catholic league and Imperial forces seem to have been supplied with uniform casaques and sometimes breeches, often decorated with contrasting 'Burgundian' crosses. No other evidence of this sort exists, either for that campaign or in the numerous other paintings the artists painted over the next thirty years.

Plate One

A. Dress of a Senior Officer, in this case Adam Trcka, who did sterling service for the Imperial cause, particularly at Lützen, Wallenstein's brother-in-law, and loyal to the Generallissimo, he was murdered with him, at Eger in 1634. Dating from the mid 1620s, he wears a suit of, probably, red silk, decorated with gold braid, beneath a sleeveless buff coat decorated similarly. Buff coats were often worn with cloth or leather sleeves, either sown or 'pointed', i.e. tied, to the coat! But the cut of this infers that it has a separate doublet worn underneath. He wears the red scarf of the Emperor's Army, with a falling ruff and large hat, both in vogue, at this time.

B. Reconstruction of a trooper of Wallenstein's Lifeguard by K.A.Wilke. Details on this body of men is limited and this reconstruction maybe rather speculative. Its size means it doesn't appear on any orders of battle and may have had a limited military role. The gold-braided casaque seems to be that of an officer. Harqubusiers and halberdiers might also have been part of this body, or the Guardsmen might have undertaken multiple roles.

C. Cuirassier, taken from Johann J. Von Wallhausen's *Kriegskunst zu Pferdt,* of 1616. The classic heavy cavalryman, of the time, the wearing of the full three-quarter armour seems to have been on a gradual decline, through this period. There does seem to have been a defining of roles, based on the battlefield role and training of a unit, rather than its armour class, with companies equipped as harquebusiers, often taking on the front-line cavalry role as time passed. Numerous small differences would have been present in the quantity and quality of the armour worn, with 'half armours', shortened paltrons and qualities differences being apparent.

Also shown are a range of helmet types, including the fearsome 'Death's head' Savoyard (iii) and (vi). The Continental *Zischagge*, see Plate 2 B (i), would also have been common.

Plate Two

A. Dragoons were intended to be able to be deployed in foot 'divisions', and this dragoon pikeman, taken from Wallhausen's 1616 manual and Wilhelm Dilich's *Krieg's Schule* of 1647, is the mounted version of the infantry pikeman. The used of Pikemen in Dragoon formation does not appear to have been extensive and would have certainly seemed outmoded by the time of Dilich's publication.

A(ii) Alternate headgear in the form of a cabasset of the type shown in Jacob de Gheyn's *Exercise of Armes* 1607. Interestingly there is some discussion as to whether this design ever actually existed. There are no, confirmed, extant items, at this time, and despite the same helmet being used in de Gheyn (1607), Wallhausen (1615), Lostelneau (1647) and Boxel (1668), there is a thought that if might be an elaborate artistic joke, perpetrated by the writers of drill manuals (i).

A(iii) Guidon of an unknown Imperial dragoon regiment. From the Arméemuseum Stockholm. Various shapes of flag were carried by dragoons, including different styles of 'swallow tailed' guidons and square infantry flags.

B. Harquebusier, medium cavalry, after Flaminio delle Croce's *L'Essercitio Della Cavalleria* of 1625. Wearing what appears to be a fully leather 'sleeved' buff coat, by no mean universal at this time, this cavalryman also sports a 'main gauche', as protection for his rein arm, also sometimes missing from continental harquebusier armours. Traditionally tasked with 'shooting in' the heavier cavalry, Richard Brzezinski, in his excellent Osprey on Lützen, has speculated that Wallenstein was making efforts to 'upgrade' this arm of his cavalry and make its actions more 'robust'.

B (ii) alternative version with an infantry helmet and armour worn over a short wool or leather doublet. This type of Infantry 'pot' was probably more extensively used than sometimes thought and along with the burgonet, a common variant in harquebusier armours.

Plate Three

A. An amalgam of various figures from Pieter Snayers' battle paintings, notably the battle of Lützen in the Austrian Army Museum, Vienna, this unarmoured Pikeman must have been a common sight. Brzezinski comments on the Swedes' habit of dumping the heavy armour at the earliest opportunity and this may well be the case for their enemies too, certainly the visual sources support this notion.

B. Standard Northern European pikeman's armour, there is a case for the wearing of 'Allemaine Rivet'-style corselets, which derived from the popular 16th century-type and were worn extensively in Southern Europe as well, worn here over the ubiquitous ropilla.

C. Common wearing of overhose to protect the finer ones beneath, together with a casaque or ropilla with 1620s 'cloak bag' breeches.

D. At the other end of the equipment level, a Pikeman in half armour, after a painting by Sebastian Vrancx, these can also be seen in Snayers' works on German troops.

Plate Four

A. Sergeant of either musket or pike, with armour, a sleeveless buffcoat and brown wool doublet.

B. An update of the 'de Gheyn' musketeer of 1607, to fit the 1620s.

C. Musketeer in natural undyed wool or linen ropilla and breeches, probably a common sight in Imperial armies.

D. Decorated ropilla from a 1630s representation of the battle of Fleurus 1628, note the 'de Gheyn' pot.

E. Marching musketeer from Matthaus Merian's engraving of Imperial troops in Regensburg, in 1634. Casaque, probably leather, snapsack and no rest.

F. Soldier wearing ruff, used extensively by commentators to distinguish Spanish troops as outmoded, in illustrations of the 1640s, ruffs were probably a common form of neckwear throughout the period. Dutch Art shows them as 'second hand' or 'hand me down' items, worn by the poor (see the works of Frans Hals and Jan Miense Molenaer for examples), and as late as the 1640s they are present in large numbers in the works of Hollar, such as his engraving of the Corn Exchange in London.

Plate Five

A. Colours of the infantry regiment Savelli (iii), maybe the Colonel's colour, or one a different set used during the regiment's long existence. All captured by the Swedes and present in the digital archives of the Arméemuseum in Stockholm. The attribution is the work of Dr. K.A. Wilke and is subject to the caveats described in the introduction.

B. Three regiments from the family Breuner served in the Imperial army, all three together at Lützen. Which regiment these belong to is unknown, there is an association with these flags and the Battle of the White Mountain, in 1620, so 'Alt Breuner' is the likeliest candidate. Again, although these are based on extant captured flags the attribution is from the 20th Century 'Zinnfiguren' group. The different borders appear to differentiate the companies.

C. Probably the Colonel's colour of Adolf Von Schleswig Holstein Gottorf, who was killed at Breitenfeld, and this colour probably captured there, the regiment continued to exist under Wallenstein and may have carried a similar colour.

D. Three unknown Imperial colours from the Arméemuseum, Stockholm. After the double-headed eagle, Burgundian crosses are the commonest decoration on Imperialist flags.

Plate Six

A. Unidentified Imperial infantry colour, a dragoon guidon of a swallow tail type, also exists with this design.

B. A colour from Johann Graf Von Aldringer (or Aldringen). Once a valued 'sidekick' of Wallenstein, Aldringer was amongst those who turned on his former employer, corresponding with those whose plotted to bring him down.

C. Colours associated by the Zinnfiguren group with Aldringer's, more believing of C(i) than the other two, which look to be in a series of their own.

D. Three of a set of four extant Imperial colours in the Arméemuseum, Stockholm. Gore Goransson 'Gustav II Adolf, Och Hans folk' attributes them to a Spanish unit serving with the Imperial Army at Lützen.

Plate Seven

A. Two of four flags of Graf Hardegg's regiment, reconstructed from the Hardeggsches Archiv by the Zinnfigurenist Pahle and Mell. This had earlier been Wallenstein's Regiment.

B. Two colours from an unknown regiment, in the Arméemuseum in Stockholm. Clearly from the same regiment using numbers to difference the companies.

C. Reconstructed colours of Graf Heinrich Von Holk, a Danish Protestant in Wallenstein's service, his efforts at Lützen cannot be underestimated, and his loss in 1633, to illness, hit Wallenstein hard. These flags are the work of Pahle and Sollner. The white flag, bearing Holk's arms, is the Colonel's.

Plate Eight

A. Holk's cavalry cornet, the other, (reverse) side, carries a representation of 'Fortuna'. Another, possibly earlier version, has has the motto shown (ii), a plain red border and a golden snake. Similar designs were present on the white Colonel's cornet.

B. Unknown cavalry cornet of white damask, clothing implies a 1630s date. From the Arméemuseum, Stockholm.

C. As B.

D. Unknown dragoon guidon, the 'Gott Mutter' design is on the reverse.

E. Unknown dragoon guidon, the Eagle is on the reverse.

Note (i) refers to conversations and debates on social media with David Evans, among others.

Bibliography

Archival Sources

Armémuseum, Stockholm

Volumes of drawings of captured regimental colours, by Olaf Hoffman

Original captured regimental colours

Bavarian Main Archives

Kurbayern Ausseres ms 2883. Clothing issued to sick soldiers

Bibliothèque Nationale

FR14166, Drapeaux et Etendant pris depuis le commencement du regne de Louis 14 jusqu'en 1688

British Library

Harl no. 6844 A short military treatise concerning all things needful in an army

Heeresgeschichtlichen Museum, Vienna

Display, Gallas' order for clothing

Niederösterreichische Landesarchiv

LA 5/- Archives of Julius von Hardegg's Regiment

LA 6/- Archives of Julius von Hardegg's Regiment

LVR Archivberatung and Forbildungszeitum at Pulheim, Germany

Correspondence of Field Marshal Count Melchior von Hatzfeldt

Schonst 4, Correspondence from Torquanto Conti to Hatzfeldt

Schonst 35, Correspondence from Landgrave Georg von Hessen Darmstadt to Hatzfeldt

Schonst 49 Correspondence from Maximilian I of Bavaria to Hatzfeldt

Schonst 172, Correspondence for Count Rudolf von Colleredo to Hatzfeldt

Schonst 206, Correspondence from Dietrict von Steinheim to Hatzfeldt

Schonst 357, Correspondence from Franz Mercy to Hatzfeldt

Schonst 386, Correspondence from Johan Pluckhardt to Hatzfeldt

Shakespeare Birthplace Trust Library

Reference no. DR762/332, Fragment of a green cornet

Statni Oblastni Archive in Zamrsku

Piccolomini Nachod, Piccolomini Papers

The National Archives, Kew, England

SP9	State Papers, Williamson Collection, pamphlets and miscellaneous
SP 16	State Papers, Charles I
SP 63	State papers, Ireland
SP 77	State Papers, Flanders
SP 78	State Papers, France
SP 80	State Papers, Holy Roman Empire
SP 81	State Papers German States
SP 84	State Papers, Holland
SP 94	State Papers, Spain
SP 95	State Papers, Sweden
SP 101	State Papers, Foreign newsletters
E351	Exchequer papers

Printed Primary Sources

Anon., *A True Relation of the Affairs of Europe*, 4 October 1622

Anon., *Keyserliche Kriegssverfassung oder ArticulsBrieff: Darauff der Römischen Keyserliche, auch zu Hungarn und Böheimb Königlichen Mayestät, etc. zu Soldatesca so wol zu Ross als zu Fuss bei Auffrichtung eines jeden Regiments gelobt und geschworen* (1626)

Anon., *The Great and Famous Battle of Lutzen ... faithfully translated out of the French copy* (1633)

Anon., *The Battel of Lützen, 1632 when the King of Sweden was Slain with circumstances preceding the same.*

Abelin, Johan Philip, *Theatrum Europaeum* (Frankfurt, 1643)

Angang, 'Piccolominis bref om Slaget vid Lutzen', in *Historisk Tidskrift* vol. 14, 1894

Barry, Gerrat, *A Discourse of Military Discipline* (Brussels, 1634)

Billings, John D., *Hardtack and Coffee or the unwritten Story of Army Life* (Boston: George M. Smith & Co., 1887)

Boas, Frederick (ed.), *The Diary of Thomas Crosfield* (Oxford: Oxford University Press, 1935)

Ceckova, *Gabriella et al., Documenta Bohemia Bellum Tricennale Illustrantia* (Prague: Academia Naklanntelstui Ceskoslovenske Akadamie, 1977), vol. 5

Cruso, John, *Militarie Instructions for the Cavalrie being a facsimile of the edition* (Kineton: The Roundwood Press, 1972), ed. Brigadier Peter Young

Davies, Edward, *The Art of War and England's Trayning* (1619)

Dilich, Wilhelm, *Kriegsbuch darin die Alte und neu Militia eigentlich beschrieben un alle Krigssneulinge, Bau und Büchsenmeistern zu nutz und guter anleitung in Druck geben und verfertigt* (Cassel: Wilhelm Wessell, 1607)

Drexel, Father, *Father Drexel's diary in Sigmund Riezler, Kriegstagebücher Aus Dem Ligitischen Hauptquartier, 1620* (München: G. Frans'chen, 1908)

Dudik, Dr B., *Waldsteins Correspondenz* (Vienna, 1865–1866)

Estienne, Henry, Lord of Fossez, *The Art of Making Devices treating of Hieroglyphicks, Symboles, Emblemes, Aenigma's, Sentences, parables, reverses of medalls, Arms Blazons, Cimiers, Cyphres and Rebus* (London 1646), translated by Thomas Blount

Fitzsimon, Father, 'Father Fitzsimon's Diary of the Bohemian War of 1620', in *Words of Comfort to persecuted Catholics* (Dublin: M.H. Gill, 1881)

Glanville, John, *The Voyage to Cadiz* (London: Camden Society, 1883)

Grimmelshausen, Hans von, *The Adventurous Simplicissimus* (Lincoln: University of Nebraska, 1962)

Hanauer, Auguste, *Trente Guerre Ans a Haguenau* (Colmar: H. Hufel, 1907)

Heath, John, *Observations upon military and Political Affairs written by the Most Honourable George, Duke of Albemarle* (London: Henry Mortlocke, 1671)

Heidenreich, Tobias, *Leipzigische Chronicke: Nebst der Continuation* (Leipzig, 1635)

Hexham, Henry, *The Art of War* (1638)

Hinds, Allen B. (ed.), *Calendar of State Papers Relating to English Affairs in the Archives of Venice, vol. XXI* (London: HMSO, 1916)

Hollaender, Albert E.J., 'Some English Documents on the End of Wallenstein', Bulletin of the John Rylands Library, 1958, p.382.

Hoppe, Israel, *Israel Hoppe's Burggrafen zu Elbing Geschichte des ersten schwedischpolnischen Krieges in Preussen nebst Anhang* (Leipzig: Duncker and Humblot, 1887), ed. Dr M. Toeppen

Khevenhüller, Franz Christoph, *Annales Ferdinandi* (Leipzig 1727), vols. 11, 12.

La Noue, Francois de, *The Politicke and Militarie Discourses of the Lord de La Noue, whereunto are adjoined certain observations of the same author, of things happened during the three late Civil Wars of France ... Translated out of the French by EA* (London, printed for Thomas Cadman and Edward Aggas by Thomas Orwin, 1588)

Le Laboureur, Jean, *Histoire du Mareschal de Guébriant* (Paris, 1676)

Liva, V., *Prameny k Dejinam Tricetilete Valky, 1618–1648* (Prague, 1951), 5 volumes

Lorenz, Gottfried, *Quellen zur Geschichte Wallensteins* (Darmstadt: Wissenschaftliche Buchgesellschaft, 1987)

Lovell, Archibald, *The Military Duties of the Officers of Cavalry Containing the Way of Exercising the Horse according to the Practice of this Present time* (London: Robert Harford, 1678)

Machiavelli, Niccolo, *The work of the famous Nicholas Machiavelli, citizen and secretary of Florence written originally in Italian and from thence newly and faithfully translated into English* (Henry Neville)

Mansfeld, Count Ernst von, *The Appollogie of the illustrious Prince Ernestus, Earle of Mansfeld etc. ... Translated out of the French copie, by SW* (Heidelberg, 1622)

Markham, Francis, *Five Decades of Epistles of Warre* (London: Augustine Matthews, 1622)

Markham, Gervase, *The Second Part of the Soldiers Grammar* (London: A. Matthews, 1627)

Markham, Gervase, *The Souldiers Accidence* (London: printed by John Dawson for John Ballamie, 1625)

Markham, Gervase, *The Souldiers Exercise* (London, 1643)

Markham, Gervase (ed. Michael R. Best), *The English Housewife* (Quebec: McGill-Queen's University Press, 2003)

Medick, Hans, and Marschke, Benjamin, *Experiencing the Thirty Years War: a brief history with documents* (New York: Bedford/St Martins, 2013)

Monluc, Blaise de, *The Valois–Habsburg Wars and the French Wars of Religion* (London: Longman Group Ltd, 1971), ed. Ian Roy

Mungeam, Gerald, 'Contracts for the Supply of equipment to the New Model Army', *The Journal of the Arms and Armour Society*, 1968.

Monro, Robert, Monro, *His Expedition with the Worthy Scots Regiment (called Mac-Keyes Regiment) levied in August 1626* (London: William Jones, 1637)

Norton, Robert, *The Gunner's Dialogue with the Art of Great Artillery* (London: John Tap, 1628)

Poyntz, Sydnam, *A True Relation of these German Warres from Mansfield's going out of England which was in the year 1624 until this last year 1636 whereof myself was an eyewitness of most I have here related as followeth* (Tonbridge: Pallas Armata, 1992)

Preissac, Lord Du (transl. John Cruso), *The Arte of Warre, Or, Militarie Discourses* (1639)

Priorato, Count Galleazzo, *An History of the Late Warres and other State Affairs of the Best Part of Christendom beginning with the King of Swetlands entrance into Germany and continuing in the yeare 1640, translated by Henry Carey* (W. Wilson, 1648)
Rushworth, John, 'The Battle of Lützen', *Historical Collections of Private Passages of State*, vol. 3, 1639–1640 (London, 1721)
Turner, Sir James, *Pallas Armata* (London, 1683)
Tadra, Ferdinand, Briefe Albrechts von Waldstein an Karl von Harrach (Vienna: K. Gerold's Sohn, 1879)
Wallhausen, Johan Jacob von, *L'Art Militaire pour L'Infantrie* (Uldrick Balck, 1615)
Wallhausen, Johan Jacob von, *Kriegkunst zu Fuss* (Oppenheim, 1615)
Ward, Robert, *Animadversions of Warre; or a Military magazine of the truest rules and ablest instructions for the managing of war...* (1639)
Watts, William, *The Swedish Intelligencer* (London: Nathaniel Butter and Nicholas Bourne, 1633)
Wilson, Peter, *The Thirty Years War: A Sourcebook* (Basingstoke: Palgrave MacMillan, 2010)

Printed Secondary Sources

17th Century War Weaponry and Politics 10th Swedish Conference, 1984 (International Association of Museums of Arms and Military History, 1984)
Anon., *European Arms and Armour, mainly XVI and XVII Centuries* (New York: American Art Association Inc, 1926)
Ailes, Mary Elizabeth, *Courage and Grief, Women and Sweden's Thirty Years War* (Lincoln: University of Nebraska, 2018)
Asbach, Olaf, and Schroder, Peter (eds.), *The Ashgate Research Companion to the Thirty Years' War* (Farnham: Ashgate Publishing Ltd, 2014)
Allmayer-Beck, J.C. and Lessing, E., *Die Kaiserlichen Kriegsvölker, 1479–1718* (Munich, 1978)
Barker, Thomas, *The Military Intellectual and Battle: Raimondo Montecuccoli and the Thirty Years' War* (Albany: State University of New York Press, 1975)
Barker, Thomas M., *Army, Aristocracy, Monarchy: Essays on War, Society and Government in Austria, 1618–1780* (New York: Columbia University Press, 1982)
Bellander, Erik, *Dräkt och Uniform: den Svenska Arméns beklädnad från 1500-talets början fram till åara dagar* (Stockholm: Norstedt och Söners, 1973)
Bireley, Robert, *Ferdinand II, Counter Reformation Emperor* (New York: Cambridge University Press, 2014)
Blackmore, David, *Arms and Armour of the English Civil Wars* (Royal Armouries, 1990)
Brzezinski, Richard and Hook, Richard, *The Army of Gustavus Adolphus, 1 Infantry* (London: Osprey, 1991)
Brzezinski, Richard, *Lützen 1632: Climax of the Thirty Years War* (Oxford: Osprey Publishing, 2001)
Dahlgren, E.W., *Louis de Geer, 1587–1652: Hans Lif und Verk* (Uppsala: Almqvist och Wicksell, 1923)
Daniel, Howard (ed.), *Callot's Etchings* (New York: Dover Publications, 1974)
Danielsson, Arne, 'Det Kejserliga kyrassiarregementet Alt Piccolomini trofeer I Statens Trofesamling' in *Meddelande* vol. 49 (Stockholm: Armemuseum, 1989) ed. Jan von Konow
Danner, Dr Adolf 'Der Kommierzienrat in Bayern im 17 Jahrundert' part 1, 'Under Maximilian I' *Oberbayerisches Archiv fur Vaterländische Geschichte* (München, 1910)
David, G. (ed.), *Autobiography of Thomas Raymond* (London: Royal Historical Society, 1917)
Droysen, G., *Die Schlacht bei Lützen 1632* (Göttingen, 1865)
Ebner, H., et al., *Festschrift Othmar Pickl zum 60 Geburtstag* (Leykam Verlag, 1987)
Engerisser, Peter, *Von Lützen nach Nördlingen* (Weissenstadt: Spathling, 2007)

Ernstberger, Anton, *Wallenstein als Volkswirt in Herzogten Friedland* (Reichenberg i.B. : Sudetendeutscher Verlag Franz Kraus, 1929)

Ernstberger, Anton, *Hans de Witte, Finanzmann Wallensteins* (Wiesbaden: Franz Steiner, 1954)

Elster, Otto, *Die Piccolomini-Regimenter Während des 30jährigen Krieges* (Wien: L.W. Seidel & Sohn, 1903)

Forster, Dr Friedrich Wallenstein, *Herzog zu Mecklenburg, Friedland und Sagan* (Potsdam: Ferdinand Riegel, 1834)

Grunzel, Joseph, 'Die Reichenberger Tuchindustrie', in *Vereines Für Geschichte der Deutschen in Bohemia* (Prague, 1893), no. 5

Gush, George, *Renaissance Armies, 1480–1650* (Cambridge: Patrick Stephens, 1975)

Hallwich, Herman, 'Matthias Graf von Gallas', in *Allgemeine Deutsch Biographie* (1878), vol. 8

Hallwich, Herman, *Briefe und Akten zur geschichte Wallensteins (1630–1634)* (Vienna: Hölder, 1912)

Hanlon, Gregory, *Italy 1636: Cemetery of Armies* (Oxford: Oxford University Press, 2016)

Hanlon, Gregory, *The Hero of Italy, Odoardo Farnese, Duke of Parma, his soldiers, and his subjects in the Thirty Years War* (Oxford: Oxford University Press, 2014)

Harte, Walter, *The History of the Life of Gustavus Adolphus* (London: G. Hawkins, 1759)

Hausmann, Friedrich 'Das Regiment hochdeutscher Knechte des Grafen Julius von Hardegg', in *Der Dreissigjährige Krieg: Beiträge zu seiner Geschichte* (Vienna: Militarwissenschaftliches Institut, 1976)

Hawley-Grynsell, Dudley, *Armourers' Marks* (London: Thorsons Publishing Ltd, 1959)

Heilmann, Johann, *Kriegsgeschichte von Bayern, Franken, Pfalz und Schwaben von 1506 bis 1651* (Munchen, 1868)

Higham, Robin, 'Some Thoughts on the 30 Years War', in *Bellum Tricennale* (Prague, 1997)

Hoft, Thomas, et al., *Shiny Shapes, Arms and armour from the Zeughaus of Graz* (Vienna: Springer, n.d.)

Hogland, Lars Eric, *Från Karl Knutsson till Kristina, Svenska Fälttecken och beklädnad från senmedeltid till Trettioåriga Kriget* (Karlstad: Acedia Press, 2012)

Holmes, Richard, *Wellington, the Iron Duke* (London: Harper Collins, 2003)

Hopkins, David and Hopkins, Hillary, *The Tale of a Soldier's Coat* (Stuart Press, 2000)

Huf, Hans-Christian, *Mit Gottes Segen in die Hölle: Der Dreissigjährige Krieg* (List Taschenbuch, n.d.)

Jany, Curt, *Geschichte der Königlich Preussischen Armee bis zum 1807* (Prussia: K Sigismund, 1928)

Jespersen, Leon (ed.), *A Revolution from Above? The Power State of 16th and 17th Century Scandinavia* (Odense: Odense University Press, 2000)

Konze, Marlies, et al., 'Der Stralsund Laufgraben von 1628 – Verschüttette Söldner und Waffen in sit. Festungsbau im Süden der Hansestadt (Quartier Frankenhof) im Spiegel archäologischer Befunde und historischer Quellen', in *Forschungen zur Archaologie im Land Brandenburg* (2014), vol.15

Krause, Andreas, *Maximilian I: Bayerns Grosser Kurfürst* (Graz: Styria, 1990)

Krenn, Peter and Karcheski, Walter J., *Imperial Austria, Treasurers of Art, Arms and Armour from the State of Styria* (Art Exhibitions Australia Ltd, 1998)

Lindegren, Jan, *Utskrivning och utsugning: Produktion och reproduktion i Bygdeå, 1620–1640* (Stockholm: Almqvist and Wiksell International, 1980)

Lockhart, Paul, *Denmark in the Thirty Years' War, 1618–1648: King Christian IV and the Decline of the Oldenburg State* (Selinsgrove: Susquehanna University Press, 1996)

Loewe, Dr Victor, *Die Organisation und Verwaltung die Wallensteinschen Heere* (Freiburg i.B.: J.C.B. Mohr, 1895)

Lucht, Antje and Lucht, Jurgen, *Fahnen und Stardarten aus der Zeit der Dreissigjährigen Krieges, 1618–1648* (Freiberg: Antje and Jurgen Lucht, 2015), 4 vols.

Lugs, Jaroslav, *Firearms Past and Present: a complete review of firearm systems and their histories* (London: Greville, 1973)

McNair, Don, *The Struggle for Stralsund, 1628–1630* (Farnham: The Pike and Shot Society, 2012)

Mann, Golo, *Wallenstein, his life narrated, transl. Charles Kessler* (London: Andre Deutsch Ltd, 1976)

Mann, Sir James, *Wallace Collection Catalogue, European Arms and Armour* (London: William Clowes and Son Ltd, 1962)

Mortimer, Geoff, *Wallenstein, the Enigma of the Thirty Years War* (Basingstoke: Palgrave Macmilian, 2010)

Neubur, George Philipp Anton, *Geshichte der under des Herzogs von Friedland Oberbefehl von der Kayserlichen Armee uebernommene belagerung Der Stadt Stralsund* (Stralsund: Christian Lorenz, 1772)

Oelsnitz, A.C. von der, *Geschichte des Königlich Preussischen Ersten Infanterie-Regiments* (Berlin: E.S. Mittler and Son, 1855)

Parker, Geoffrey, *The Thirty Years' War* (London: Routledge and Kegan Paul, 1987)

Parrott, David, 'The Military Enterpriser in the Thirty Years War', in *War, Entrepreneurs and the State in Europe and the Mediterranean, 1300–1800* (Leiden: Brill, 2014)

Perjes, G. 'Army provisioning, logistics and strategy in the second half of the 17th Century', in *Acta Historica Academiae Scientiarum Hungaricae*, vol, 16 (1970)

Petrelli, T.J. and Liljedahl, E.S. 'Standar och dragonfanor' in *Antiqvarisk Tidskrift for Sverige*, vol. 14 issue 3 (1895)

Pyhrr, Stuart W., *European Helmets, 1450–1650, Treasures from the Reserve Collection* (The Metropolitan Museum of Art, 2000)

Redlich, Fritz, *The Germany Military Enterpriser and his Workforce* (Wiesbaden: Franz Steiner, 1964)

Redlich, Fritz, 'Contributions in the Thirty Years' War', *English Historical Review*, Dec 1959 vol. 12, issue 2

Reitzenstein, *Karl von, Der Feldzug des Jahres 1621* (München: Zippner, 1891)

Richardson, Thom and Rimer, Graeme, *Littlecote, The English Civil War Armoury* (Leeds: Royal Armouries, 2012)

Roberts, Michael, *Gustavus Adolphus, a History of Sweden 1611–1632* (London: Longmans, Green and Co., 1958)

Sandstedt, Fred and Sandstedt, Lena, 'Proud Symbols of Victory and mute witnesses of bygone Glories', in *Hoc Signo Vinces* (Helmstand: National Swedish Museums, 2006)

Schurger, Andre, 'The Archaeology of the Battle of Lützen: an examination of 17th century military material culture' (University of Glasgow, Ph.d Thesis, 2015)

Sombart, Werner, *Studien zur Entwicklungsgeschichte des Modernen Kapitalism* (Munich and Leipzig, 1913)

Sommeregger, 'Duke Friedrich von Savelli', *Allgemeine Deutsche Biographie 53* (1907)

Stadler, Barbara, 'Pappenheim und die Zeit des Dreissigjährigen Krieges' (Winterthur: Gemsberg-Verlag, 1991)

Sennawald, Ronald, *Das Kursächsische Heer im Dreissigjährigen Krieg 1618–1648* (Berlin: Zeughaus, 2013)

Spring, Laurence, *The Bavarian Army During the Thirty Years War, 1618–1648* (Solihull: Helion and Co. Ltd, 2017)

Swedish Army Staff, *Sveriges Krig 1611–1632* (Stockholm, 1936–1939)

Swedish Army Staff, *Sveriges Krig, Bilagsband, 1611–1632,* vol.1 (Stockholm, 1936)

Turek, Eva, *Under False Colours* (Stockholm: Armémuseum, 1996)

Vogel, Hans, 'Arms Production and exports in the Dutch Republic, 1600–1650' in M Van Der Hoeven, *Exercise of Arms*

Upland, H.K.H. Prins Gustaf, Duke of, *Arkiv till upplysning om Svenska Krigens och Krigsinrattningarnes histori*a (Stockholm, 1854)

Wallace, A.V.B. Norman, *Wallace Collection Catalogue, European arms and armour supplement*

Zober, Ernst Heinrich, *Geschichte der Belagerung Stralsund durch Wallenstein im Jahr 1628* (Stralsund: W. Trinius, 1828)

Watson, Francis, *Wallenstein, Soldier under Saturn* (London: Chatto and Windus, 1938)

Wertheim, Dr Hans, *Der Tolle Halberstädter Herzog Christian von Braunschweig im Pfalzischen Kriege, 1621–1622* (Berlin: International Bibliothek GMBH, 1929)

Wilson, Peter H., *Lützen, Great Battles series* (Oxford: Oxford University Press, 2018)

Wilson, Peter H., *Europe's Tragedy, A History of the Thirty Years War* (London: Penguin, 2009)

Wittrock, G., 'Fyra Relationer om Slaget vid Lützen', *Historisk Tidskrift*, vol. 52, p.304

Wrede, Alphons Freiherr von, *Geschichte der K. und K. Wehrmacht* (Vienna: L.W. Seidel, 1898), 5 vols.

Websites

Engerisser, Peter,'Matchlock Musket, Suhl approx, 1630' <http://www.engerisser.de/Bewaffnung/weapons/Matchlockmusket.html> (accessed 8 May 2015)

German Biography <http://www.deutsche-biographie.de> (accessed November 2015)

Horse feeding <http://ecoquine.wordpress.com> (accessed December 2015)

Nichlisch, Nicile, et al., 'The Face of War: Trauma analysis of a mass grave from the battle of Lützen,' PlOS 2017 12 (5) <www.ncbi.nlm.nih.gov/pmc.articles/PMC5439951> (accessed 28 March 2018)